Outcast

"NOTHING IS LEFT BUT THE WALLS, THE BARBED WIRE, THE CONTROLLED GATES, THE ARMED GUARDS. BETWEEN THEM THEY DEFINE THE REFUGEES' IDENTITY—OR RATHER PUT PAID TO THEIR RIGHT TO SELF-DEFINITION. ALL WASTE, INCLUDING WASTED HUMANS, TENDS TO BE PILED UP INDISCRIMINATELY ON THE SAME REFUSE TIP. THE ACT OF ASSIGNING WASTE PUTS AN END TO DIFFERENCES, INDIVIDUALS, IDIOSYNCRASIES. WASTE HAS NO NEED OF FINE DISTINCTION AND SUBTLE NUANCE, UNLESS IT HAS EMBARKED FOR RECYCLING; BUT THE REFUGEES PROSPECTS OF BEING RECYCLED INTO LEGITIMATE AND ACKNOWLEDGED MEMBERS OF HUMAN SOCIETY ARE, TO SAY THE LEAST, DIM AND INFINITELY REMOTE. ALL MEASURES HAVE BEEN TAKEN TO ASSURE THE PERMANENCE OF THEIR EXCLUSION. PEOPLE WITHOUT QUALI-TIES HAVE BEEN DEPOSITED IN A TERRITORY WITHOUT DENOMINATION, WHEREAS ALL THE ROADS LEADING BACK TO MEANINGFUL PLACES AND TO THE SPOTS SOCIALLY LEGIBLE MEAN-INGS CAN BE AND ARE FORGED DAILY, HAVE BEEN BLOCKED FOR GOOD."

Zygmunt Bauman,
Wasted Lives: Modernity and its Outcasts, 2004

OUTCAST

The Plight of Black African Refugees

Edited by
Yilma Tafere Tasew

With Introductions by
Christopher LaMonica
Shelly Dixon

AFRICA WORLD PRESS

TRENTON | LONDON | CAPE TOWN | NAIROBI | ADDIS ABABA | ASMARA | IBADAN | NEW DELHI

AFRICA WORLD PRESS
541 West Ingham Avenue | Suite B
Trenton, New Jersey 08638

Copyright © 2011 Yilma Tafere Tasew
First Printing 2011

Book design: Saverance Publishing Services
Cover design: Emily Fletcher and SPS

Library of Congress Cataloging-in-Publication Data

Outcast : the plight of Black African refugees / edited by Yilma Tafere Tasew ; with introductions by Christopher LaMonica, Shelly Dixon.
       p. cm.
ISBN 978-1-56902-349-5 (pbk.)
1. Political refugees--Africa. 2. Blacks--Africa. I. Tasew, Yilma Tafere, 1959- II. Title.

HV640.5.A3O98 2011
362.87096--dc22

                                        2011006320

To all black African refugees, who have the integrity and the courage to stand up for justice and to those refugees who are wasted in the middle of nowhere in African refugee camps.

Especially to my fellow refugees of Oda, Walda and Kakuma refugee camps from 1991- present. You are always in my thoughts no matter what.

I love you all!

ALSO BY YILMA TAFERE TASEW

Disaporic Ghosts: A Discourse on Exile and Refugee Issues, First Edition Ltd. 2005, New Zealand.

Agonizing Wounds, First Edition Ltd. 2006, New Zealand.

Thank You! "Thank You!", Volume 1, Steel Roberts Publisher, 2010, New Zealand.

Thank You! " Thank You!", Volume 2,3, and 4, Steel Roberts Publisher, 2011, New Zealand.

CONTENTS

ACKNOWLEDGEMENTS

I want to acknowledge the following people: Elise Goodge, for the editing, designing, typesetting this book and for putting up with my outrageous demands; Dr. Ramon Das, Prof François Ugochukwu, Andrea Useem, Dr. Marion Maddox, Dr. Teresia Teaiwa, Valerie Morse, Kathy Jackson, Sacha Green, Amanda Calder, Mel Downer, Dr. Christopher LaMonica, Dr. Shelley Dixon, Fantaye A. Keshebo, and Lewis Scott for their enormous contributions to this book; my publisher Kassahun Checole of Africa World and Red Sea Press for publishing this book; Susan Pearce, Emily Fletcher, KanyInda Lewis, John Anderson, Keith Lees, Jacqui McDougall, Etaferahu Tachebele, My brother and friend Abera Tilahun, Senait Kassahun, Eyerusalem Bobosha for all your help and support.

FOREWORD

Elise Goodge

I first met Yilma some years ago. We were colleagues and discovered we had a mutual affection for poetry. Yilma noticed that I was a fairly fast typist and asked me if I would type some of his poems up for him. I obliged and through his poetry and our conversations I thought I had learned something about him. Some time later Yilma asked me if I would edit his next book, again I agreed and began an almost two year, literary journey through Kenya, Nigeria, Ethiopia and back to New Zealand. I realised that before embarking on this journey I had barely scratched the surface of who Yilma is.

I have been raised on an isolated island at the bottom of the Pacific and though, like most New Zealanders, I consider myself to be some-what worldly I have come to learn, through editing this book, that my life has been one of naive tranquillity and security.

I have not known war, civil unrest, dictatorships, starvation, torture, imprisonment, confinement, hopelessness or disease. While I wouldn't say I take my fortunate position in the world for granted I cannot walk a day in Yilma's shoes, as I am incapable of imagining, or even speculating about, much of his experience.

What I can do, however, is edit a book. I can assist in making it available to others; I can help to facilitate the sharing of information and experience. Though this is but a small gesture, compared with the wealth of knowledge I have gained from being Yilma's friend, I hope it is received with the love, tenderness and passion with which it is offered. I say this on behalf of all those who have contributed to this publication.

INTRODUCTION

Christopher LaMonica

Once again Yilma Tafere Tasew has done a marvelous job of bringing together a group of refugees, scholars, activists, and professionals to discuss the very important matter of African refugees. He has also provided his own contribution to the book, this time providing more details of his own experience as a refugee at the Kakuma Camp, in northeast Kenya. For those interested in the circumstances surrounding refugee life, Tasew's contribution is heartfelt, blunt and revealing. Many of us encounter refugees in our own comfortable developed country context, scarcely giving a thought to the pain and suffering that took place in refugees' lives prior to their arrival. Yilma describes his pain, his efforts to survive, his having to sleep under a sheet, the camp environment, his challenges with the UN High Commission for Refugees (UNHCR) and the sights, sounds and people he encountered along the way. Of all his recent publications this just might be the best one yet.

Dr Ramon Das starts the book with a discussion of humanitarian intervention in Darfur. Once again, the world has been all too slow at responding to this African humanitarian crisis. Stuck in their traditional pursuits of national interest, individual states have proven inadequate to the task. And, despite United Nations Security Council resolutions and years of peace agreements amongst the various factions involved, tragically little has been done. In fact, many argue that matters there are only getting worse. Das explores these circumstances amidst a growing environment of critique against all humanitarian efforts.

As we all know, in recent decades 'aid' has been criticized for a variety of reasons; many have argued that aid has only helped to worsen conditions, including a 'dependency' on that aid. In other words, the well-intentioned contribution of free clothing or dairy products, for example, can have tragic developmental consequences for, respectively, the local clothing entrepreneur or farmer. After all, how can a local entrepreneur or farmer compete against free goods? The obvious answer is that they cannot. And where markets have been suddenly saturated with ocean freight container loads of these goods—a common sight in today's African markets—the local entrepreneur has been devastated. Essentially what this means for those of us who would like to 'help' is that 'aid' is much more complicated than previously thought. Today, before sending large quantities of any goods to any market, a careful consideration of existing markets and conditions is required. This, in fact, is the critical 'anti-aid' environment within which organizations, such as the World Food Programme, must now operate.

For a time, amidst this growing critique of 'aid,' the response would often be that 'humanitarian aid' was a different matter—put simply, in times of crisis, there could be no real debate and we must simply do what we can for humanitarian reasons. In recent years, however, even humanitarian aid has come under attack. Within academia, for example, there is a growing literature on the unintended consequences of humanitarian aid, as had been the case with other forms of aid just a few years ago. One of the first books on this was written by Fiona Terry, entitled *Condemned to repeat? : the paradox of humanitarian action* (2002) that carefully looked at some of the practical realities of humanitarian aid work "on the ground." Terry surveys the challenges faced by Afghan refugees in Pakistani camps, Nicaraguan and Salvadoran refugees in camps in Honduras, Cambodian refugees in Thai camps, and Rwandan refugees in camps located in the eastern regions of the Democratic Republic of Congo. What Terry suggests, which is repeated in other works of a similar genre, is that the camps are exceedingly difficult to manage, in constant need of resources and often become places of harassment or worse. Further, the lethal rivalries that had existed prior do not simply disappear when the same groups of people move to these camps; in many cases they become the new base of operations for some of the world's worst gangs and thugs. Put simply, even humanitarian aid has recently come under great scrutiny of late.

At the same time, of course, we are being told by the UN Secretary General, Ban Ki-Moon, that today's rising food prices will cause unprecedented suffering in developing country contexts. "If not handled properly," Ban stated in April 2008, "this crisis could result in a cascade of others ... and become a multidimensional problem affecting economic growth, social progress and even political security around the world." As this is being written, food riots are being reported on both the African and Asian continents. Time and again, development economists tell us that there is enough food to feed everyone on this Earth and that the problem is one of distribution. More than ever, food is being used as a political weapon, with tragic human consequences. Citing clear statistics on the maldistribution of food throughout the world, and the real impacts on human welfare and security, are a growing number of critics of free trade and globalization. Large corporations, who have growing influence on the global price and distribution of foods are "likely to reap the benefit of modern-day economic growth and liberalization," argues John Madeley in Hungry for Trade (2000), "free trade has enslaved the hungry rather than freed them." Since 2005, food prices have risen 83%, and while the human consequences continue to be dutifully reported by NGOs and others, many continue to argue that change, if it is to take place, must occur "over there," in developing country contexts.

All the while individuals and families do what they have to do to survive; if this means going to refugee camps and risking their lives and livelihoods they go, because they must; and if there is an opportunity to move out of a conflict-ridden region to a safer place they go, because they can. Here in Outcast we have several presentations of these lived experiences: Yilma Tafere Tasew describes the combined emotions of joy and bitterness of having to live as a refugee in a new home with the memories of his life in Ethiopia, away from all of his family. "Thank you, thank you!" he declares in one of his poems with both great sincerity and real cynicism; Teresia Teaiwa recounts her deeply felt emotions and practical thoughts on what it is like to be "far away from the homeland"; while Sacha Green, Amanda Calder and Mel Downer describe the efforts that are undertaken to reunite refugee families in New Zealand, by family members, government agencies and others. Kathy Jackson similarly addresses the challenges of African refugee families in New Zealand, with a particular focus on the experiences of the children.

In circumstances such as these it hard not to think 'what if' and several contributions contemplate exactly that. Valerie Morse, for example, considers what a world without borders, without nations, might look like. Her piece makes us wonder how issues such as immigration might look if borders did not exist! Free movement of people might be the result, without reference to immigration, i.e. there would only be migration of peoples! Is the abolition of state borders the only solution? Similar concerns are addressed in the chapter on liberalism and the refugee, where the reader is asked: Might there be a contradiction between the purported aims and 'merits' of liberalism (made by economists, development practioners promoting change "over there," and politicians) and policy? If there are contradictions should they be exposed?

In a world where policy options seem not to work, regardless of intentions, where policy statements are possibly contradictory or possibly entirely wrong due to the nature of the state system—or other—is it any wonder that, for many, religion becomes a place of solace? In a world that sometimes seems hopeless, religious figures and institutions play an important role for many hoping for positive change. In a thought-provoking chapter, Dr Marion Maddox considers the plight of refugees and the role of religion. And Fantaye Keshebo considers that same issue from a sociological perspective. Like Tasew, Keshebo discusses the particular challenges of an individual struggling for survival in refugee camps—in her case as a female. Her description is not only one of frustration; Keshebo also expresses an ongoing concern for others still in harsh camp circumstances.

Indeed, throughout *Outcast* the reader will find that all of the contributors share a concern over how to improve the lives of those who, for understandable reasons, have, at times, experienced a sense of hopelessness. This concern and compassion is found in the chapters by Françoise Ugochkwu and Andrea Useem, who consider how refugees and people in exile are treated in literature. By looking at some of the early Nigerian literature, Ugochkwu reminds us that issues like this are certainly not new but that, perhaps, attitudes toward people in exile have changed over time. Certainly, today, there are strong reasons to believe that refugees are often placed in the position of "the other," that their views are not adequately heard or acted upon in policy circles—Useem points out how this is also true in some of the literature and that

descriptions of "the strange" can, wittingly or not, lead to dehumaniza-
tion of those who are simply struggling for a better life, albeit with the
label of "refugee." Similarly reminding us of our common humanity is
L.E. Scott, who has written a very thoughtful chapter on the fear of
HIV/AIDS and African immigrants. Yilma Tafere Tasew completes
the book with his most comprehensive discussion, to date, of his own
experience of a refugee. His focus is on the early years of his experience,
how he not only survived but thrived, from the perspectives of others,
in the challenging refugee camp environment of Kakuma. Along the
way, on a more personal level, Yilma was struggling with his own fears,
angers, and other emotions. He addresses these often complex, often
contradictory, thoughts and emotions, in the best way he knows how:
through poetry.

INTRODUCTION 2

Dr. Shelly Dixon

A multitude of refugees and exiles of various kinds inhabit the pages of this collection—either as writers or as participants in the human drama described by the volume's contributors. The authors draw from a diverse range of knowledge and experiences, which reflect both the various histories of refugees and also the many responses to the issues surrounding states of exile. The pieces they have contributed are equally diverse. Poetry sits proudly amongst academic analyses, discussions concerning immigration policy choices and changes, and personal narratives of varying exilic states. This volume is one small but significant example of a growing and important body of research, debate and writing about the experiences, effects and implications of exilic states in their various forms. I trust that readers of this collaboration will be prompted to reflect on our individual and collective roles in welcoming, comforting and assisting those who need to belong.

Many of these writings are from men and women who have lived the trauma the majority of us are spared. The willingness and often, determination, to tell their stories is testimony to their courage and strength. Many of us more privileged members of society have joined this community of storytellers, artists and activists in order to contribute in some small way to the telling of the narratives of exile. Each of the contributors in this collection has his, or her, own reasons for doing so. For some, it is the need to change government policy that is the driving force. Other writers merely tell their story. What links each of these contributors is their desire to participate in the ongoing conversation about the exilic experience. Whether or not you consider yourself a refugee, this collection of varying voices, perspectives, and experiences offers an opportunity for the reader to join the conversation about exilic states.

To be exiled is an act of dispossession, of home, land and belongings. More importantly, and more painfully, it is to experience a state of not belonging, to be cast out, rejected, abandoned or ignored, to be cast adrift. This disconnection is often from the most intimate of ties— both true blood ties, and those who are a 'chosen' family' of friends and supporters. The severance of familial links is often the cruelest result of exile. Regardless of whether the exile returns home, this feeling of not belonging echoes throughout the lives of those who have lived at a remove from those they love. This is perhaps one of the most challenging of the hardships experienced under exile, for it is one that funding and resources cannot resolve.

In the playground, a child often sits on the fringe of activity. S/he is friendless, alone, ostracized. S/he may be 'different' in terms of ethnicity, gender, sexual orientation, language, physical characteristics or beliefs. S/he may simply be 'antisocial' in that s/he is unwilling to follow the crowd and behave in a certain way. This child symbolizes all those who we witness in states of exile throughout our lives. S/he represents the lonely and all too common position of the ostracised. S/he may ultimately join with others whose beliefs or behaviours are deemed offensive to the dominant group, but even in the company of similar people, this person still experiences a state of exile. I believe that we have all experienced minor states of exile during our lives and the pain associated with such rejection and shame.

From the playground, through our schooling, at social events, dating and making friends, and in our working environments, there is pressure and an innate desire to 'belong,' to be a part of a community. Unfortunately, many times throughout our lives, we are shunned to some degree. For the exile, the refugee, the dispossessed, this exclusion from privilege is often long lasting, severe, and produces scars that never fully heal.

Acts of abandonment and encouraged or enforced exile—whether literal or figurative—are historical markers of humanity's failure to be inclusive of all. We have not learnt the lessons of our past. Historically, human societies have abandoned and excluded those who challenge that society's 'norms'.

The historical rate of infanticide in many communities is but one example of humanity's desire to expel those who offend: "[i]nfanticide allowed for selection of the fittest or most desirable offspring, with sick, deformed, female, or multiple births targeted for disposal" (Moran 1978). Many societies have permitted the manslaughter of twins, for example. Throughout history, twin babies have frequently been exposed of at the edge of the community and left to perish. The superstitious believed that twins would bring ill luck to the larger group because of their 'difference' and thus parents were driven to ostracise their own kin—the ultimate sacrifice—in the name of an ostensible greater good. The birth of female children has been associated with similar feelings of shame in many patriarchal societies. In environments where maleness was favoured, it was common for female infants to be neglected or exposed to the extent that they would perish, or for them to be simply murdered. Disturbingly—by today's standards, at least—these acts of infanticide were usually not merely ignored, but rather 'endorsed' by the society of the time.

Our mental institutions are further evidence of our desire to quarantine those who may 'taint' us with their difference. Arguably, many of those labeled 'insane' (especially those who may harm themselves or others) may benefit from appropriate care and treatment. However, the label of insanity, and the various levels of quarantine or ostracism that such labeling endorses, also demonstrates a societal drive to maintain standards of 'normalcy' which are based on dichotomies (sane/insane, healthy/unhealthy) which are at best problematic. Arguably, the institutionalised are further evidence of humanity's intolerance and fear of difference and of our inadequate means of absorbing such difference into the fold.

Likewise, in the medical field, historical and contemporary analogies of exile are evident. We have favoured quarantine for those who may 'infect' a larger 'healthy' community, as was evidenced most notably during the various outbreaks of the plague. Entire communities exiled themselves, or were cut off from afar, in the hope that others may be spared infection. Again, the pragmatic reasons for quarantine are, in this case, clear and valid, and yet the exile of our fellow humans during a most horrific time of suffering is also an example of our prejudicial and sadly inhumane attitude towards those who may threaten our status quo.

In the political arena, the same strategies of containment apply. Historically, dictators of various kinds have identified, monitored and often removed individuals and groups who putatively posed a threat to the reigning authority. Others have had to flee the places they consider home, in order to avoid violence, imprisonment or death at the hands of their governments. There is significant evidence to suggest that agitators for social and/or political change have often suffered for their views and for their outspokenness. As is the case for at least one contributor to this collection, these types of actions have been punished by imprisonment, torture, and the need to flee the activist's home country (an extreme form of exile indeed).

In apartheid South Africa, the focus of my own research, those who spoke out against the apartheid government were subjected to increasingly harsh punishments. Official and unofficial forms of censorship, police brutality, imprisonment and the removal of passports from citizens wishing to travel into or out of the country are just a few examples of the human rights abuses the apartheid government subjected 'its own' citizens to. In this sense, even those who were not denied re-entry into their country were at least metaphorically exiled from their civil rights and their ability to speak out against a harsh and unjust system of government.

This discussion of historical and contemporary exilic behaviours, in a range of arenas, is not exhaustive, but merely indicative. It is not necessary for me to list every historical example of literal and metaphorical exile: I will leave it to others more qualified than I to speak about gender imbalances, religious persecution (see Marion Maddox's contribution), and the prejudicial and exilic implications surrounding issues of sexuality. It should be clear, from the few brief examples referred to above, that we humans have proven ourselves to be prejudicial and unjust, and that the many different exiles who inhabit our world are the victims of our repeated failure to be truly 'human' in an humanitarian sense.

Clearly, for the benefit of us all, we must move beyond the childish negotiations of power and privilege practiced in the playground and act more justly, but humanely. It is only when we examine the prejudicial and horrific decisions of our past that we can hope to avoid similarly unjust acts in the present and the future. The contributions that follow allow us the opportunity to do this reading and reflection and to decide what our own individual and collective roles in this process will be. The preceding discussion has been made in the hope that readers may approach the following contributions with the thought in mind that it is not merely the traditional refugee who is victimised and worthy of our attention and assistance, but rather a multitude of men, women and children who have experienced a range of exilic states. With this in mind, readers may see themselves or someone they love reflected in the words on these pages. It is my hope that this connection with the voices speaking here will set the scene for a more just and humanitarian future for us all.

Chapter 1

HUMANITARIAN INTERVENTION IN DARFUR?

Ramon Das

INTRODUCTION

Judging by the coverage in major newspapers, one could be forgiven for thinking that the current situation in Darfur is far and away the worst in the world from the standpoint of violations of basic human rights. Hollywood movie stars have joined high ranking officials at the UN in condemning Sudanese government abuses in Darfur and have joined the US government (though not the UN) in labelling the situation in the region a genocide.

Undoubtedly the situation in Darfur is dire. Current estimates are that more than 200,000 have died and some 2.5 million are either internally displaced within Darfur or refugees who have fled across the border to Chad. A large share of responsibility for the situation (not all) lies with the Sudanese government. Its indiscriminate campaign against an ongoing rebellion in the region, including its support for the horseback militias known as the Janjaweed, is the main reason why there are today some 150 squalid camps housing millions of villagers who have fled the violence. A renewed bombing campaign in early 2008 has driven tens of thousands of additional villagers into the camps in Darfur and there can be little doubt that many of these people would welcome assistance from the outside world. In anything approaching a perfect world, the international community would have long ago decisively intervened, in some way or other, to stop the bloodshed and suffering.

The real world, of course, is far from perfect, and in this world it is far less clear whether, and if so how, the international community should intervene in Darfur. First and foremost, it is important to be clear about which segments of the 'international community' are likely to intervene. In the first instance, there is the United Nations Security Council, which, as I write, has just deployed an armed force of some 9000 peacekeepers to Darfur—much smaller than was originally anticipated. There is also the possibility of regional alliances outside the UN framework, such as NATO's intervention in Kosovo in 1999. Indeed, another examples provided by Darfur quite recently: the African Union had a lightly armed force of 7000 or so soldiers in Darfur, which has now been integrated into the UN force just mentioned. Finally, there is the possibility of unilateral intervention in Darfur. One of the African states neighbouring the Sudan, or perhaps a non-African state, might decide to intervene militarily.

These three possibilities share an important feature in common. All of them are certain to enjoy the tacit support, if not the explicit backing, of one of the major powers—above all, the United States. I shall argue here that in thinking about the ethics of humanitarian intervention in Darfur, this fact must be kept uppermost in ones mind. More generally, it is a mistake to think about potential 'humanitarian' intervention cases (such as Darfur) in isolation from other cases where potential interveners could prevent comparably bad or even worse outcomes. In the real world those countries most likely to fill the role of 'humanitarian' interveners are themselves often directly or indirectly responsible for substantial human rights abuses—abuses that they are in a position to prevent much more readily than they are in a position to prevent the abuses occurring in the 'humanitarian' case in the spotlight. In short, our thinking about the ethics of humanitarian intervention in the real world should pay at least as much attention to the prospects—and track records—of potential interveners as it does to the predicament of those in need.

To be clear, my argument does not rest on the fact that potential interveners typically lack pure motives, or on the claim that they shouldn't act at all unless their actions meet some overall standard of 'consistency'. Rather, the force of the present argument rests entirely on a comparison of likely consequences, in particular, the likely consequences of intervening in the highlighted humanitarian case versus the likely consequences of doing something else. In general, there are two ways that military intervention, in a given country C, could be the wrong thing to do. First, it might be that intervention into C actually produces more harm than good, in which case (other things being equal), clearly it would be best not to intervene in C. Second, it might be that intervention into C, though it would produce more good than harm, would produce (far) less good, on balance, than would some alternative course of action. It is important to see that the truth of either of these possibilities is sufficient (again, other things being equal) not to intervene in C. A consequence worth highlighting is that even if intervening in C will likely produce more good than harm, it still may not be the right thing to do.

Applied to the case of Darfur, I shall consider the two elements of the argument just sketched in reverse order. First, I shall argue that the most likely great-power interveners that would lead or decisively influence any intervention—I focus on the US, but others are Britain and France—all are in a position to end or exert considerable influence on ending comparable (indeed, substantially worse) abuses in Iraq. In the case of the former two powers, this is relatively straightforward: it mainly involves pulling their military forces out of that country, followed by reparations for the massive damage and suffering that they have caused. In the case of France, although it does not have this direct option, it has other potential options at the UN, given its permanent veto, such that it could apply substantial pressure on the US and Britain to withdraw from Iraq.

The second part of the argument focuses on Darfur itself. Here I shall suggest that it is far from clear, particularly given the past track records of the great powers in intervening in Africa, as well as their likely motives, that they would make the situation in Darfur any better than it currently is. There is considerable reason to think they would make it worse. I specifically take up the issue of the UN force that has just been deployed to Darfur, and argue that its success or failure depends upon a number of factors that are just starting to become clear, crucially including which state or organization is in command of the operation and the size and armed strength of the force. However,

I don't want to rest too much on the claim that an armed intervention led by one of the Western powers would not improve the situation in Darfur. Again, the present argument is mainly a comparative one. The reason that Western powers, such as the US, should be focusing on trying to end the catastrophe in Iraq before even thinking about intervening in Darfur is simply that it is much easier for them to achieve comparable humanitarian and human rights outcome in the former country than in the latter.

The remainder of the paper is structured as follows. First, I outline what I take to be the conventional approach to the ethics of humanitarian intervention. This view tends to emphasize the plight of persons suffering abuses in the target country and to downplay questions about the moral and practical fitness of potential 'humanitarian' interveners. In section two, I lay out the basic facts about the humanitarian situation in Iraq and argue that there is a fairly clear way for Western powers to alleviate the human rights abuses and suffering occurring there—namely, end the occupation and make reparations for damage and suffering caused to the Iraqi people. In the final section I address the situation in Darfur itself in more detail, and argue that it would be much harder for Western powers to achieve humanitarian outcomes in Darfur than it would be to achieve comparable outcomes in Iraq.

I

My first task is to outline the conventional view about HI. I call the view 'conventional' not only because it is so often defended in theory, but also (and more importantly) because it is typically assumed in practice. I am not so concerned that it 'is the' conventional view as I am to use it as a foil for the position I shall defend. In any case, I believe the view has two parts, one that focuses on the plight of those in the target country; the other that focuses on the practical and moral fitness of likely interveners. The first part of the conventional view tends to emphasize the plight of people in need in an 'absolute' sense, rather than a comparative one. By this I mean that the focus tends to be on members of a specified country or group that fall below some minimal threshold of well-being or justice, rather than on whether there are others comparably worse off who could be helped more easily. The second part of the conventional view, meanwhile, typically merits far less discussion. The dominant tendency is simply to assume that some international actor, or combination of actors, meets the required moral and practical standard of fitness and is therefore a legitimate potential intervener. Most mainstream commentary pays little attention to the potential intervener's likely motives or track record.

Consider, as an example, the military intervention by NATO in Kosovo in 1999. Defenders of that intervention have tended to focus on the plight of Albanian Kosovars considered apart from—rather than in comparison to–other cases of suffering or human rights abuses. Indeed, many commentators rested their argument on what was 'likely' to happen in Kosovo (in early 1999) based on Milosevic's track-record from the early '90's, rather than on facts about what had actually happened in the period immediately preceding the NATO bombing. Michael Walzer provides a typical example:

> In some parts of Kosovo the harsh realities of ethnic cleansing were already visible before the decision to hit the Serbs with missiles and smart bombs was made. And given the Serbian record in Bosnia, and the mobilization of soldiers on the borders of Kosovo, and the refugees already on the move, military intervention seems to me entirely justified, even obligatory. (Michael Walzer, *Arguing about War*, Yale University Press, p.99.)

Walzer's commentary is representative in that it does not discuss the actual numbers of Kosovars killed or displaced in relation to other contemporary cases. Nor does he discuss the context in which those deaths and other casualties occurred—namely, an armed insurgency (the Kosovo Liberation Army, labelled a terrorist organization by the US State Department in 1998) facing an admittedly brutal counter-insurgency led by the Serbian government.

In contrast, well-known critics of the intervention, such as Noam Chomsky, have focused on the actual numbers of Kosovars killed in the year preceding NATO's intervention, taking pains to compare these to other relevant cases. Chomsky notes, first, that the actual figures in the case of Kosovo hardly warranted use of the term genocide. For the year preceding the bombing, the death toll from all sides was about 2000 persons, with about 200,000-300,000 internal refugees. Second, and just as important, these figures were comparable to other death and casualty tolls for the same period in other countries, notably Turkey and Colombia.

Chomsky's focus on these latter two countries is not arbitrary. Colombia was at the time (and remains today) the leading recipient of US military aid in Latin America. Turkey, in addition to being a major recipient of US military aid, is a long standing member of NATO. The significance of these facts for the question of 'humanitarian intervention' in Kosovo should be clear. If NATO, and in particular its dominant member, the US, were truly interested in preventing serious human rights abuses, then it should have focused on countries over which it had considerable control (Turkey and Colombia) rather than one over which it had very little control (Kosovo). Again, the point is not to criticize the US/NATO for its lack of consistency; rather, the point is that it could have prevented comparable abuses much more easily—indeed non-violently—in Colombia and/or Turkey than in Kosovo. As Chomsky argues, in part with reference to the then-contemporary case of Indonesian aggression against East Timor, it is likely that this goal could have been accomplished simply by threatening to cut off arms supplies, or perhaps, in Turkey's case, to expel it from NATO. In any event, there was no need for any sort of military intervention to achieve results comparable to those it claimed to be pursuing in Kosovo.

The second part of the conventional view addresses the moral and practical fitness of potential 'humanitarian' interveners. As suggested, this question is rarely taken up in any detail when considering actual cases. Consider, for instance, a recent and comprehensive discussion by Brian Orend of just war theory for 'non-classical' wars, including humanitarian intervention. Reflecting a commonly held view, Orend holds that cases of humanitarian intervention, although they present a special case for the question of just cause, nonetheless must meet all of the other criteria for any just war. In particular, the proposed intervener (whether it be a state, a collection thereof or an international body such as the UN Security Council) must meet the criteria of being 'minimally just.' These include:

- Being recognized as such by their own people and the international community
- Not violating the rights of other countries; and

- Making every effort to satisfy the human rights of their own citizens

These are sensible minimal criteria. The first question that any serious discussion of a proposed humanitarian intervention must consider is whether the proposed intervener meets the criteria. Unfortunately, although Orend's theoretical discussion of these criteria is illuminating, his discussion of actual cases tends to ignore this crucial question. In particular, in a discussion of the first Gulf War Orend blithely asserts that "most Western societies, including America, satisfy the criteria of minimal justice."

In fact, Orend's assertion is demonstrably false of the United States—and probably of every other major power—even at the time of the first Gulf War. Today, years into the aggressive wars against Afghanistan and Iraq that have killed over one million innocent persons, it is very hard to see how even to begin to make the case that the US meets criterion 2, above. Orend, of course, is hardly alone in assuming that the US and other Western powers are minimally just. The basic mistake he and others make, I think, is that they put an inordinate emphasis on a state's domestic laws and institutions and basically ignore its foreign policy. There is no other way one could regard, say, the US, the UK, and Australia as minimally just states. Yet there is no justification for this difference in emphasis. A state that violates the basic rights of other states fails to be minimally just even if it treats its own citizens in an exemplary manner.

In the real world, it is hard to think of any minimally just Western state that is at the same time a plausible candidate to lead an armed humanitarian intervention in Darfur. A similar point applies to those international organizations that are most likely to lead such an intervention, the UN Security Council and NATO. Arguably, no permanent member of the Security Council meets Orend's criteria for being minimally just. And NATO, of course, is totally dominated by the United States. Although the present argument does not depend on such facts, they are well worth bearing in mind in what follows.

HUMANITARIAN INTERVENTION IN IRAQ?

In this section I focus on the current war in Iraq. I begin by high-lighting two aspects of that conflict for purposes of comparison to the crisis in Darfur. The first is the extent of the humanitarian and human rights crisis in Iraq. The second is how that crisis might best be alleviated if not resolved—specifically, whether Western powers have an important role to play in bringing this about. These issues are of course controversial. However, for present comparative purposes I think the relevant facts and proper responses are clear enough.

The Iraq war has received considerable coverage in the media, yet it is probably fair to say that the extent of the human rights and humanitarian crisis caused by the war is not widely known in the West. The most widely-discussed statistic in the US is the number of US soldiers killed (about 4000); the US military explicitly does not keep track of Iraqi civilian casualties. The relevant facts for Iraq are particularly striking in comparison to the crisis in Darfur: Iraq constitutes a markedly worse catastrophe than Darfur when measured in terms of civilian casualties and refugees created. Since 2003, the war is responsible for somewhere between 1 and 1.3 million violent deaths. By comparison, estimated deaths for Darfur during the same period are between 200,000-450,000. The Iraq war has also forced over 4 million persons from their homes, about half of whom have fled into other countries (mainly Syria and Jordan). This is roughly 65% more than the number of refugees and internally displaced persons created by the Darfur conflict (2.5 million). In short, and without trying to put too fine a point on it, from a humanitarian and human rights point of view the situation in Iraq is substantially worse than the undoubtedly horrific situation in Darfur. Other things equal, an omniscient, omnipotent 'humanitarian intervener' would select Iraq as a target for intervention first.

Given that no such intervener exists, how, in the real world, is the crisis in Iraq to be resolved? There are two answers usually given to this question, often in tandem. The first is simply that there are no good solutions to the situation in Iraq, only less bad ones. On this point it is hard to disagree. The current situation is far worse even than it was before the war under Saddam, when Iraqi society had already been devastated by twelve years of crushing sanctions following the first Gulf War. The second answer, which concerns the continued presence of US troops, is far more contentious. The claim usually put forward is that whatever can be said against the continued presence of coalition troops, they are the only thing standing between the current bad situation and the total collapse of Iraqi society into civil war. In short, however bad things are in Iraq now, they would deteriorate even more were coalition troops to withdraw.

An honest assessment of this last claim must begin by acknowledging that it could turn out to be correct. No one really knows what would happen were US troops to withdraw from Iraq, and certainly one possible outcome is that it could make a bad situation worse. The second thing to be said, however, is that there are many good reasons to believe the contrary, most based on the evidence, some based on common sense. I turn to these directly. Third, and most important for present purposes, whatever can be said about the uncertainty of the situation in Iraq applies 'a fortiori' to Darfur. It is a serious, if common mistake to believe that a Western-led solution to ending the violence in Darfur is somehow straightforward as compared to a Western-led solution to ending the violence in Iraq. If anything, the reverse is true. Support for this last claim will be provided mainly in the following section.

What is the evidence that the continued presence of US troops in Iraq is good for Iraqis? Despite the repeated assertion of this claim, it is hard to find good reasons to believe it and easy to produce arguments against it. For a start, the US did, after all, invade the country, and has effectively occupied it for the past five years. Invasions and occupations have been known to be resisted with armed force, and it is the height of arrogance to suppose that American invasions/occupations are for some reason immune to this sort of natural reaction. Second, consider the fact that of the three main ethnic groups in Iraq (Shia, Sunni, and Kurdish) the US has fought major battles against the first two, which comprise an overwhelming majority of the population. Although it is a now-familiar mainstream argument that the recent 'surge' of troop strength (mostly confined to Baghdad), has led to a significant drop in violence, informed observers believe this is a negligible factor. Far more important are, first, that the US has effectively been bribing Sunni 'Awakening' militias (for the considerable sum of some US$10 per fighter per day) not to attack American troops, and second, that the largest Shia militia, the Mehdi Army, has been temporarily commanded by its leader, Moqtada al Sadr, to stand down. Neither of these developments can be expected to continue for long, and when they end the violence can be expected to pick up once again.

Another important source of evidence concerning the likely effects of a US troop withdrawal is the opinion of Iraqis. What do they think are the main causes of violence in their country? As it turns out, there is considerable polling evidence on this question, conducted mostly by reputable Western polling organizations, yet barely reported in the Western media. The Iraqi view, repeated consistently, including in the most recent poll, is that the presence of US troops is itself the chief cause of the violence in Iraq: most appear to believe that violence would diminish if the occupying forces were to leave. For instance, in the most recent poll taken in March 2008, a large majority of Iraqis believe that the presence of US forces in Iraq makes the security situation in the country worse (61%) not better (27%). American sociologist Michael Schwartz has provided a detailed analysis of why Iraqis might believe this, showing how standard operating procedures of US troops in conducting door-to-door searches may be directly responsible for most of the violent deaths suffered in Iraq since the start of the war.

So there is good reason to think that the withdrawal of US troops would improve, perhaps greatly improve, the human rights and humanitarian situation in Iraq. Of course, from a moral point of view no one should advocate 'simply' withdrawing US troops, i.e., doing nothing else. To the contrary, minimal justice dictates that the US owes the Iraqi people massive reparations for the devastation it has caused. (The fact that this claim is politically unthinkable does not make it untrue). Bear in mind that the US is currently spending 275 million dollars 'per day' on the war. There can be little doubt that six months or one year's worth of that money (50 to 100 billion dollars), invested in rebuilding Iraq's shattered infrastructure, would go a considerable way toward improving the lives of ordinary Iraqis and further decreasing the chances of violence.

In short, if the US and other Western powers truly wish to redress a bona-fide humanitarian and human rights catastrophe—one that happens to be of their own making—there is no better place to start than Iraq. It is an interesting question (one that we must set aside here) why Darfur, not Iraq has dominated discussion of 'humanitarian intervention' in recent years in Western countries.

DARFUR

In mainstream commentary the conflict in Darfur is usually presented in morally clear-cut terms: a case of ethnic cleansing, perhaps even genocide, perpetrated by Arab, government-backed militias against black skinned Africans. Like many other greatly simplified stories, this one has a grain of truth to it. For the most part, however, it is little more than a caricature of the actual conflict which, like most others, has an interesting and pertinent history. Although we cannot delve into this history in detail here, knowing a bit of it constitutes a useful antidote to the over-simplified account one usually encounters.

Most analysts have traced the current conflict in Darfur to a prolonged struggle between nomadic tribes and more settled farmers, mainly over fertile land and exacerbated by drought. After nearly 20 years of this struggle, and facing a growing insurgency from Darfur's peasant farmers, the Khartoum government in 2003 began arming some of the poorest nomadic tribes, incorporating them into the already existing *Janjaweed* militias as part of a counter-insurgency campaign. These militias then began a concerted and brutal attack against their more settled neighbors. It is chiefly these attacks that the UN has classified as 'ethnic cleansing' and which many commentators have seized upon as a case of genocide. The truth is considerably more complicated. According to Gerard Prunier, who has explored the complexity in detail, the attacks are best understood in the context of a government counter-insurgency campaign against a guerrilla-type enemy. Prunier notes, first, that the government sponsored campaign was "... not an attempt to kill everybody; rather, it was a matter of large-scale attacks and massacres aimed at terrorizing and displacing the population.'" He goes on to compare the Sudanese government's actions in Darfur to other cases where a militarily dominant force has tried to subdue a guerrilla army by concentrating and containing the civilian population from which the guerrillas draw their support. To be sure, according to Prunier the *Janjaweed* attacks did contain 'genocidal elements,' insofar as victims were often verbally derided during attacks as 'blacks' or 'like slaves' by their attackers. Yet it is clear from his account that those attacks fall well short of actual genocide.

Prunier is relatively sympathetic to the idea that genocide may be taking place in Darfur. Other informed observers take a different view. Noted Africa scholar Mahmood Mamdani has described the violence in Darfur as mainly a civil war, arguing that the application of the term 'genocide' to the conflict says more about the politics of the conflict than it does about the actual character of the violence. While conceding that the worst abuses have been committed by the *Janjaweed*, Mamdani points out that the insurgents have been accused of gross human rights violations as well. He compares Darfur to Iraq on grounds similar to those offered in this paper, noting that the term 'genocide' is frequently applied to the violence in Darfur but almost never to the violence in Iraq, despite the fact that the two countries are comparable in this respect.

In a more recent article, Mamdani emphasizes the complexities and uncertainty surrounding the conflict in Darfur, and the dangers these pose to the new UN force, indeed, to any outside force that would try to end the fighting. His remarks are especially relevant to the question whether an armed 'humanitarian intervention' in Darfur is likely to succeed. The only lasting solution to the conflict, Mamdani argues, is a political one yet the main political agreement—the Darfur Peace Agreement of May 2006—was never signed by key rebel groups. This, according to Mamdani, is the crux of the problem for any foreign-led intervention. In a conflict, such as the one in Darfur, an outside intervening force that is anywhere close to the proposed size of the UN force (26,000) can do little more than try to enforce an existing political agreement. It cannot hope to impose such an agreement on the population by force.

For those who are skeptical, bear in mind that Darfur is nearly the size of France. It is larger than Iraq, a country in which 150,000 of the world's most highly trained and equipped troops have proven woefully inadequate to the task of defeating a local insurgency. There is no good reason to think that a much smaller, less well-trained and equipped force in a larger and ethnically more diverse country would do any better. Given the history of colonialism in Africa and the likelihood that any Western-led force would be seen as occupiers, there is considerable reason to think that such a force would make things even worse.

Moreover, the current behavior of the major Western powers toward the hybrid UN/AU force does not exactly inspire confidence in their humanitarian motives. Perhaps the most important question regarding the UN force is who controls it? In particular, should the force be under African command, or should it, ultimately, be under the command of a Westerner or at least a non-African? On the face of it, there are good reasons to prefer the former rather than the latter. Similar to what can be said about the composition of the troops themselves, African commanders are less likely to be viewed with suspicion by the warring parties and, other things being equal, probably have a better chance of succeeding in stopping the violence. This important point, however, is obscured in Western media reports, which generally lay the blame for the delay in deploying the UN force at full strength at the doorstep of the Khartoum government. The key problem, according to mainstream reports, is that there are not enough troops because Khartoum refuses to allow non-Africans into the force. Moreover, it is said that the African troops on the ground lack the training and experience to do the job properly.

To support this view, news reports invariably allude to the fact that the AU force ran into problems after some of the rebel groups refused to sign the Darfur Peace Agreements. However, the reports usually neglect to mention that the EU began withholding money just at this crucial juncture when things were beginning to get difficult. In fact, informed observers have praised the AU force for doing a good job in the circumstances, and there is more to tell than a tale of African incompetence. Vijay Prasad reports:

> For a while the African Union was able to stabilize the situation, although it did not succeed in crafting a political solution to the problem. The African Union, created in 1999, has neither the financial ability to pay its troops nor the logistical capacity to do the job. The European Union, which paid the troops' salaries, began to withhold funds on grounds of accountability, and this gradually killed off the peacekeeping operations. (Vijay Prasad, *Destination Darfur*, August 13, 2007.)

Unfortunately, the same sort of thing is happening today. The UN force currently in Darfur lacks badly needed equipment, crucially including military transport helicopters and other logistical support. These can only come from the US or European countries, neither of which have provided them nor show any indication of doing so. The obvious question is: why not?

One answer is suggested by Mamdani. In a recent interview, he notes that "there is a concerted attempt being made to shift the political control of any intervention force inside Darfur from inside Africa to outside Africa." Expanding on this idea, Prasad comments:

> In other words, the U.S. and Europe are eager to control the dynamics of what happens in Africa and not allow an indigenous, inter-state agency to gain either the experience this would provide or the respect it would gain if it succeeds. The African Union has been undermined so that only the U.S. can appear as the savior of the beleaguered people of Darfur, and elsewhere.

Doubtless some will dismiss this idea as conspiracy theory. Yet it is not easy otherwise to explain the Western reluctance to provide the UN force with the means that would at least give it a chance to succeed. It is not as if they are requesting cutting-edge military technology. Nor can money be a serious factor: the cost of providing the helicopters is a tiny fraction of what the US is spending on the war in Iraq. Further evidence in favor of Prasad's suggestion comes from the fact that the US and Europe began dragging their heels on helicopters, etc. only after it became clear that Khartoum would not accept a non-African commander.

As I have said above, I don't wish to rest too much on the claim that a Western-led 'humanitarian' intervention in Darfur would be unlikely to improve the dire situation there. Although I have tried in this section to show that there are good reasons to believe this, it is not in the end my main claim. Rather, my main claim is a comparative one, the argument for which is contained in this section and the previous one. The Western powers most likely to lead a full-fledged armed intervention into Darfur—above all the United States—could bring about comparably good or better outcomes in Iraq by withdrawing their forces and making reparations for the massive damages they have caused. This claim rests entirely on a comparison of likely consequences; it does not depend in any way on the idea that humanitarian interveners should act 'consistently' if they are to act at all.

CONCLUSION

To conclude, I shall briefly try to summarize the main claims made in this paper. First, I have argued that our thinking about the ethics of armed humanitarian intervention must be grounded in the real world. In particular, we should pay at least as much attention to the prospects and track records of likely interveners as we do to the predicament of those in need. In the present case, this means that we should focus on those Western powers—above all the United States—that are the most likely candidates to lead a full-fledged armed intervention into Darfur. I have argued that when we focus on the US, we find that, if it sincerely wishes to end a humanitarian catastrophe, it is able to do so much more easily and directly in Iraq than in Darfur. Finally, this claim rests entirely on a comparison of likely consequences; it does not depend in any way on the idea that humanitarian interveners should act 'consistently' if they are to act at all.

Chapter 2

FAR AWAY FROM THE HOMELAND

By Teresia Teaiwa

Could our ancestors have dreamed of this land? A place beyond the New World, a destination without a Middle Passage? This is New Zealand and we are not the first direct descendants of Africa to land here. Centuries ago many a black man sailed and whaled these seas. Some brothers and sisters even toured, entertaining antipodean audiences long before mass media. Some even settled. In 1916, the New Zealand census registered 95 'Negroes' and 6 Africans. In 2001, (no more 'Negroes') but almost 6,000 from Africa. No, we are not the first direct descendants of Africa to land here, so why does it feel so strange?

❧❧

Congo, Ethiopia, Ghana, Kenya, Nigeria, Somalia, South Africa, Zimbabwe...there could be more, but these are the ones whose children have found their way across my path in New Zealand. Ones who are on their way to becoming 'black kiwis.' in a land where the only real kiwis are brown or spotted. There is something quite arresting about a lanky young Somali speaking English with a Kiwi accent.

❧❧

Who am I? Prodigal daughter of Africa? Often mistaken for an African, even by Africans. "Are you Ethiopian?" "Maybe Libyan?" "Egyptian?" "South African? (Coloured, of course.)" "No, I'm from Fiji, but my mother is African American. Does that count?"

❧❧

My husband's Tokelauan-Samoan-Irish-New Zealand nephew wants to know if I am from Africa. I say, "Well, I guess, yes. I am African American." My grandmother from Washington, DC would beg to differ. "We are not African. We are African American."

❦

As early as 1822, African Americans had been moving "back to Africa." Liberia was founded then as a colony for freed American slaves. Just under 100 years later, Marcus Garvey launched his Black Star Line—the first international shipping company owned and operated by Blacks. The Black Star Line ran a trans-Atlantic trade route from Africa to the Caribbean and the USA's eastern seaboard states. Black Star vessels also took passengers back to Africa, until the state and other enemies of Garvey, African liberation and black separatism engineered the company's demise in 1922. Somewhere in between the founding of Liberia and the floundering of the Black Star Line, my great-great-grandparents decided they would join a "back to Africa" movement. A story is told in our family of the family (two parents, three sons) packing up all their belongings in Guthrie, Oklahoma and catching the train (a couple or more days' travel) to New York City. I imagine my great-great-grandparents, great-grand-uncles and great-grandfather all starched, pressed and brylcreamed, brimming with excitement. But in that time between the founding of Liberia and the floundering of Black Stars, my family's dreams were dashed on the docks of New York City. The ship had left without them. There would be no refunds. The return to Oklahoma must have been darker than the *Trail of Tears* for my great-great-grandmother. She was not even African! And yet she had agreed to move her family to Africa. For a better life? Guthrie, Oklahoma is located in the Red River Valley. Just under 100 years later, the eldest great-granddaughter of a boy who did not get to go to Africa, would learn to sing in Fiji:

> Come and sit by my side if you love me
> Do not hasten to bid me adieu
> But remember the Red River Valley
> And the one who has loved you so true
> As you go to your home by the ocean
> May you never forget those sweet hours
> That we spent in the Red River Valley
> And the love we exchanged mid the flowers...

🐉🐉

Black is the colour of solidarity. Some of us wear it on our skins; others of us speak it with our tongues. Maori once were black. Pacific Islanders too. Some time between the eighties and the nineties, they started calling themselves brown, severing the chord—political, if not umbilical—declaring their independence from this particular struggle. Declaring their independence from blackness. Declaring their independence from Africa. Maybe that is a good thing.

🐉🐉

There is an "I am African" advertisement campaign. Spin-off from Live 8, Make Poverty History, etc, etc. The ads feature quintessentially white celebrities (Gwyneth Paltrow, Richard Gere, David Bowie, Liz Hurley, Liv Tyler, Sarah Jessica Parker, Elijah Wood), a few celebrities of colour (Imam, Lucy Liu, Alicia Keys, Lenny Kravitz, Tyson Beckford), and even an interracial couple (Heidi Klum and Seal). Tribal markings painted over their black and white portraits, the ads exhort viewers, consumers, to help buy drugs for AIDS-ridden Africa:

> Each and every one of us contains DNA that can be traced back to our African ancestors. These amazing people traveled far and wide. Now they need our help.

The ads appear in magazines like GQ, Fashion Rocks, and other venues far, far away from the homeland.

🐉🐉

The 'Fro': symbol of Afrocentricity, big in the 1960s and 70s and enjoying a revival in the double 'O's.' But find me the place in Africa where the 'Fro' is indigenous. Where people wear their hair like a halo, in all its kinky unbraided, untwisted, uncurled, unbeaded, unscarfed, unshaven glory. Stars of the Black Power movement in America share with me a secret: the 'Fro' came from Fiji. Someone saw a picture of a man in National Geographic, his hair worn proudly as the *bui ni ga*. That someone said, "That brother looks cool," and a new icon was born. They say the 'Fro' came from Fiji: far away from the homeland.

🐉🐉

The Fijians repeat a legend that says their ancestors came from Africa. Lutunasobasoba, sailed from a land called Taga ni Ika (Tanganyika?), so they say, but academics assert this cannot be true. It was a myth introduced by missionaries whose thinking was clouded by the discourse of racial phenotypes. The similarities between Fijians and Africans, academics say, are otherwise really superficial. The Fijians repeat their legend anyway.

❦❦

Other academics elsewhere (mainly in Canberra, Australia), less interested in myths of historical connection, suggest that in fact there are significant similarities between the (Black) Islands of the Pacific (aka Melanesia) and the (Black) Nations of Africa in the present day: coups, conflicts, crises, corruption... The 'Africanization of the Pacific,' is a serious, un-ironic, unapologetic, discourse. Africanization, of course, is a bad thing.

❦❦

Let me tell you a different story of Africanization. Let me tell you a story of secondary school children in many Pacific Island nations studying Chinua Achebe's novel *A Man of the People* for their university entrance exams. Let me tell you a story of Papua Pocket Poets and the visual artists of Papua New Guinea being inspired by a German who exposed them to Nigerian poetry and painting. Let me tell you a story of one Samoan and one Hawaiian who have befriended and promoted the ideas and books of their Kenyan friend, Ngugi Wa Thiongo. Let me tell you a story of a young woman deejay in Fiji who filled her graveyard shift with the sounds of Johnny Clegg and Savuka. Let me tell you the story of a high chief of Fiji who ordered that the choir at his wedding sing a South African hymn. Let me tell you how popular the South African reggae star, Lucky Dube was in Fiji, Vanuatu, and the Solomon Islands. This is a different type of Africanization, of course. This Africanization is political and poetic. It is liberating and empowering. This Africanization does not register on the indices or matrices of analysts in Canberra: for them Africanization can never be a good thing.

❦❦

Will Africa recognize all her children? Will the smells of the Pacific make sense to her? Will an accent from Aotearoa be understood by her? Or will she rank us all according to the distances of not just space, but time spent away from her? Pity those of us who have known her only as an idea.

❦❦

And so I grew up in Fiji. Could my ancestors have ever dreamed of a place so far, far away from their homeland? I did not know how Fiji had been preparing me for a return to my roots until, while visiting family in Washington DC in 2001, a friend invited me to dinner at Bukom, a West African Restaurant in the Adams Morgan district. The motto at Bukom is "Savor the flavor of West Africa." I can't remember what I ordered, but I remember wanting to taste fufu. I think I may have ordered the Komi Ke Kenan (I don't have a photographic memory, I have just called up the menu on the internet!) because the fire that was lit on my tongue almost gave me a fever. But thanks to Fiji, being raised on Indo-Fijian curries and learning to eat almost all my hot meals with a side of chillies, I survived that dinner at Bukom. For Fiji introduced me to an Indian Diaspora and that Indian Diaspora has prepared me for a variety of reunions within the Africa Diaspora.

❧

An Indo-Fijian taxi driver in Wellington warns me not to be too quick to ask every Indian driver I come across if he's from Fiji. "Why?" I ask. "They don't like being mistaken for Fiji Indians," he says. "Especially the ones from Africa."

❧

Welcome to Little Africa. The blackest corridor of central Wellington: *Hair Afrik*, at the top of Pigeon Park; *Kwanzaa*, the African gift shop, diagonally across; and possibly the longest single line of back to back African immigrant driven taxis. On weeknights—Tuesdays, Wednesdays— around 9 and 10pm, check out *Nando's* restaurant where Somali and Ethiopian men gather for spicy chicken after soccer. At times this particular stretch of Wellington reminds me of 1980s Adams Morgan, Washington, DC!

❧

I learned most of what I know about Africa in Washington, DC, because my best friend at university was Ethiopian. Daughter of a former General in Haile Selassie's army, who had been held as a political prisoner for ten years, released by Mengistu in an amnesty, accepted by the USA for political asylum. My friend taught me a lot about loss and recovery, about once having had privilege and then having none. She had gone from pampered princess to Goodwill shopper and survived. In 1987, while we were at university, Fiji's first Labour government was ousted in a military coup. My friend was uncomfortable with

21

my Marxist analysis of the coup. I was unappreciative of her particular sensitivities. But our bond transcended politics. It was unexpectedly cultural. It was not my African American blood, but my Fiji culture that linked me to my African friend:

1. We had both grown up listening to the Caribbean disco music of Boney M. (Enough said.)
2. My people ate raw fish, her people ate raw meat. I made the transition from kokoda to kitfo with relish!
3. Most Americans—and most disappointingly—many African Americans considered us exotic exports from primitive lands. We both routinely got asked by small-talking strangers if our families lived in mud huts.

As a result of our shared strangeness in America, I felt closer to Africa. As far as I was concerned, Ethiopia could have been home. I listened to Aster Aweke albums. Wrote a research paper on the political history of Ethiopia. Ate regularly at a restaurant named Meskerem. Learned how to say "Ameseginalhu."

༅

I censor myself in Wellington taxis. Wanting to make connections (like saying, "My best friend at university was from Ethiopia")—but then stopping myself, thinking, "Maybe the driver is Eritrean, not Ethiopian, and then what would he think of me?" Most of the Amharic phrases my girlfriend taught me were for conversations among females...I never learned the words for addressing males...and I've forgotten how to say thank you. The taxi driver, with the name like an archangel, reads my mind and tells me "Ameseginalhu."

༅

Kinship is insufficient. It cannot compete with charity. World Vision brings others closer to Africa than you: a dollar a day saving someone's life, rock concerts promoting the belief that we can reduce Third World debt by increasing First World consumption.

༅

Celebrity consciences become clichés of themselves. Brad and Angelina shut down Namibia so that their daughter could be born in privacy. Malawi is landlocked but news of Madonna's suspect adoption of a boy there flows to the Pacific on media waves that know no boundaries. Celebrity colonialism is courted by countries so poorly led that sovereignty is simply another commodity.

❦

Who doesn't want to reach out and touch Africa these days? But how do we like it when Africa reaches out to touch us? More precisely our bank accounts? Via email? Welcome to the age of SPAM from Africa: where widows of statesmen and their doctors and lawyers tantalize us plebes on cyberspace with promises of wealth beyond our wildest imaginations: all we have to do is send them our bank account details. Who wants to reach out and be touched by Africa in this way?

❦

Once were Third World? Our survival in the First World seems simply selfish. If we cannot raise funds then we must raise consciousness. Wellington newspapers and national television reports: Yilma Tafere Tasew, Ethiopian survivor of Kenyan refugee camps refuses to celebrate World Refugee Day by performing his ethnicity. Believes instead he must perform his politics.

❦

Somali schoolgirls scheduled to feature in a program of folk dances, fail to appear. Death in the family, back in Somalia. Send only their musical instruments to the concert at Te Papa. Their feet and hearts are elsewhere.

❦

African youth draw fire from skinheads for their dress and confidence: too American too Black, not Kiwi enough, not Kiwi enough.

❦

Winter on Courtenay place and Somali women Kiwi-up their dress. Long veils and long skirts, punctuated by fake fur-lined hooded jackets. Look warm.

❦

Africans in the New World don't expect shoppers to see them or smile.

❦

Ethiopian woman has tattoos on her face. Walks through Farmers. Looks hard.

❦❦

Kenyan boy spoke no English. Within a month spoke Kiwi well. Ka pai!

❦❦

The Pacific is not that far away from Africa. We are technically only separated by one ocean...on either side. To our left, across the Indian Ocean: linguists tell us we even have Austronesian cousins in Madagascar! Somalia, Kenya, Tanzania, Malawi, Mozambique, South Africa, just an ocean away. To our right, the Atlantic: so we get to see South Africa from two angles, Namibia, Angola, Zaire has a small Atlantic coast, Congo, Gabon, Cameroon, Nigeria, Benin, Togo, Ghana, Cote d'Ivoire, Liberia, Sierra Leone, Guinea, Guinea-Bissau, Gambia, Senegal, the Cape Verde Islands. Distance is such a relative concept. Africa is not that far away.

Chapter 3

AFRICAN CHILDREN AND THEIR FAMILIES IN NEW ZEALAND

Kathy Jackson

New Zealand accepts variable numbers of immigrants from countries around the world each year, a few of whom are Africans. Within the total is a relatively fixed number of refugees, about 750 each year, some of whom are also Africans. However, as Rousseau and Drapeau (2004) have pointed out, a high percentage of people who emigrate from countries where there is repression, social disruption and war have experienced traumatic events. Thus, we cannot assume that Africans who arrive in New Zealand as refugees are the only ones who have been traumatised in their home country, some who arrive as immigrants may also have been.

The initial selection and resettlement processes differ for African immigrants and refugees. Like other immigrants, Africans who want to immigrate to New Zealand must meet pre-set criteria. Although these criteria change from time to time according to government policy the general expectation is that immigrants will have skills needed for New Zealand's economic well-being. They are expected to be financially independent from the time of arrival and cannot access the unemployment benefit or other benefits until they have lived in New Zealand for at least 1 year and often more.

Refugees come because New Zealand governments want to meet their humanitarian and treaty obligations in a suffering world. Over the past 20 years New Zealand has accepted groups of African refugees from countries such as the Democratic Republic of Congo, Ethiopia, Eritrea, Somalia, Sudan, Rwanda and Burundi. Very small numbers have also come from other countries, including Algeria, Liberia, Nigeria, Kenya and Tanzania. Some of these have arrived as asylum seekers and have been accorded refugee status once in the country. Although many African refugees have come from traditional village societies, where about 80% of Africans still live, not all of them have come from this setting. Refugees come from all walks of life and some from African countries, like others from the Middle East and elsewhere, are well-educated and have held important positions in their home country.

Because many New Zealanders do not know how refugee status is determined or how refugees are chosen to resettle in this country, it is important to clarify these issues. A refugee is a person who is living outside his or her country and who cannot return there because of a well-founded fear of persecution (UNHCR, 1996). Refugees who are selected for resettlement in New Zealand come from refugee camps run by the UNHCR, and have been identified by UN staff as meeting this criterion. New Zealand Immigration Service staff travel to the camps, interview possible candidates for resettlement themselves, and recommend certain families and individuals for acceptance here. One of the aims of the selection process is to build up communities of refugees from the same ethnic group, so that families are not isolated from people like themselves.

This chapter outlines some African beliefs and values that are different from those of most New Zealanders and discusses a few of the difficulties and challenges faced by Africans in New Zealand because of these differences. Because a significant proportion of Africans who come to New Zealand arrive as refugees it also outlines some of the special difficulties they experience and describes some of the services provided to help them during the resettlement process. Much of what is included also relates to immigrants and refugees from other parts of the world, but material relating specifically to Africans is reported as far as possible.

AFRICAN REFUGEES: SPECIAL ISSUES

As immigrants, refugees face the same challenges and difficulties as other immigrants, but because of their history, typically have some additional challenges to overcome. Irrespective of their country of origin, refugees who are not well educated, widows or women alone or with children only are known to find the resettlement process more difficult than better educated people or those who have the support of a spouse. Young people who arrive during adolescence are another group for whom resettlement has been repeatedly shown to have poorer outcomes (Abbott, 1997: J R McKenzie Trust, 2004).

REFUGEES' INITIAL RESETTLEMENT

Refugees arrive in New Zealand in groups of around 150 and spend 6 weeks at the Mangere Refugee Resettlement Centre. During the first few days they undergo complete health checks. Besides checks for infection, this screening includes assessment of some genetically determined disorders like sickle cell anaemia and thalassaemia which are more common in African peoples than in some other ethnic groups.

Once health checks are completed all refugees attend the pre-school or school to learn English, from beginner level to more advanced depending on previous knowledge of the language. The school is run by the Auckland University of Technology.

Psychologists at the Auckland Refugees as Survivors Centre (RAS) undertake individual and group assessments of adults and children to determine their mental health status and needs, and provide some initial treatment. Part-time psychiatrists assess and treat the few refugees with more severe disorders. A part-time nurse has recently been appointed to oversee medications and participate in health education.

Psychologists at the agency work with interpreters to ensure a quality assessment is made. At present these include people who speak Somali, Kirundi, Kinyarwanda, Arabic, French, Swahili, Amharic, Tigrean, and Dinka. In most instances female interpreters are provided to work with women clients, who also see a female therapist, however this is not always possible.

In addition RAS has a team of community facilitators from various ethnic groups who also work in a support and educational role with the refugees. Staff in this team teach refugees about health services and healthy eating, the impact of smoking on family health, and other health related topics. Again, some of this team are Africans. Because research shows that immigrant and refugee mental health is improved if individuals gain employment and integrate into the wider society, the community team also provides optional instruction in the NZ Road Code (so that at least one member of each family may leave the centre with a Learner licence). Soccer training and soccer games for the men will begin soon. In addition to her clinical role, a body therapist runs a dance group for women.

While at MRRC, refugees are also interviewed by social work staff from Refugee and Migrant Services to determine possible issues and difficulties specific to each family. At the end of the six-week period at the centre African and other refugees are resettled in the community where they have continued support from the Refugee and Migrant Service for a period of at least 6 months. Trained volunteers work with each family to help them learn how to cope with the demands of New Zealand life (e.g., using buses, going shopping, taking children to the park). These volunteers are themselves supported by experienced social workers who provide supervision and work with any families who are experiencing greater than usual difficulty in adjustment.

Finally, housing and finance are arranged. Housing New Zealand (HNZC) works with families to find homes for them typically in public housing, again with an emphasis on placing people from the same ethnic group in the same community as far as possible. Thus, for example, there is a significant community of resettled Somalis in Auckland, another in Hamilton and a third in Christchurch. Families from Sudan have resettled in Auckland and Wellington. Families do not have a choice of housing and must accept what they are offered if they wish to access public housing. A few are offered private sector rentals but only if public housing is unsuitable or unavailable. Work and Income New Zealand interview families and arrange for them to receive the same levels of financial support as other New Zealand families in adverse situations receive.

THE REFUGEE EXPERIENCE

Refugee children and their families around the world have similar experiences before and during flight to safety. Before flight there is often increasing insecurity and fear. People know that they are being watched, that their behaviours are being reported on to others, Sometimes they lack food, not just because of drought, but because corrupt governments ensure that food aid only reaches people of their own majority ethnic group. In Africa health services to minority groups may also have been markedly poorer than those available to more powerful groups in the community (UNDP, 2000).

Before and during flight, Africans have witnessed the death of loved ones, gone without food, water and shelter, and may have been beaten, whipped or shot. Permanent head and bodily injury, loss of sight and hearing from these kinds of assaults may occur. People who have been imprisoned may have been locked in tiny spaces, deprived of sleep, tortured with various implements, experienced mock drowning and other similar trauma. Sexual assault of men and women, boys and girls is common, and very young children may have witnessed the gang rape of their mother (Naslund, 1997).

Despite these kinds of experiences African refugees are a resilient group who have been creative in their problem-solving in order to survive (Pavlish, 2005) and this psychological strength needs to be valued as they resettle. Africans in New Zealand have solved many problems and may only need help to obtain the resources that will let them solve the problems they face in this country. Alternatively, some of the approaches and strategies that have served them well during their time in refugee camps may no longer be useful during resettlement, for example, being really pushy in order to obtain resources has been a valuable survival technique but it is not well tolerated by the bureaucracies that refugees have to deal with once they arrive in this country. Similarly, solving problems on a day-to-day basis without having long-term goals is an appropriate way of coping with life when there is no security, but can limit one's options once security has been attained. Experience at Auckland Refugees as Survivors has shown that interactive group work discussing these matters can be beneficial.

CORE CULTURAL VALUES OF AFRICANS

Regardless of whether Africans arrive as immigrants or as part of the annual quota of refugees they are similar in many ways. In general terms, their cultures can be described as collective and masculine, with some differences between different ethnic groups in the extent to which they are also uncertainty avoidant and/or have high power distance (Jackson & Abosi, 2006). The terms used here come from a framework for describing preferred patterns of interaction between members of a culture which was developed by Geert Hofstede in 1980 and has led to a great deal of subsequent confirmatory research in countries around the world.

At first glance, the idea that African cultures are so similar as to meet the criteria for Hofstede's model seems surprising. But, although there are a vast number of African cultures, some core cultural values and beliefs are widespread. Often the difference between one ethnic group and the next relates more to the way core values express themselves behaviourally than to difference in the values themselves. Much of the research into the core beliefs of Africans was done in the 1980's and early 1990's but culture changes slowly and we can still conclude that "An African is not American or European or Asian and cannot be. An African is unique in every aspect of his or her life...." (Jackson & Abosi, 2006, p.3) and should be understood in this way.

HOW ARE CORE VALUES EXPRESSED?

1. Collectivism

In collective cultures individuals learn to take account of the needs of the group when interacting with others and making decisions about their own lives. African children are actively taught to think and behave in this way from an early age. Their group typically includes not just the nuclear family but also the wider kinship network and at the widest range includes other members of the same tribe and family connections through marriage to members of other tribes. Children typically spend all their time with members of this group (Jackson & Abosi, 2006). In general, members of collective cultures are uncertain about interacting with members of other groups and suspicious of their motivations (Hofstede, 1980).

In these cultures there is an emphasis on maintaining the group, which requires that confrontation is avoided and emotions, especially negative emotions, are controlled. Training in moderation of emotional expression begins very early, during the first year of life (e.g., Dixon, Tronick, Keefer, & Brazelton, 1981). Conflict is avoided through indirect communication when there is disagreement. One of the ways in which conflict is avoided is by not raising any one child above others. This means that individual praise is rarely, if ever, given. In this way, the envy of individual success that leads to curses and accusations of witchcraft can be avoided (Nsamenang, 1992).

2. *Masculinity*

This term relates to the extent to which male roles (and hence, by exclusion, female roles) are clearly defined. In traditional African cultures what men do and don't do is defined in this way. For example, men in many traditional communities dig over the ground when new land is being broken in, but they do not do planting or weeding. Men do not carry water. Boys and men look after the domestic animals. This separation of roles is associated with separation of activities from an early age. Once they are past the age of about 6 or 7 boys spend increasing amounts of time in male company only and girls and women also spend much time together (Barley, 1986,1994; Mackey, 1981; Mazrui, 1986).

3. *Power distance*

This concept refers to the gap in status between a high status member of any group and an individual of lower status. Many, but not all, African cultures are very hierarchical, with status differences valued by both the more high status member of any interaction and by the person with lower status (Jackson & Abosi, 2006).

Status increases with age and occupation. Within families this has the effect of making participants in a conversation unequal. Parents typically give instructions to their children, and children follow these instructions without comment (Dixon et al., 1986). Teachers are accorded high status, irrespective of whether they are competent at their work or not. Parents typically believe that there is nothing they can tell the teacher about their child that will help the child at school (Hofstede, 1986). In NZ this may be one of the factors that contribute to an African parent's decision not to attend parent-teacher meetings.

4. *Uncertainty avoidance*

This Refers to the extent to which individuals can cope with situations that are ambiguous or unclear. This is another area where cultures varied from each other. In societies where people have been farmers for many generations there is likely to be less tolerance for ambiguity. Children of farmers learn that they need to follow the seasons if they are to have enough food, rather than deciding to take the risk of planting or harvesting at some unusual time and children, from much of Africa, have this heritage. But in cattle-herding cultures people need to be able to cope with the unexpected or ambiguous, such as the appearance of a predator, in order to keep the animals safe. Cultures where there has been a long nomadic history or valuing of the warrior tradition (e.g., Somalia) also need to be able to cope with situations whose outcome is unclear. This culturally based experience with uncertainty may facilitate or hinder adaptation to the changed situation of life in New Zealand.

5. *Spiritual values*

An additional feature of culture that seems to be important for Africans generally relates to the centrality of personal spiritual values (Schwartz, 1994). Africans may be Christians, Moslems or animists and Africans with all of these beliefs have settled in New Zealand. In many African countries there is a long history of conflict between Christians and Moslems. These differences may influence behaviours of Africans who resettle in New Zealand.

Christianity and Islam both arrived in North Africa very early. Over the centuries some non-Christian and non-Islamic beliefs have become attached to the core beliefs of the faith. For example, many Moslems believe that female genital mutilation is required by Islam but, in fact, the practice is a pre-Islamic one. Both the older form of Christianity, practised in Ethiopia, other North African cultures and Islam require periods of fasting. What is meant by the term 'to fast' differs from one group to another with the prolonged fast during the Islamic period of Ramadan putting the greatest demands on believers.

Some more general features of culture besides those identified by Hofstede have long been known to be important for Africans. Some of these are outlined below.

6. *Gender hierarchy and family life*

In African societies, men have much higher status than women and are the decision makers when any matter of public importance arises. Men have the right to hit their wives, although, as in many other cultures, there are sanctions if beatings are more severe than the limits defined within the culture. Children belong to the father's family in much of Africa, although in matriarchal cultures of West Africa they may belong to the mother's family. If the parents divorce or one dies these beliefs can determine who has subsequent responsibility for the children and who inherits the land and other goods. In most of Africa inheritance is through the male line. This increased during the colonial period in some areas because of British beliefs about inheritance rights and the status of women in the West at that time. Some African women consequently have fewer rights today than their forebears did prior to the colonial period (Boulding, 1992; Okeyo, 1980).

7. Marriage and child-bearing

For Africans, marriage is important, and involves the creation of a relationship between families, not just the two individuals concerned. Dowry, paid by the man to his wife's family, cements this relationship. Because the whole family is committed to this new relationship parents of the young couple have a lot invested in helping them to stay together, thereby reducing the risk of divorce.

Because of social change and the many stresses of poverty and war, increasing numbers of women raise their children alone. Some may never have married others may be widowed or have had a husband who has worked away from home for long periods to earn money for the family.

Continuation of the lineage is important and in many cultures a person is not considered to be truly adult until he or she has become a parent. Thus, child-bearing is important and many young women have their first child while still in their teens. Large families are valued as protection of the lineage, since there are many reasons why any one newborn may not actually reach adulthood (Jackson & Abosi, 2006).

8. Adulthood

As in other cultures, the age at which a person becomes an adult is an important staging post in life. Traditional African rites celebrating girls' first menstruation and boys' first wet dream acknowledge that the young person is entering the adult world. Thus, there may be a conflict between traditional ideas about maturity and the western pattern where post-pubertal adolescents are still studying and are treated, in some ways at least, as children.

9. Ideas about tradition and modernity

When people have not had much schooling and have continued to live as their ancestors did for many generations, traditional ways of doing things are important (LeVine et al., 1996; Nsamenang, 1992). But all Africans have been influenced by modernity to some degree. This can create conflict for them; educated Africans may have given up many traditional ways of behaving but may find that they cannot, or do not want to, give up other values, such as responsibility for the well-being of their kinship group. Similarly, an individual may be very 'modern' in his or her understandings about their particular area of expertise but retain much more traditional ideas about other matters that they haven't had to think about very deeply.

10. Ideas about time

In traditional African cultures people believe that there is existence before life and after death as in Maori culture. Ancestors influence the living and should be treated with respect. Failure to meet obligations to ancestors can annoy them, so that they interfere in harmful ways in the experiences of the living (Barley, 1986, 1994; Taylor, 1992).

Socially, clock time is less important for many Africans than it is for majority culture New Zealanders. For example, an Ethiopian colleague of the present author has said that if she invites a mixed group of people to her home, she will ask Africans to come about 2 hours earlier than New Zealanders, then both groups arrive at about the same time. She has also noted that obligations to the person she is with outweigh other obligations. Thus, if she is going to an appointment and someone arrives at her home just as she is ready to depart, she cannot just say "Hello" and explain about her need to rush away. Culturally, she must invite the person into her home, offer tea and food and spend time talking with her visitor. Only when the visitor notices that she is dressed neatly and was probably going out can she mention her appointment but she is expected to say that what she was going to do was not important and can wait. This cultural difference can create problems for newly arrived Africans, although if the New Zealand way of doing things is explained to them, they accommodate it as much as possible.

11. Intelligence, learning and schooling for boys and girls

Traditional African beliefs about intelligence focus on what have been called the "socio-affective" aspects of intelligence (Kagitcibasi,

1992).This refers to the child's skills in dealing with the social and emotional demands of village life. A child who is obedient, reliable and cooperative is considered to be an intelligent child (Berry, 1984). Today, parents may be aware of the difference between a child who is 'intelligent at school' and one who is 'intelligent at home'. School intelligence is not valued in African villages unless the child is able to use that intelligence to promote the well-being of the broader family and group (Dasen, 1984).

Traditionally in most cultures children were expected to learn important skills without direct teaching and this still happens today. Children learn by observation and practice within the peer group setting. In addition, they learn about the behaviours expected of them as adults by some direct teaching around the period of puberty. Much of this direct teaching relates to behaviour around sexuality, but some also learn specific trades, such as metal-working, during this period.

Parents and teachers typically believe that girls are less intelligent than boys and the children themselves agree (Davison & Kanyuka, 1992; Davison, 1993). Despite intensive efforts in some countries to change this attitude, male teachers continue to act on the belief that girls are stupid especially once girls reach puberty. As a consequence of this and other beliefs, girls are far less likely to be sent to school than boys. Girls are also less likely to continue with education once they reach puberty because of parents' fears that they will become over-educated and therefore unmarriageable and fears about the risk of sexual assault. Girls in village schools in Africa generally do more chores than boys, both at school and after school. This means that they may be out of class more often than boys with reduced opportunities to learn and that they also have less time for homework.

12. Praise and punishment of children

Less educated Africans see physical punishment as a valuable aid in child-rearing (Kilbride & Kilbride, 1990; Nsamenang, 1992; Zeitlin, 1996). But ideas about praise and punishment of individual children may differ from one ethnic group to another. University students in Botswana, for example, reported high frequencies of physical punishment, whereas hitting children was much less acceptable in Malawi.

In traditional communities all children are the responsibility of all adults, so that children may be reprimanded or punished by any adult for culturally unacceptable behaviour or for lack of respect towards adults. Many teachers still believe in the use of corporal punishment even although it is banned in most African countries. Some teachers 'get around' the requirement not to use the strap or cane by pinching, hair-pulling and other forms of physical punishment (Jackson & Abosi, 2006).

13. Ideas about health and mental health

Unless they have been well-educated and have lived in a major town or city, Africans generally have very limited access to health services and rely on treatments available from the traditional healer or shaman. These treatments generally involve the use of herbal and other plant extracts, some of which have a beneficial effect although others may not be effective in real terms. Africans attribute some ill-health to natural causes but may believe that other problems have been caused by witchcraft, magic or curses (Jackson, 2006).

As is well known, many children die before the age of 5 years from preventable diseases. A large number of the Africans who come to New Zealand have probably experienced the death of at least one child and perhaps more than one. Some surviving children may have long-term health problems as a result of accidents, or untreated eye and/or ear infections.

Like many other refugees, Africans have had even less access to psychological services in their home country than they have had for physical health (Koinange, 2004). They typically describe the psychological distress in terms of physical indicators. They may complain of general malaise, aches and pains, a bad back, sore stomach and so on. They respond well to body therapy, which includes massage and a range of other complementary body treatments. Many African women enjoy attending regular dance groups. African beliefs about the nature and causes of their psychological distress differ from those of Western medicine. For example, a person suffering with physical health problems, stress and distress may have their ailments attributed to witchcraft, curses or spirits. Preferred treatments may include the use of herbs, prayer, reading the Bible or the Qur'an (Jackson, 2006).

WHAT DO THESE AFRICAN CULTURAL VALUES MEAN FOR AFRICANS IN NEW ZEALAND AND FOR OTHER NEW ZEALANDERS?

Clearly, the expectations held by African adults about 'correct' behaviour differ from the expectations of the majority of New Zealanders. New Zealand pakeha children are raised as individualists, which means that they are taught to make decisions independently of the needs of other people and to take care of their own needs. In general they do not have obligations to relatives outside their nuclear family. They belong to many different groups and therefore have experience in entering and leaving groups and dealing with people with different interests and priorities to their own. The child 'belongs' to his or her nuclear family and parents protect their child from other adults who might chastise them.

Besides being individualists pakeha New Zealanders are egalitarian, so do not value differences in status. They show moderate levels of flexibility about the roles of men and women, and also tolerate uncertainty reasonably well. But there is quite a lot of similarity between the values of Africans and those of New Zealand Maori people and Pacific Islanders. The emphasis on family (whanau), the hierarchical nature of the cultures and the definition of roles for men and women are similar. The emphasis, since 1988, on recognition and valuing of Maori culture can help New Zealand pakeha to understand and accommodate to features of African culture and behaviour.

Difficulties can arise within immigrant families, including African families, when members of the family acculturate to New Zealand ways of doing things at different rates. An African mother who is at home with young children may not have much contact with non-African New Zealanders and may continue to adhere strongly to values and behaviours from her country of origin. Her husband, who is at work or studying with other New Zealanders may find his values and behaviours changing. An African teenager who is trying to fit in with his or her peer group may change even more rapidly and come into conflict with one or both parents about their expectations for appropriate behaviour.

Some of the challenges faced by Africans in New Zealand relate partly to the current age of the child, partly to the age at which each individual has arrived, partly to on-going family beliefs, values and patterns of interaction and partly to the reaction of other New Zealanders to their presence in our community. The remainder of this section of the chapter describes some of the challenges faced at differing ages although it cannot deal with all of the challenges. Again, some of the research cited here is rather old, due to the lack of more recent studies in this area.

Birth to age 5 years

Women from rural Africa and from war zones may not have had good access to information about pregnancy and child birth but research there shows that they are quick to take advantage of new information in this area (Gray, Baudouy, Martin, Bang & Cash 1990; Palmer, 1993). In some East African countries particularly, men were traditionally kept away from their newborn child for some days after the birth (Munroe & Munroe, 1992) and were not expected to attend their wife during labour. Women who have undergone extensive genital circumcision may need special medical procedures to prevent damage to the mother as she gives birth (Lightfoot-Klein, 1989). Traditional beliefs about abstaining from sexual relations with their partner, before and after the child's birth, may place strain on marital fidelity, although the traditional expectation that birth should be followed by a long period of sexual abstinence is weakening today. Most African women have not had good information about family planning.

Traditional ideas and ideas about modernity influence the African mother and her child from the moment of conception but because of the high value put on child-bearing African women are usually well-supported during pregnancy. Today, many African women associate bottle-feeding with modernity and prefer not to breast feed because it is seen as old-fashioned. More traditionally oriented women in some African ethnic groups may still not feed new-born children during the period when they are producing colostrum, which was traditionally considered to be harmful to the newborn (Konner, 1977). In some ethnic groups the introduction of solid foods is delayed until late in the first year with negative effects on children's growth (Palmer, 1993;

Zeitlin, 1996). These are clearly important educational issues which need to be sensitively addressed by health professionals in this country.

A common problem for pre-schoolers in many African countries is that ear infections remain untreated and about 1 in 20 children begin school with sufficient build up of wax in their ears to cause some hearing loss, with active ear infection or scarring from earlier infection (e.g., Hatcher et al., 1995; Minja & Machemba, 1996). This reflects the lack of health resources available to African families, who will take advantage of the better health services in this country. But in Africa sharing of medications and failure to complete a course of antibiotics once symptoms abate are both common. Parents may need education about this. Pre-school and primary school teachers especially should also be aware of the possibility that children born in Africa may be at risk of having some hearing loss and should discuss this with parents if necessary.

African children may experience discrimination based on skin colour from about the time they begin to attend pre-school. Research (e.g., Aboud, 1988; Brown, 1995, Hirschfeld, 1996) has repeatedly shown that, by about the age of 4 years, children have a well-established preference for spending time with others like themselves. Pre-school teachers and African parents need strategies to help their children deal with any discrimination that occurs.

The primary school years

The impact of African values on children's behaviour depends in part on the age at which they begin to interact with Kiwi children. Children who are born to African parents in New Zealand or arrive here early in their lives enculturate to both cultures. They learn that when they are in school or with Kiwi friends they can behave in certain ways and that when they are among other Africans they should behave in other ways. But even for these children some patterns of behaviour are so ingrained at an early age that it is difficult to learn a new behaviour. A typical example of this problem relates to eye contact. Belief in the harmful impact of prolonged eye gazes is common among people from North Africa and among peoples from the Horn of Africa. Adults should not look at a small child for too long. In this regard, African children resemble Maori children and teachers need to accept that lack of eye contact does not show lack of respect or attention; in fact, the opposite is true.

Traditionally, positive attention to the individual is also believed to be harmful to group well-being because it makes the child proud (Nsamenang, 1992). African parents often do not give the high levels of praise that are emphasised in Western parenting and teaching guidelines. For example, a university student in Botswana explained to the present author that he only found out that his father was very pleased with his school results in a very indirect way. His father told the father of another pupil, who then told his son, who reported back to the first boy. Positive attention that emphasises the success of the whole group is more acceptable and individual praise may feel uncomfortable for African children especially during the initial phase of resettlement.

Because they have learnt to spend all their time with a small group of others, African children who arrive in New Zealand during their primary school years may show an initial preference to behave in this way in schools here. The constant changing from working alongside one child for one activity and with another child for another activity may induce feelings of discomfort until children have settled and acculturated to some degree. Teachers may need to accommodate this preference for stability in work groups initially.

Some children of all ages will not have attended school at all before arriving in NZ. Thus, they arrive in their local school having had only 6 weeks of school experience and may need help to adjust to the routines of a New Zealand school day. Others will have attended schools where the practice has been based on traditional nineteenth century teaching, where there has been a shortage of qualified teachers, texts, desks, chairs and pencils. In such schools children have typically chanted responses as a large group (Chapman, et al., 1993; Fuller & Snyder, 1991). Basic skills such as doing pencil and paper tasks, answering hypothetical questions about events or possibilities outside their personal experience, and working independently while the teacher helps other children may all be very new.

The prejudice and preference for one's own group that begins during the pre-school years continues through the primary school years, peaks at around 8 years and drops away sometime during the two years at intermediate school, as children begin to develop the capacity to take others' perspectives along with their increasing skills in abstract thought (Aboud, 1988; Brown, 1995). This is not to say that African children will then no longer be a risk of race-based prejudice because a small number of children continue to hold prejudices and act in discriminatory ways throughout the teenage years and into adulthood. But it does mean that parents and teachers can draw on children's capacity to think more abstractly when trying to educate them about these behaviours.

Adolescence

Adolescence is a time when individuals are beginning to form an adult identity. Adolescents everywhere do this by becoming more involved with their peer group as they try new roles. Adolescent refugees also want to be like their peers and they may reject the values of their parents in order to gain acceptance. But language barriers may prevent these young Africans from being fully accepted into the New Zealand peer group so that, having given up their culture of origin, they cannot fully adopt New Zealand culture. Young people in this situation are referred to as marginalised. The implications of marginalisation for mental health are not good, this group of people is most likely to experience considerable psychological distress. Special efforts are needed if these young people are to be able to retain their culture of origin and take up useful aspects of NZ cultures. Developing English language competence may be a key factor here.

African boys who would have undergone initiation into adulthood around puberty in their home country may find it difficult to cope with being under the control of female teachers. In their home village such boys would not be answerable to women in day to day matters. Methods of solving interpersonal problems may also be unacceptable in New Zealand. For example, some African boys get into physical fights because this is the way they would have coped with challenges to their masculinity or rights in their village of origin. In Botswana, for example, it is considered better for a man to fight another man than to shout at him; shouting is a sign that one is completely out of control, indeed that one is quite mad.

African girls who are Moslems may find that their parents are unhappy about any interaction with boys. This is because the honour of a Moslem family is closely tied to the pre-marital chastity of their daughters. Teenage Moslem girls may be expected to live with restrictions that are not applied to their brothers or to the other adolescent girls in their school. Experience at RAS suggests that some parents demand to know everything about phone calls and text messages. For Moslem girls who have grown up in New Zealand this level of intrusion into privacy may seem excessive.

For adolescent Moslem boys there may be conflict with parents about alcohol use and sexual behaviour. Wearing ear rings or body studs may also cause conflict with parents because of religious requirements that the body be treated with respect.

Refugee parents will often say that they have chosen to resettle outside their own country in order to provide for the future of their children. This may result in undue pressure on adolescents to succeed academically. Village Africans may not know much about the wide range of study and career options available to young people in this country, so they may expect their children to study only for the narrow range of professions that they know—often medicine, accounting or law. In their home culture it is normal for parents to decide what career path children should follow but in NZ this can be a stressor for young people who have not been in this country long enough to have the English skills needed for such a course. Schools can play an important role here, helping families to learn more about the range of trades and other occupations open to adolescents with specific language and other competencies.

The Adult Years

Ideas about correct behaviour mean that African adult relationships differ from those of mainstream New Zealanders. The potential for misunderstanding, when members of collective and individualistic cultures meet, is normal. Pakeha New Zealanders may not understand the obligations that Africans have to others in their in-group. This includes responsibility for providing financial and other kinds of assistance to those in need. Africans here are culturally required to provide financial and any other assistance to kin who are still in their home country and often living in very poor conditions. This obligation exists even when the African in New Zealand is struggling to make ends meat. For example, one colleague of the present author has said that she did not feel she could ever refuse a request for money from her family in Africa until she had the support of her sister who came to live in New Zealand and learnt about the cost of living here.

Beliefs about the age at which one can learn new things may also hinder the resettlement of some Africans. People in many cultures believe that childhood and youth are the times for learning and that once one is an adult further learning will be very difficult.

Older African adults, usually grandmothers, sometimes come to NZ as caregivers of orphaned children and teenagers in refugee families. These women face particular difficulties in adjustment and can easily become socially isolated and unwell.

SPECIAL ISSUES FOR REFUGEE FAMILIES

1. Children in refugee families may be traumatised by their experiences.

During their flight from danger children have experienced a great deal of loss. In total, this represents a loss of childhood. They have not had the security or safety to which children are entitled, have missed play and schooling, have been exposed to the worst kinds of damaging behaviours on the part of adults and have often been hungry, thirsty and unwell. They may have come to physical harm as they ran from danger or they may have had to steal or prostitute themselves in order to survive (Kilbourn, 1995).

Even during flight parents try to protect their children from the worst events and commonly believe that they have managed to do so. However, children have typically witnessed a great deal more violence than parents believe. Sometimes children have been forced to choose which members of their family will live. If captured and imprisoned, they may have been subjected to the same tortures inflicted on adults.

The consequences of these experiences vary according to some characteristics of the children and their families. Very young children who do not have enough language to talk about their experiences and feelings so can only show their distress behaviourally. They may regress to earlier forms of behaviour, such as wetting themselves during the day or night even though they had previously established bladder control. Some soil themselves. They may become clingy and anxious, wanting to be in constant physical contact with their mother, whining and unsettled.

Primary school aged children may think that they should have been able to protect other members of the family, even though the situation did not allow them to do so. They may have anger or sadness about what happened and show a lot of aggressive play. Older adolescents have learnt about the worst of human behaviour at an early age. They are capable of understanding some of the events but often lack the information they need in order to think through what has happened to them. Shame and self-disgust for using sex or stealing to survive make them at risk of self-destructive behaviours, such as misuse of alcohol, sexual promiscuity or drug taking (Monahon, 1993, Jackson & Harrison).

Their reaction to traumatic events also reflects the child's personality and general way of coping. A child who is temperamentally more anxious may respond with anxiety, one who gets angry over small things may show increased anger. The parents' response to horrific stressors is also important to children's response. If parents are psychologically disorganised or deeply anxious as a result of their experiences their children will be more likely to show these responses as well.

2. Children in refugee families may have parents who are deeply traumatised.

A small percentage of African parents may not be able to parent optimally because they, themselves, are suffering from the long-term effects of trauma. Like their children, refugee adults have frequently experienced or witnessed acts of horrific violence, have lost all material goods, including irreplaceable items such as photographs, birth and marriage certificates, and may themselves have been tortured. Women who have been raped often cannot mention this because of cultural taboos and therefore they are unable to seek help for physical or psychological harm from this event. Some men have also been raped, an experience which has an extremely negative impact on their male identity.

These events may have triggered symptoms of post-traumatic stress disorder (PTSD), depression and/or anxiety. Parents who have post-traumatic stress may be emotionally very volatile and become extremely angry with minor provocation. Some become violent towards their wives and children. Recurring nightmares may leave them unable to sleep and constantly exhausted. Avoidance of places and events that remind them of trauma may mean that some cannot easily leave the safety of their home. Some avoid joining activities with others from their ethnic group, thus isolating themselves from an important potential source of social support. For others, common local events such as a car back-firing or crackers exploding on Guy Fawkes Night will trigger a re-experiencing of past events, which is so vivid that the individual acts as if the event is happening in present time. Emotional flatness, that is, a lack of normal emotional response, is another common symptom of PTSD. A person may describe the most horrible events without showing any emotional reaction to what he or she is talking about.

Men and women who have lived in villages where their ancestors lived for many generations may experience what has been called cultural bereavement. This develops when a person's sense of their own identity is closely tied to being in a specific place. Being torn away from that place reduces the individual's sense of themselves as a whole person. The term relates to the loss of dreams for the future, for present and future roles and status for themselves and their children. While it is clearly impossible to restore the old life, resettled refugees may gain status and social support within community groups which helps with this grief to some degree. Cultural bereavement is not the same as depression, although it is sometimes mistaken for it. Research from non-African cultures suggests that people who are mistakenly identified as being depressed may reject the medicalisation of their grief and sadness and refuse treatment for it (Dossa, 2002).

Adults (and children) whose relatives have died during flight may not have had time to complete burial rituals. As noted earlier in the chapter, the deceased have an important role in African cultures. Incomplete rituals may mean that the spirit of the dead person cannot move on to the next phase of his or her life and the living person may believe that the spirit of the dead is harming or restricting them. This unresolved and complicated grief can impede the adjustment of refugees to their new environment. Having Christian or Moslem faith does not preclude this belief (although religious leaders may not be happy about this), so that African refugees' mental and physical health may be improved if it is possible for them to complete rituals in some way (Jackson, 2006).

Sometimes parents try to protect their children by not talking about past experiences. But their secrets influence their behaviour and children become aware of gaps in the family history which leave them puzzled and feeling unsafe. In particular, it is impossible for most African women to deal with their reactions to rape because acknowledging rape may lead to desertion by their husband. Husband and wife relationships are likely to be harmed by such secrets and their children's' development is adversely affected where these and other secrets exist.

Children's lives are adversely affected when parents are still trying to resolve their own reactions to traumatic events, even if the children themselves have been born in New Zealand and have never experienced trauma first hand. A mother who is deeply depressed or has post-traumatic stress symptoms may not be able to provide the loving, secure environment that her child needs. A father may lash out at his children or regularly drink too much to avoid thinking of the past. In this situation we say that there has been cross-generational transmission of trauma.

3. Risk of re-traumatisation.

Finally, there is always the risk of re-traumatisation. Like immigrants from all over the world, African refugees maintain contacts with family members and friends in their home country. They closely monitor news about events there. Because civil war is often still ongoing in their country of origin they are constantly at risk of being re-traumatised if they learn that friends and family members back home have been bombed out of their home or have disappeared in suspicious circumstances. African communities in New Zealand are small, with the result that there is constant rumour and gossip about what is happening in their home country. This in itself adds to the stress experienced by some refugees.

4. Young people without any caregivers.

A minority of refugees who are still legally minors or who are very young adults arrive in New Zealand without the support of older family members. Such separation adds to existing trauma for these young people because they continue to need their family as a support while they establish adult identity (Rousseau, Mekki-Berada & Moreau, 2001). These isolated individuals are usually young men, in their teens, and they need considerable additional support and guidance if they are to make a satisfactory adjustment. However, differences between ethnic groups may occur. Children from nomadic families may be more used to separation from their family and rely more on their peer group for support. In resettlement countries this close association with the peer group may be seen as deviant (Rousseau, Said, Gagne & Bibeau, 1998).

PROVISION OF SERVICES TO AFRICANS
IN NEW ZEALAND

New Zealand is providing a number of services that help promote successful adjustment of African immigrants in this country. Most services, apart from schooling and basic health care, are provided by volunteers or non-government agencies, which means that there is a constant struggle for resources, especially finance. Many services, such as the various ethnic community support groups, have been set up by Africans themselves. Over time some of these groups may have split into smaller special interest groups. Splitting is often an indication of growing confidence in their ability to cope with New Zealand systems rather than a failure of the resettlement process, although it may be either. A group of Somali women in Auckland, for example, concluded that their interests were not being met entirely in the general Somali community group and have set up their own women's group.

ON-ARRIVAL PROVISIONS FOR REFUGEES

The initial resettlement programme offered at the MRRC is highly regarded by the UNHCR (Karen Read, personal communication, 2004). The range of services provided during the 6 weeks that newly arrived refugees are at the centre has already been briefly outlined. Information obtained during the provision of these services goes with the refugee family to their new home. This includes:

1. Education records

Records of language assessments and school achievement are given to each family to take with them when they leave the Centre, so that they can pass this information on to teachers in any school or educational facility they or their children might attend. It is worth noting that parents often do not remember to take these records with them when enrolling their children at school. Some also do not want their child to be identified as having a refugee background for fear of discrimination, despite being told that if their children are identified as refugees the school can obtain additional funding to support them.

47

2. Physical health records

Records relating to physical health screening, vaccinations and treatments while at Mangere go with each patient to be taken to the treating GP when the family resettles in the community. Again, it is unclear how often records are handed on to a GP.

3. Mental health records

A very brief summary outlining a refugee's contact with RAS is included with the general medical records. Because of the extent to which poor mental health is stigmatised in African communities (Jackson, 2006) detailed reports by psychologists, psychiatrists or the body therapy team are not routinely included. However, information is provided which would enable a health professional to contact the agency for further details if needed.

COMMUNITY BASED SERVICES FOR REFUGEES

Once refugees are resettled in the community the amount of support available to them varies from city to city and this is where the New Zealand programme for refugees needs improvement. People themselves form community support groups, which provide the basis for much social interaction within their own ethnic group, and other services are available on the same basis as they are available to all immigrants. This fails to recognise the special needs of some refugees.

1. Access to health services

Research around the world shows that the percentage of resettled refugees who experience poor mental health once they have moved to a new country reflects not only the extent of trauma they have experienced before arrival, but also the impact of events in the receiver country. Poor integration into the host community, lack of social supports within their own ethnic group, long periods of unemployment, lack of recognition of work experience and qualifications gained in their home country, limited acquisition of English all contribute to poor mental health after immigration. While various non-government agencies and tertiary institutions try to meet some of these needs they struggle constantly to get support from the broader community and from government funding agencies.

The quality of medical services and dental services that refugees can access vary from place to place. For refugees who are dependent on Work and Income New Zealand (WINZ) for income the cost of accessing these services, especially dentistry, means that they may not be able to get the level of health care they need. Similarly, lack of funds may make it difficult for parents to pay the club membership fees and provide the sports equipment children need for both their own physical well-being and for integration into the broader community. This is especially likely to be the case for refugee families who are supporting members of the extended family still living in war zones or refugee camps. Because refugee unemployment remains high for long periods, this may influence the development of some children.

Problems are experienced because of difficulties in communication and differences in religious practices and health understandings. The Code of Health and Disability Services Consumers' Rights (Health and Disability Commissioner, undated pamphlet), however, requires that New Zealand residents should be able to access services which "take into account [their] cultural, religious, social and ethnic needs, values and beliefs" and that these services should provide information in "a form, language and manner which [they] can understand". The services should provide "a competent interpreter if [they] need one" although this statement is weakened by the fact that this has only to be 'reasonably' practicable. Currently the need to provide an interpreter is not considered to be 'reasonably' practicable when patients visit their GP.

Specialist provision of mental health services for traumatised refugees is very limited. Unless a refugee meets the criteria for services from a Community Mental Health Centre (CMHC), he or she can only access services through their GP. Very few meet criteria for assistance from their local CMHC although they may be extremely disabled by a combination of symptoms of post-traumatic stress, depression and anxiety, which frequently co-occur. Because interpreters are not available at general practices this has meant that refugees may struggle with unresolved trauma issues in the longer term (Cheung, 1994; Liev, 1995). To date, there have not been any specific studies of Africans in New Zealand but there is no reason to expect that their need for specialist services will differ from the needs of other refugees.

In Auckland, the Refugees as Survivors Centre is currently not funded to provide ongoing counselling for African or other refugees in the community, so the role of psychologists is limited to an assessment of mental health. A transition counsellor follows up any refugees who have been identified as needing continuing support for poor mental health but is only able to check on whether the identified individual has been able to access community health services. The agency is currently seeking funding to expand psychological services into the greater Auckland community. The role of Wellington Refugees as Survivors differs from that of the Auckland RAS but again the level of service they can provide is insufficient to meet the mental health needs of refugees who have resettled there. Hamilton and other cities where there are refugee communities provide some services but each district health board makes its own decisions about the extent to which the special needs of refugees are acknowledged.

2. Access to education

Many African immigrants, like others, find it difficult to access education in English and in skills which might increase their chances of obtaining employment. The High fees of courses contributes to this difficulty.

Young adults who are keen to join the workforce often cannot do so because they lack the English needed for their special interest, such as English for the building trade. General English courses lack relevance to their personal goals so they are at risk of dropping out of study and becoming permanently marginalised.

African women with young children cannot easily access education. The outcome is that they become increasingly isolated from their children's learning because children learn many new concepts in English, some of which do not exist in their first language. They cannot translate some of these concepts for their mother because of their still developing first language skills.

3. Access to employment

Skilled professionals from African countries, as from other parts of the world, experience discrimination in the job market. Relevant skills and experience fail to counter the "lack of New Zealand experience" which is often given as a cause for rejection (J R McKenzie Trust, 2004; Tan, 2006). Even one's name serves as a barrier to employment. But this is not necessary. One supermarket in Auckland, whose manager recruits immigrant and resettled refugee staff finds that they make committed and careful employees and that staff turnover is low.

An example of what can be done comes from outside Africa. An Afghani colleague of the present author, who is a medical doctor and managed a district health system in his home country, has commented that all his friends, who were accepted as refugees to Sweden, are now working as doctors there. At first they worked there under close supervision and as their skills were recognised were gradually accepted as the professionals they are. Clearly, this approach could also apply to African doctors and other skilled refugees in this country if helpful systems were put in place.

OTHER FORMS OF DISCRIMINATION

Like other refugees, African families are sometimes actively discriminated against by neighbours in their street. On occasion, this has been so extreme as to result in the relocation of the African family to another address. Disadvantaged people who live in public housing may be generally angry and upset about their situation and, more specifically, upset when they know that family members are waiting for public housing and refugees "jump the queue" as they see it. Education about refugees and special efforts to encourage a greater understanding are needed.

CONCLUSION

Like other immigrants, people who come to New Zealand from Africa face many challenges and cope at least reasonably well with most of them. Well-educated Africans have the skills and attitudes that help them to make the adjustment to New Zealand society and to accommodate New Zealand values but New Zealanders still discriminate against them. Africans who are not well-educated and who have suffered traumatic experiences may not settle so well unless New Zealanders, in general, and government, in particular, help them to access the supports and services they need. In this way African immigrants, refugees and their families are just like other immigrants and indeed like other New Zealanders.

Although Africans may express their core values differently from the ways mainstream New Zealanders express their values, the values themselves are very much the same. Parents want health and safety for their children and themselves, access to education and employment and the social supports that enable them to solve problems and grow in confidence and well-being. New Zealand can afford to meet their needs and should continue to improve services to Africans and other refugees in order to build a truly multicultural society.

References

Abbott, M. (1997). Refugees and migrants. In P. M. Ellis & S C D Collings (Eds.). *Mental health in New Zealand from a public health perspective, (pp.250-264).* Wellington: Ministry of Health.

Barley, N. (1986). *A plague of caterpillars: Return to the African bush.* Harmondsworth, England: Viking.

Barley, N. (1994). *Smashing pots: Feats of clay from Africa.* London: British Museum Press.

Boulding, E. (1992). *The underside of history: A view of women through time.* (Rev. ed., Vol. 1). Newbury Park: Sage.

Cheung, P. (1994). Post-traumatic stress disorder among Cambodian refugees in New Zealand. *International Journal of Social Psychiatry, 40(1),* 17-26.

Dasen, P. R. (1984). The cross-cultural study of intelligence: Piaget and the Baoule. *International Journal of Psychology, 19,* 407-434.

Davison, J. (1993). School attainment and gender: Attitudes of Kenyan and Malawian parents toward educating girls. *International Journal of Educational Development, 13,* 331-338.

Davison, J., & Kanyuka, M. (1992). Girls' participation in basic education in southern Malawi. *Comparative Education Review, 36,* 446-466.

Dixon, Tronick, Keefer, & Brazelton, (1981).

Dossa, P. (2002). Narrative mediation of conventional and new "mental health" paradigms: Reading the stories of immigrant Iranian women.

Hatcher, J., Smith, A., McKenzie, I., Thompson, S., Bal, Il, macharia, I., Mugwe, P., Okoth-Olende,C., Oburra, H., Wanjohi, Z., Achola, N., Mirza, N., & hart, A. (1995). A prevalence study of ear problems in school children in Kiambu District, Kenya, May 1992. *International Journal of Pediatric Otorhinolaryngology, 3,* 197-205.

Health and Disability Commissioner Te Toihau Hauora, Hauatanga (undated pamphlet). *Your rights when receiving a health or disability service.* Available: www.hdc.org.nz

Hirschfeld, L. A. (1996). *Race in the making: Cognition, culture and the child's construction of human kinds.* Cambridge Mass: MIT Press.

Hofstede, G. (1980). *Culture's consequences: International differences in work-related values.* Beverly Hills, CA: Sage.

Jackson, K. (2006). *Fate, spirits and curses: Mental health and traditional beliefs in some refugee communities.* Auckland: Auckland Refugees as Survivors.

Jackson, K. & Abosi, O. (2006). *South of the desert: A teacher guide to child development in sub-Saharan Africa.* Pretoria: University of South Africa Press.

Jackson, K., & Harrison, L-.R. (2001) *Companion House Children's Program: A guide for counselor-advocates.* 46pp.

J. R. McKenzie Trust (2004). *The journey to work: Jobs for refugees.* Wellington, NZ.

Kagitcibasi, C. (1992). Research in child development, parenting and the family in a cross-cultural perspective. In M. R. Rosenzweig (Ed.).*International psychological science: Progress, problems and perspectives (pp. 137-160).* Washington: American Psychological Association.

Kilbourn, P. (1995). The impact of war on children: A kaleidoscope of experiences, emotions and traumas. In. P. Kilbourn (Ed.), *Healing the children of war: A handbook for ministry to children who have suffered deep traumas.* Monrovia, CA: MARC.

Kilbride, P. L., & Kilbride, J. E. (1990). *Changing family life in East Africa: Women and children at risk* (pp. 133-146). University Park, PA: Pennsylvania State University Press.

Koinange, J. W. (2004). Psychology in Kenya. In. M. J. Stevens & D. Wedding (Eds.) *Handbook of International Psychology,* (pp.25-41). New York: Bruner-Routledge.

Levine, R. A., Dixon, S., Levine, S., Richman, A. Leiderman, P. H., Keefer, C. H., & Brazelton, T. B. (1996). *Childcare and culture: Lessons from Africa.* Cambridge: Cambridge University Press.

Liev, M. H. (1995). Refugees from Cambodia, Laos and Vietnam. In S. W. Grief (Ed.). *Immigration and national identity in New Zealand: One people, two peoples, many peoples?* Palmerston North, Dunmore Press.

Lightfoot-Klein, H. (1989). *Prisoners of ritual: An odyssey into female genital circumcision in Africa.* New York: Harrington Park.

Mackey, W. C. (1981). A cross-cultural analysis of adult-child proxemics in relation to the plowman-protector complex: A preliminary study. *Behaviour Science Research, 16,* 187-223.

Mazrui, A. A. (1986). *The Africans: A triple heritage.* London: BBC.

Minja,B. M., & Machemba, A. (1996). Prevalence of otitis media, hearing impairment and cerumen impaction among school children in rural and urban Dar Es Salaam, Tanzania. *International Journal of Paediatric otorhinolaryngology, 37,* 29-34.

Monahon, C. (1993). *Children and trauma: A guide for parents and profession-als.* San Francisco: Jossey-Bass.

Munroe, R. L., & Munroe, R. H. (1992). Fathers in children's environments: A four culture study. In B. S. Hewlett (Ed.). *Father-child relations: Cultural and biosocial contexts (pp.213-230).* New York: Aldine de Gruyter.

Naslund, M (1997). *An investigation of war related trauma experiences and psychological symptomatology of young refugees.* Unpublished master's thesis. Monash University, Melbourne, Australia.

Nasmenang, A. B. (1992). *Human development in cultural context: A third world perspective.* Newbury Park, CA: Sage.

Okeyo, A. P. (1980). Daughters of the lakes and rivers: Colonization and land rights of Luo women. In M. Etienne & E. Leacock (Eds.). *Women and colonization: Anthropological Perspectives.* New York: Praeger.

Pavlish, C. (2005). Action responses of Congolese refugee women. *Journal of Nursing Scholarship, 37(1).* 10-17.

Rousseau, C., Said, T. M., Gagne, M-J., & Bibeau, C. (1998). Resilience in unaccompanied minors from the north of Somalia. *Psychoanalytic Review, 85(4),* 615-637.

Rousseau, C., Mekki-Berada, A., & Moreau, S. (2001). Trauma and extended separation from family among Latin American and African refugees in Montreal. *Psychiatry, 64(1),* 40-59.

Rousseau, C., & Drapeau, A. (2004). Premigration exposure to political violence among independent immigrants and its association with emotional distress. *Journal of nervous and Mental Disease, 192(12),* 852-856.

Tan, L. (27 Nov 2006) *Heritage warped by arrogance and cultural ignorance.* New Zealand Herald, Section A, p.15.

Taylor, C. C. (1992). *Milk, honey and money: Changing concepts in Rwandan healing.* Washington: Smithsonian Institution Press.

UNDP (2000). *Human development report 2000.* Oxford: Oxford University Press.

UNHCR (1996). *1951 convention and 1967 protocols relating to the status of refugees.* Geneva: UNHCR.

Zeitlin,M. (1996). My child is my crown: Yoruba parental theories and practices in early childhood. In S. Harkness & C. M. Super (Eds.), (pp175-188). *Parents' cultural belief systems: Their origins, expressions and consequences.* Thousand Oaks, CA: Sage.

Chapter 4

IMAGINING AFRICA WITHOUT BORDERS, WITHOUT NATIONS

By Valerie Morse

Do you imagine Africa? I do sometimes. I imagine a land of amazing beauty, of unspeakable exploitation, of fantastic civilisations, of disappearing species, of contrasts. I seldom imagine a continent of nation-states, contained and bounded by the artificial lines of colonial administration. Yet it is these lines, imagined, yet sharp, defended and believed in, that now define the landscape, the history and the people.

Without these lines, these borders, would it be possible to be a refugee? To be exiled? If you could be at home anywhere on the planet then could you really be cast out or forced out? 'Home' is a nebulous idea, a combination of comfort and security borne of family relations, cultural/linguistic affinity and geographical familiarity. Yet all human cultures share many of the same basic rituals and relations, albeit with plenty of variation. So much of what we associate with 'homeland' is a construct that is useful. It is useful because it links people, it gives them a sense of unity where none may exist; it creates myths of common history and shared experience. People rally in its defence, fight and die for its survival. Others oppress and exploit in its name.

The nation-state, of course, does not do this—it is created by those who rule it. The strength of the myths the unity of any nation-state is not accidental. They are manufactured, contrived and invented, all to a greater or lesser extent. The nation-state is also externally defined by those with control over the discourse on state relations—a 'failed state', a 'powerful state', a 'rogue state'—often with serious, sometimes fatal, consequences.

Nation-states are, however, inherently exclusive. The very definition of borders and citizens suggests that there are those that do not belong. It is, for example, possible to be a 'stateless person', a bureaucratic term that conjures up images of an exile, forced to walk the earth unable to ever rest or return home. It is this inherent exclusive characteristic of nation-states coupled with exploitative capitalism that creates refugees and exiles.

So I argue here against these artificial lines, against the nation-state and for an Africa unbounded, ultimately for a world without borders. I argue that without nation-states we can have no true refugees, no exiles.

It must be said at the outset that administratively determined nation-states should not be confused with the natural grouping of peoples based on shared culture, language, history or belief systems. It similarly must be said that a definition of 'homeland' is not an idea that is singularly imposed by such an administrative entity. Moreover, it is as often as not an environmental or cultural force rather than a political one that creates refugees and exiles. Nevertheless, the modern phenomena of mass expulsion whether as a result of political, cultural or environmental forces can certainly be intimately, if not exclusively, linked to the existence of nation-states.

Under the current capitalist system of exploitation, a stateless Africa, one without borders, would be little better than under the present configuration. The development of modern capitalism progressed hand in hand with the evolution of the Westphalian idea of a nation-state. The two are linked by history and mutual dependence. Neo-liberalism, the most current manifestation of capitalist economics, contributes its own unique misery to the refugee situation. This wider context must not be ignored when considering how refugees are created in the first place.

THE MODERN AFRICAN NATION-STATE

African nation-states provide particularly poignant examples through which to examine the hypothesis that without artificial boundaries, there would be no refugees or exiles. Nearly every modern African state dates its formation to post-WWII. Thus the state-building exercises typical of young states (e.g. myth-making and institution building) are still in ascendancy, rather than in stages of consolidation or decline. Furthermore, the extreme exploitation of the continent's resources and people by European and American colonial powers are still clearly discernible. It is therefore easier to see the hand of, the manifestation of the state and of exploitative capitalism. On the other hand, both the pre-nation-state circumstances and the alternative possibilities of societal/political organisation can be easily examined.

Where did these imagined borders come from? The Berlin Conference, called by German Chancellor Otto von Bismarck at the request of Portugal in 1884 in order to sort out colonial possessions, was the beginning of the real 'scramble for Africa.' This conference, attended by 14 Ambassadors of various colonial powers, was the forum for dividing up the spoils of Africa and the imposition of artificial boundaries. At the time of the conference, 80% of Africa remained under traditional and local control. What ultimately resulted was a gerrymandered map of geometric boundaries that divided Africa into fifty irregular countries. This new map of the continent was superimposed over the one thousand indigenous cultures and regions of Africa.

The Berlin Conference was Africa's undoing in more ways than one. The colonial powers superimposed their domains on the African continent. By the time independence returned to Africa in 1950, the realm had acquired a legacy of political fragmentation that could neither be eliminated nor made to operate satisfactorily.

The physical occupation of Africa by colonial powers continued for nearly another century after the conference. In that time, the people of many of these colonial inventions were subject to ceaseless exploitation and ideological proxy wars waged by both the East and the West. European and US colonial powers installed capitalist economic systems in Africa. African colonial possessions became the resource-rich periphery that contributed to enhancing the wealth of the core, i.e. the first world. In that time, many of these colonial states developed highly stratified class systems, often characterised by the accessibility of education to a small select group. By 1900 colonial powers controlled nearly 100% of African land with the exception of Liberia and Ethiopia. Thus the ability of indigenous Africans simply to survive was seriously compromised.

Widespread national liberation struggles across the continent during the 1960s and 1970s did result in a marked shift in power away from the past colonial masters. Unfortunately, in many cases, this did not mean widespread democratisation. Rather, foreign models including socialist and neo-liberal economic ideas were imported and imposed by a western educated ruling class. As an example, following independence from the British in 1961 the socialist government of Tanzania nationalised considerable landholdings and financial institutions. But rather than embracing egalitarian possibilities, the bourgeoisie Tanganyika African National Union chose instead to ally 'national interest with foreign capital."

These new nation-states have been engaged in post-colonial myth making and institution building that is mutually reinforcing, and is, naturally, a tool of elite power. One of the most horrifying examples of this exercise was the genocide of nearly 1 million people in Rwanda. Up until independence in 1962, the Belgian colonial government had classified the Tutsi people as superior to the larger population of Hutu people and issued identity cards to that effect. This was in spite of the cultural similarities between the two peoples and the relative lack of conflict between them. Nevertheless, Tutsi enjoyed the privileges of this higher class including access to jobs and higher education. This institutional racism set the stage for the mass slaughter of Tutsi people in 1994 by the Hutu government, which was intent on securing its primacy and redefining one of its national myths. After the genocide, nearly 200,000 Hutu people fled Rwanda to avoid United Nations troops and subsequent prosecution. This precipitated one of the largest refugee disasters in modern history and caused protracted conflict between neighbouring states.

Today it is difficult to see any African state as even nominally egalitarian. Power sharing, decentralised government, worker and/or peasant control and significant social equity are the lost dreams of a generation of revolutionaries. Instead, independence has seemingly brought only greater class stratification, underdevelopment, corruption and political instability. The formation of post-colonial states did not alter this even in situations where significant socialist agendas were advanced and fierce national liberation struggles were waged. Africa was too much a part of the global economy and its resources far too valuable and too lucrative for the people to be allowed to assert any true autonomy by the ruling class, i.e. former colonial powers, other would-be interventionists and local elites. This is the legacy of the imposition of capitalist economic and racist political models on African society.

THE REFUGEE REALITY IN AFRICA

In addition to military actions, conquest involved the forceful ejection of natives from their lands, which were then seized by the colonialists. And this seizure was protected through the violent suppression of all forms of dissent by the coercive apparatus of the colonial state.

This forceful ejection is the reality now for some 5 million Africans who were at the start of 2006 people 'of concern' to the United Nations High Commission for Refugees (UNHCR) including refugees, asylum seekers, returned refugees, internally displaced people (IDPs) and stateless people. The High Commission's founding mandate defines refugees as people who "are outside their country and cannot return owing to a well-founded fear of persecution because of their race, religion, nationality, political opinion or membership of a particular social group." Thus by its definition a refugee is created by the societal constructs which make existence no longer tenable in one's own home.

World-wide, the origin of five of the ten largest refugee populations is Africa: Sudan, Burundi, Democratic Republic of Congo, Somali and Liberia. The four largest refugee movements of people occurred in African nations in 2006. At the start of 2006, there were an estimated 23.7 million internally displaced people world-wide. The UN refugee agency was helping 6.6 million IDPs in 16 countries, a 22 percent jump compared to the previous year. Clearly there is a refugee crisis in Africa. There is a political crisis in Africa.

AGAINST ALL NATION-STATES

In the words of Kwame Nkrumah, who spearheaded the formation of the independent nation-state of Ghana, the task was to "Seek ye first the political kingdom, and all else shall be given unto you." In order to achieve this goal, nationalists argue that it is necessary to unite all classes within the oppressed nation against the imperialist oppressor. Nationalists tend to deny the importance of class differences within the oppressed nation, arguing that the common experience of national oppression makes class divisions unimportant, or that class is a 'foreign' concept that is irrelevant. Thus, nationalists seek to hide class differences in a quest to found an independent nation-state.

The reality, however, is that local elite' often have far more common interest with their colonial masters than they do with their fellow citizens. The class system in Africa has been described as 'truncated' comprising only administrative and working/peasant classes. This characterisation is true to varying degrees throughout Africa where there is a distinct absence of the 'growing middle class' that typifies other underdeveloped economies that are engaging in the neo-liberal global economy. There are examples of African states in which this class division is further exacerbated by cultural or racial divisions, the most obvious example being South Africa. Rigid class divisions give rise to political instability and the use of blunt political instruments to ensure adherence to the nation-state project. These often include a high degree of state-sanctioned violence.

While generalising, it is reasonable to observe that expatriate colonial masters were replaced by indigenous masters with few material changes to the masses. Colonial governments perhaps had a higher degree of choice about the extent of the exploitation of African peoples than do post-colonial independent states. Two primary factors account for this phenomenon: The first factor is the legacy of colonialism: the overt and covert methods of colonising that have been imprinted on the minds of generations of Africans and which continue everyday throughout the continent. The second is the imposition of global neo-liberal economic policies on African nations, leaving little room for autonomy let alone fundamental societal change.

Many on the political left would conclude that the rise of modern capitalism is co-extant with that of the modern nation-state. The consolidation of these geographical units (Germany and Italy) into unified nations, Marx and Engels believed, was a *"sine qua non"* for the development of modern industry and capitalism. While the transition from a feudal world to a capitalist one was contemporaneous with the manifestation of the modern European nation-state, the former is not reliant on the latter. That said, in the current manifestation of capitalism, as exemplified by neo-liberal economic policies, the nation-state aids and abets capitalists in their exploitative ways and substantively exacerbates the refugee situation.

In what manner, you may ask. Neo-liberalism is characterised by: the privatisation of public assets; deregulation of trade, finance, investment, education and healthcare by nation-states in favour of trade management through a global rules-based system; the growth of multinational financial institutions (such as the IMF and World Bank); the rise of foreign direct investment; the development of intellectual property as a commodity, and a focus on individualism and societal atomisation. Indeed, neo-liberalism has been called 'capitalism with the gloves off' because business forces are stronger and more aggressive, and faceless organised opposition than ever before.

Under the rubric of so-called 'free trade,' multinational corporations have vastly expanded their rights to move production across borders in a ceaseless quest for the cheapest wages and the least obstructive labour and environmental laws. Similarly such 'free trade' has created whole new markets for essential public services previously provided ostensibly under terms of reasonable equity. The privatisation of water is but one example.

While theoretically a system of rules-based trading would put all nation-states on a level playing field, the reality is that it serves to entrench the power of first- world nations that heavily subsidise their ruling classes through tax incentives and subsidies. Former colonial powers that have had 400 years of nation-state building are at a significant advantage over those that have emerged as cohesive entities in the past 50 years. Put simply, the former have highly developed capitalist economies that have been recipients of state largess for those centuries. The neo-liberal model disallows any such state intervention in the emerging countries of today

Anarchism does not argue in favour of state intervention as a theoretical solution to the limitations of neo-liberalism. Suffice it to say, neo-liberalism assumes the equality of all nation-states, an egregious, if convenient, error of reasoning, one with devastating consequences for the less developed members of the world community.

Moreover, while neo-liberal economic theory advocates the free movement of goods and services, there is a deafening silence from its champions regarding the free movement of people. This is where the sharp edges of capitalism and nation-states converge to create refugee crises.

The neo-liberal reality for much of Africa is unprecedented environmental degradation and labour exploitation at the hands of multinational corporations. A particular African reality is the inaccessibility of life-saving AIDS drugs due to ownership of the intellectual property by western pharmaceutical companies. Corporations such as Royal Dutch Shell, BHP Billiton and deBeers take every opportunity to challenge or ignore the jurisdiction of nation-states.

This exploitation is complemented by the forced implementation of fiscal structural adjustment policies by the IMF and World Bank that dictate a government based upon Western models. The results are predictable and dramatic: the people of Africa and the land are dieing, or rather, they are being quietly but brutally annihilated.

The specific effect of neo-liberalism on the creation of refugees is, I would argue, a shift from inter-state refugees, to 'internally displaced persons." Statistically, this is the trend globally. This shift is a direct result of the intensification of border controls, the centralisation of personal data including citizenship, the creation of a global surveillance state by US-friendly intelligence agencies and the more general hardening of national 'identity' against the increasingly globalised political-economic discourse.

When colonisation is viewed as systemic violence and exploitation tantamount to low- intensity warfare and post-colonial governments are populated by elite' intent on maintaining exclusive power, then it follows that the modern African nation-state exists largely to wage war on its own people for the benefit of the few in power. In this colonialism is not unique. In fact, it is not strictly speaking, the effects of colonialism, although they are particularly vicious, but that of capitalism, which casts the nation-state into this form.

Having drawn this conclusion it is but a next step that nation-states in fact create refugees. Violence is inextricably associated with the definition of both war and statehood. States evolve from conflict and out of that violence, refugees are defined, expelled, liquidated or co-opted and thus violence is the natural pre-cursor to the creation of refugees.

STATELESS PRE-COLONIAL AFRICA

Certainly pre-colonial Africa was not free from war, violence towards women, slavery, patriarchy, or coercion. Empires and emperors did exist. However, in *African Anarchism: The History of a Movement*,

Sam Mbah and I.E. Igariewey make a strong case for the prevalence of countless examples of anarchistic practices in pre-colonial Africa.

The first example is the widespread practice of communalism, which they define as both a mode of production and as a societal practice in which both individuals and communities enjoyed almost total autonomy.

> Among the most important features of African communalism are the absence of classes, that is, social stratification; the absence of exploitative or antagonistic social relations, the existence of equal access to land and other elements of production; and the fact that strong family and kinship ties form(ed) the basis of social life.

Further elements of this communalism that the authors describe included horizontal political structures with diffused power and functions, equality among members of the community and the use of both consensus and conciliation to make decisions and resolve disputes.

Mbah and Igariewey give four case studies of stateless societies. While none of them can be said to represent anarchistic organisation in its entirety (e.g. freedom from hierarchy and coercion, decisions based on consensus, equal access to power, and autonomy), all certainly have a distinct lack of 'centralisation and concentration of authority' which is a necessary pre-cursor for one.

ORGANISING AFRICA: WHERE ELSE FOR REFUGEES?

A very different shape and form of political organisation might have been possible for Africa following independence from colonial occupation. That de-colonisation occurred piecemeal, often prompted by significant, sustained and organised revolutionary action, would have made a stateless continent difficult if not impossible to conceive during that time. Unlike South America earlier, Africa had no unifying liberator like Simon Bolivar.

Nevertheless, the 'choice' of nation-states rather than a federation of national, tribal, trade union or cultural groups certainly configured African people in the distinctly Western concept of statehood. This has been disastrous for many Africans. These harsh national borders have split natural groups and united opposing forces in situations destined for conflict. Again it is this artificial creation that has created a situation where people are forced from their homes. This tension creates a situation where one group necessarily becomes the 'other'—the outsider—within their own homeland.

Anarchism proposes a world without national borders, one in which freedom from coercion and autonomy are embraced as paramount characteristics of a civilised society. Anarchism rejects both government and hierarchical methods of organising because neither serves the interests of people, but rather serve only a select few, the ruling class, who seek to maintain positions of power, privilege and domination over others. Invariably, those in power reinforce systems of domination that sustain them as the ruling class: racism, capitalism, imperialism and patriarchy, in a never-ending cycle of violence and exploitation.

An anarchist Africa is possible. By its nature, it would be part of a global anarchist world where exploitative capitalism was consigned to history and the needs of all people were met communally and sustainably.

Where might Africans begin to dismantle domination? The struggle against domination happens everywhere: at work, at school, in homes, in the fields. It is a struggle that is collective, not individual, although each person must find the most fulfilling means of destroying domination in his or her own life. It is as Milan Kundera wrote, "the struggle of humanity against power, it is the struggle of memory against forgetting."

It is not surprising that this quote was invoked by Ken Wiwa, the son of Ken Saro-Wiwa, lifelong Ogoni environmental activist, on the 10th anniversary of the murder of his father by the Nigerian government and Royal Dutch Shell Corporation. In dismantling power, we are not breaking new ground, but following in familiar footsteps we only have to remember them. His father's struggle against corporate violence, against state-sanctioned environmental destruction and forced evictions provides an example of where to begin. To begin we must only just begin, take that first step.

Dissolving the state in this post-modern or post-structuralist world is no easy ask. For the 'state' manifests its power in ways that are often invisible, subtle and insidious. More importantly, it is not the place of an outsider to define the struggle for African peoples. That said any successful struggle against oppression cannot end with simply the end of the domination of the day, but rather the deconstruction of all power over people. In particular, it must deconstruct the institutionalised power of the nation-state, which is the concentration and systematisation of all other forms of domination.

Moreover, the struggle waged by African people for autonomy, for freedom and ultimately true anarchy/autonomy is not one that is waged alone. It is a global struggle and one that can only be won ultimately on a global scale.

Six billion people inhabit the planet. Some 20 million people are refugees. Each day, each of us has the same basic needs, and many of the same basic desires. Is it not possible for us to make this finite world home for all?

There are many cynics and naysayer's among the ruling classes who disparage these ideals and who say we must deal with the refugee 'problem' by making more treaties, more courts, more deals and more camps. There are those who seek to 'make poverty history' and solve Africa's problems while they hold onto their piece of the pie, retain their privileges. They are interested only in mitigating remedies, not in addressing the fundamental stumbling blocks—nation-state borders and enforced capitalism that created the refugees in the first place. Those who dream small dreams and imagine only the do-able, the band-aid approach, rather than the ideal are destined to perpetuate injustice and misery.

For those who enjoy the privileges of nation-state borders and who accept, even embrace, the capitalist world, your days are numbered. For Mother Earth, the earth, cannot support an unsustainable system indefinitely. It is as clear as the cracks in the drought-ridden Western Sahara desert that our fate on this planet is intimately tied to each other and the health of the earth. No one gets out alive and your children shall reap the greed that you sow.

Imagine for a moment an Africa without borders, without nation-states, without war, without want and without refugees. Imagine an end to propaganda that manipulates the minds of people to create enemies based on race, religion, gender or nationality. Imagine a world based on mutual aid. Is it so extraordinary to think that we could all care for each other's health and well-being? Imagine true freedom, freedom to be who you want, where you want in the world. Imagine wandering the earth and being free to call all of it 'home.'

Chapter 5

RELIGION AS THE NEW RACE

By Marion Maddox

RELIGION AS THE NEW RACE

The final days of the 2007 Australian federal election campaign were enlivened by revelations of a fraudulent leaflet purporting to be from a non-existent Muslim group. The leaflet, circulating in the suburban Sydney seat of Lindsay, read:

> In the upcoming federal election we strongly support the ALP as our preferred party to govern this country and urge all other Muslims to do the same. The leading role of the ALP in supporting our faith at both state and local government levels has been exceptional and we look forward to further support when Kevin Rudd leads this country.

After listing some instances of alleged ALP support, such as a (fictional) move "to forgive our Muslim brothers who have been unjustly sentenced to death for the Bali bombings," the flyer concluded with the uniquely-spelled invocation, "Ala Akba." Confronted by Labor campaigners after a tip-off, the source of the leaflet turned out to be senior figures from John Howard's Liberal Party, including the husbands of both the outgoing Liberal Member for Lindsay and the candidate seeking to replace her.

The incident became a prototype of a public relations disaster, contributing to the defeat of conservative Prime Minister John Howard's eleven-year-old government. The exposé of the phony leaflet painted the local Liberal organisation as both racist and inept, and distracted attention from scheduled events which the federal Liberals had designed in a quest for last-minute momentum. It not only revealed a campaign in chaos, but implicitly demanded comparison with a similar incident in the previous (2004) federal election. Then, voters in the adjoining seat of Greenway received a leaflet bearing the ALP logo, campaign slogan and a photo of the Labor candidate, Ed Husic. The leaflet read, "Ed Husic is a devout Muslim. Ed is working hard to get a better deal for Islam in Greenway." The seat, which had been held by the ALP throughout its twenty-year history, passed to the Liberal candidate, who until her election had been an employee of the region's 15,000-strong Hillsong Pentecostal megachurch. The leaflet, in an area often referred to as "Sydney's Bible belt," may have contributed to her slim 883-vote margin. Far from distracting from the larger Liberal campaign, the Husic leaflet (for which no source was ever identified) appeared in 2004 to mesh smoothly with it and, indeed, with a long-standing theme of Howard-style politics.

One longstanding feature of what came to be known as "Howardism" was the political harnessing of racism, while denying any racist intent. Howard and his closest supporters regularly expressed sympathy for those Australians who, they said, were "not racist," but instead felt "racial resentment." Howard assured them that, while not necessarily agreeing with their demands, he nevertheless 'understood' their anger at the 'special treatment' of Indigenous Australians, refugees and other marginalized groups. Far from unique to Australia, this pattern has been widely discussed in relation to a number of countries (e.g. Mendelberg 2001; Kintz 1997; Pitcher 2006). But the Australian instances point to a distinctive aspect of how this tactic is developing, namely, targeting religion rather than race.

A defining narrative of western identity is of the passage from ignorance to enlightenment. As well as its broad historical application over six centuries, the narrative finds a myriad of micro-versions depicting the West's triumphant march from intolerance to tolerance, from autocracy to democracy and from constraint to freedom (often translated into a 'white man's burden' to share such goods with the less enlightened, whether they want it or not.) One feature of such micro-narratives is the way in which overtly racist statements by political leaders have become increasingly politically disavowed, challenging, as they do, the image of ourselves as enlightened, liberal and tolerant.

The popular story of flight from intolerance to tolerance appears natural and self-evident. In Australia, from the passage of the Immigration Restriction Act in 1901 until the early 1970s, immigration was guided by the so-called "white Australia policy." Until 1958, a blatantly discriminatory dictation test, which could be administered in any European language, effectively barred Australia's borders against anyone deemed racially or politically undesirable. As documented by Gwenda Tavan (2005), the policy had begun to unravel before its formal abolition, while traces of it lingered in public discourse and practice until the political embrace of multiculturalism, under the Whitlam Labor governments (1972-1975), and beyond. The preference for British immigrants was diluted, first with Jewish refugees from Europe, later refugees or "boat people" from Vietnam and, most recently, from Afghanistan and Iraq.

With respect to Australia's Indigenous population, during the first half of the twentieth century successive governments embraced the policy of assimilation, which was frankly described by officials as an effort to "breed out the colour" so that Aboriginal characteristics would disappear from the population over successive generations. That was the rationale for the policies of forcible removal of Indigenous children from their families which, until the early 1970s, produced Australia's Stolen Generations. By the time of Prime Minister Kevin Rudd's February 2008 parliamentary apology to the Stolen Generations, so unspeakable had such policies become that the very act of publicly acknowledging their existence became an important part of the apology. Underlining the difficulty of even acknowledging such policies in the modern, enlightened twenty-first century, Liberal opposition leader Brendan Nelson's speech endorsing the apology attempted to maintain, despite the historical record, that the children had been taken mainly for humanitarian rather than eugenic reasons.

In the USA, the abolition of slavery was mitigated by overtly segregationist 'Jim Crow' laws which persisted through the American South into the early 1960s, keeping black and white citizens apart in almost any public encounter, from schooling to transport to eating out. In the 2008 presidential primaries, a recurring hope of Democrat contender Barack Obama's campaign was that by selecting a black candidate America would demonstrate a final maturation out of its racist past and into a 'new politics' era of inclusiveness.

Such self-congratulatory narratives of the triumph of tolerance do not mean that racist sentiment and racial injustice have disappeared. Rather, the terms in which they are expressed have changed. A number of recent analyses (Pitcher 2006; Fear 2007) have pinpointed the ways in which publicly expressed racism has become less respectable, while more subtle forms of expression have allowed racist ideas to be articulated, even as their articulators deny any racist intent. Tali Mendelberg (2001) demonstrated how naming a covert race campaign for what it is neutralises its effect. White voters typically entertained negative racial stereotypes but simultaneously adhered to egalitarian norms. In place of overt racism, a political language emerged which hinted at racist stereotypes without spelling out the connection between race and supposed attributes. The new political discourse hinges on a rhetorical picture of a world divided into 'us' (safe, secure, familiar) and a racially-marked 'them' (dangerous, taking 'our' jobs, threatening 'our' children) (Kintz 1997). As Mendelberg pointed out, such:

> Implicit racial messages are ambiguous racial cues; it is unclear whether they are about race or not. The racial cue is there but it is dominated by nonracial content. This ambiguity may be the source of their power. Implicit racial messages may be more effective in evoking racial predispositions than unambiguous—that is, explicit—racial messages. Ambiguously racial messages activate racial predispositions but circumvent conflicting considerations such as a commitment to the norm of equality. (2001:126)

As long as the message is implicit, voters can be persuaded to draw on their 'racial predispositions,' which "remain ready for use when voters form and express opinions about racial matters and when they choose among candidates" (127). But making the implicit message explicit neutralizes the effect. Once voters can no longer deny that they are responding to a racist message their egalitarian norms are no longer circumvented. Racial priming loses its force with a citizenry intellectually aware that 'racism is wrong'.

New terms—"plausible deniability," "dog-whistle politics"—have entered the political lexicon to describe such ambiguous racism. Ben Pitcher pointed out, in relation to recent British politics, "The public disavowal of racism points to the success of what might be termed a language war over racial reference," with the result that "now it becomes far harder than before to challenge racist discourses that are, accordingly, obliged to find expression through the language of multi-culturalism and anti-racism" (Pitcher 2006: 537).

In 2005, UK Conservative Party election campaign materials asserted "It's not racist to impose limits on immigration," and asked, "Are You Thinking What We're Thinking?" According to Pitcher, it relied "often quite subtly, on a range of racist exclusions that typically escape the media's ethical censure." By allowing such representations through the filter of what is publicly expressible, the media's "avowed commitment to anti-racism nevertheless permits the expression of a hate that dare not speak its name."

One way that hate can more readily speak its name is by seeming to direct itself at a category other than race. The two Australian leaflet episodes, with which I began, reveal a further, less-noted feature of the new politics of race, namely, the way in which religion has come to act as race's surrogate. This development unfolded not only in Australia but in numerous Western countries. The French headscarf debates, the Danish cartoon controversy, and repeated controversies in the UK over the wearing of the niqab (face covering) by Muslim schoolgirls and teachers showed a world religion, with members from a vast array of ethnic backgrounds, occupying the place in public debate which would once have been taken by race. This development unfolded in the unique circumstances afforded by the large-scale movement of refugees seeking asylum; the 'war on terror' (described by then US President George W. Bush as a "crusade"); and the widespread (if hazy) endorse-ment of Samuel Huntington's *Clash of Civilizations* thesis. While overt, nameable racism has become, as Mendelberg and Pitcher point out, politically risky, casting aspersions on someone else's religion remains (at least in the case of Islam) a more acceptable political tactic, albeit still requiring delicate handling.

We can understand this international pattern by exploring the history of Islamophobia in recent Australian political history, against the background of world events and in the context of an allegedly global discourse.

In 1996, John Howard came to power in a campaign built, according to his then national campaign director, on the organising themes of "Us" versus "Them" (Williams 1997: 159). 'We' were being marginalised, ignored and belittled by a Labor government in thrall to 'Them,' noisy, self-serving 'special interest groups'. Just who 'They' were was never made clear. Over three terms of government, 'Them' stood, at various times, for Indigenous Australians, ethnic minorities, refugees, trade union members, churchgoers, feminists, environmentalists, and more.

From July 2001, a new 'Them' entered the Howard government's list of menaces: Muslims. The explicit casting of Muslims as a religious 'them' as best understood against the background of the concurrent public conversations about religion. One conversation, often loud and explicit, was about Islam. It portrayed Muslims as outsiders-within-the-nation, conduits of anti-Western views and potential terrorists (especially when wearing distinctive, religiously-marked dress). That conversation gained volume from the stereotypes of asylum seekers (and, later, terrorists) purveyed, and intensified, by public policy moves such as Australia's increasingly aggressive border protection against would-be refugees and later by increasingly draconian anti-terror legislation.

A concurrent conversation, often muted and carried on more between the lines than in the headlines, was about Christianity. While Australia is often said to be culturally and historically Christian, and that is true at least in the limited sense that its traditions and assumptions are more shaped by Christianity than by any other religious tradition, it could hardly be said to be actively or obviously Christian today. A country where only around nine per cent of the population claim to go to church weekly, rising to the high teens for monthly, seems unlikely soil for the kind of religious fervour which would find others' views of God a source of fear. Yet 'Christian values' were increasingly invoked in public debate during the late 1990s and early 2000s. The phrase came to mean something distinct from the Christianity which most Australians had either rejected or to which they gave only nominal adherence. 'Christian values' stood not for any specific set of beliefs, but, rather, for a general and nostalgic sense of 'tradition,' related to nationalism, civic order and public safety.

Many countries reported increases in Islamophobia in the wake of the World Trade Centre and Pentagon attacks and the accompanying national security panic which swept the USA and its allies; but Australian Muslims were already the targets of public vilification, street-level abuse and generalised fear well before these events.

As early as 1998, former High Court Judge and Human Rights and Equal Opportunity President, Ronald Wilson, drew attention to the government's rebranding of mainly Muslim asylum seekers as 'illegals,' despite their recognition under international law. Subsequent government opinion-shaping added images of those arriving on unseaworthy boats as 'queue-jumpers,' wealthy, self-serving associates of people smugglers. The message got through so well that, by July 2001, social commentator Hugh Mackay reported that, among his focus group respondents in the crucial outer-suburban marginal seats, 'Refugees previously referred to as "boat people" are now routinely described as "illegals", and said to bring 'unacceptable levels of crime and violence" (Mackay 2001: 30-31). A month later, the headlines were dominated by another story, though it was by then a year old. It concerned a series of gang rapes in Sydney's western suburbs. The police had tried to publicise the events at the time, but the story only became news after it was recast by pointing out that the perpetrators were Muslim, while the victims were mainly Anglo-Australians. By the time the year-old gang rape story made headlines in August 2001, the carefully-nurtured public mood was fertile ground for a seemingly natural association between 'Muslim,' 'Middle-Eastern' and 'criminal'. The so-called "war on terror" built upon a well-established pattern.

At that point, Howard was in the fatigue stage of his second term, dented by his Coalition parties' devastating losses in the Western Australian and Queensland elections. One factor in these State disasters had been Pauline Hanson's One Nation party, which was not delivering preferences to the Coalition. One Nation had launched its Queensland campaign with a refugee policy: "We go out, we meet [the boats], we fill them up with fuel, fill them up with food, give them medical supplies and we say, "Go [back] that way." Federally, Howard faced falling polls, a resurgent ALP and a federal election due by the end of the year. David Marr and Marian Wilkinson describe how, on 8 August 2001, Howard broached using the Navy to implement One Nation's "push off" border protection policy—an option long championed by his hand-picked department head and ally, Max Moore-Wilton (Marr and Wilkinson 2003: 45-46).

Just a week later, 345 people arrived on Christmas Island, an Australian territory in the Indian Ocean, 500 kilometres south of Jakarta. They were joined by another 359 the following week. By the end of August, Australia had more than three and a half thousand people in migration detention centres, and more were coming. Most were Iraqi and Afghani Muslims. On 24 August, the diminutive *Palapa* lost its engines, leaving its 438 passengers adrift, without even a radio or positioning equipment, until their dramatic rescue by Norwegian Captain Arne Rinnan of the *Tampa*, two days later. Rinnan's increasingly frustrated efforts to land passengers on Christmas Island, the Australian government's stalling over medical assistance while sending an SAS show of force, the tenuous 'Pacific Solution' of shipping asylum seekers to detention on Nauru, and the impact of all that on the 2001 election have been exhaustively told by Marr and Wilkinson. Our concern is the affair's part in the continuing depiction of Muslims as the latest 'Them'. The Howard government went to extraordinary lengths to prevent the *Tampa* refugees ever setting foot in Australia. One effect of the refugees' isolation was that, as Marr and Wilkinson note, the nearest image of them that Australian viewers saw, throughout the crisis, was a hazy picture of a distant ship, through a long-distance camera lens.

It was into this already heated atmosphere that the news of the 11 September 2001 attacks broke. The effect was intensified by the fact that America's 'war on terror,' in which the Howard government enthusiastically joined, was itself replete with religious overtones. From the beginning Bush seemed to be commissioning his troops for a cosmic showdown between the forces of evil and the forces of righteousness. He announced a "crusade" on terror and identified Iraq as part of an "axis of evil." Both were taken as placing his government's actions in the Middle East in a historical continuum with the medieval church's crusades against Islam, with all their overtones, for Muslims, of unprovoked, ideologically-driven Christian brutality. Two days after the "crusade" remark, Bush's office issued a retraction, saying that all the President had meant was that the response to terrorism would have the characteristics of a "broad cause."

Following the "crusade" episode, Bush took some pains to neutralise the comment, at least as far as his secular and international audiences were concerned. He was shown visiting a mosque, meeting Muslim leaders and repeatedly describing Islam as "a religion of peace." Crusades disappeared from his vocabulary, though he persisted with religious allusions such as the idea that "the liberty we prize is not America's gift to the world, it is God's gift to humanity." Bush's iconography of an anointed 'us' facing down a religiously threatening Muslim 'them' required careful crafting.

Howard's messages about Muslims were less ambiguous. In Australia, explicitly religious language cannot be relied on to carry the automatic positive vibes it does for many American audiences. Rather, religious appeals in Australian politics work more along the lines of the 'implicit' racial appeals described by Mendelberg.

Howard's portrayal of Muslims as the new 'them' picked up the half-spoken list of associations forged during the gang rape and asylum seeker panics. Muslims remained firmly other, even when he was expressing sympathy with their plight. The chasm between 'us' and 'them' was obvious, for example, in his response to the deliberate burning of a Brisbane mosque shortly after 11 September 2001. Although newspapers reported his comments under the heading "PM Outraged," his indignation proved conditional: "If it is an act of vandalism or vilification, I condemn it unreservedly." He continued, piling on qualifications:

> Islamic Australians are as entitled as I am to a place in this community. If their loyalty is to Australia as is ours, and their commitment is to this country, we must not allow our natural anger at the extremes of Islam ... to spill over onto Islamic people generally. (Shine 2001)

By purporting to know the hearts of one part of the population ('ours'), while raising doubt about the loyalty and commitment of another, he drew a sharp division between loyal and disloyal Australians; and he placed himself firmly on the righteously angry, patriotic, non-Muslim side.

Incidents like the mosque torching were the visible crest of a wave of street-level anti-Muslim harassment, with women and children the most frequent targets (Human Rights and Equal Opportunity Commission 2003). Australia's response to the October 2002 Bali bombing raised the possibility that 'acts of vandalism or vilification' against

Muslims were no longer the exclusive work of individuals, but had become official policy. Breaking into family homes during the evenings or in the early hours of the morning, handcuffing parents in front of their children and confiscating personal belongings, Australian Security Intelligence Organisation (ASIO) agents conducted highly public raids on the homes of people suspected of having attended past public lectures by Bali-implicated cleric Abu Bakar Bashir. Victims described violent methods that seemed less about catching suspects than about intimidating communities. The wider public got an impressive picture of a strong, security-conscious government. It seemed a heavy-handed form of intelligence-gathering—and, leading to neither charges nor convictions, a singularly ineffective one. That the raids took place during Ramadan made the insult seem still more calculated. As the lawyer for one of the raided families put it, "If [ASIO] had given our client the courtesy of asking him to provide information, or let them interview him or even come to his house, he would have opened his doors and made them a cup of tea" (Australian Broadcasting Corporation 2002). In fact, as the Asia Pacific Human Rights Network reported, at least one of those raided had contacted ASIO and offered to be interviewed. ASIO personnel refused his offer, only to come crashing through his front door at dawn two mornings later (Asia Pacific Human Rights Network 2003).

The depiction of Muslims as the new 'Them' had progressed so far by this time that violent images of armed men breaking into the homes of sleeping families, rather than evoking fear of government terror tactics, showed up in opinion polls as reinforcing the government's standing as strong on national security. Howard declared himself "one hundred percent" behind the raids on Indonesian Muslims:

> These raids relate to investigations concerning individuals. People who claim that this is in some way targeting Islamic sections of Australia are just, in my opinion, deliberately trying to create a difficulty that does not and ought not exist. (Riley et al 2002)

That the raids used unnecessary force and maximum family disruption, at the time of greatest potential religious offence, to obtain no evidence against people who had, in some cases, already come forward, all melted into a perfect example of Mendelberg's 'denial'.

Throughout, Howard insisted that his government's actions could not be attributed to racism. His 2004 victory speech hailed his government's Australia as "a beacon ... of tolerance ... all around the world." Again and again he reassured his constituents, "I don't find any racism in the Australian people," even as his government launched one campaign after another to encourage Australians to fear and suspect those different from themselves. In response to accusations of personal racism, he regularly replied, "There is not a racist bone in my body." Partly, this reflects Pitcher's observation that racism should not be understood primarily as a matter of 'conscious intentionality,' because "racist discourses do not by any means need to be regarded as such by either their speakers or audiences" (539).

In the Australian instances discussed above, and, arguably, in the US and UK, treatment of religious difference in the context of the 'war on terror,' religion functioned as a surrogate for race in a discourse whose effect was to implicitly question the equal citizenship of Muslims. Whatever their ethnicity, Muslims were able to be collectively portrayed as outsiders to nations represented variously as secular (and therefore upholding ideals of religion-state separation) or as Christian (and threatened by the presumed incursions of an alien, and supposedly less civil, faith). Moreover, the focus on religion facilitated the conflation of refugees with the very regimes they were attempting to escape, and against which the 'coalition of the willing' forces were engaged.

Mendelberg's analysis suggests that such tactics should be vulnerable to exposure. Once the racist subtext is revealed, her model predicts that the persuasive force would disappear. Yet this is not what happened in Australia. In 2001 and 2004, many voices announced the hidden assumptions underlying the fear campaigns. Yet campaigns heavily based on religio-racial fear saw John Howard's government returned with successive increased majorities and, in 2004, with the ultimate prize, control of the Senate. Many Australians, labeled by Howard as 'politically correct,' remained dismayed at the erosion of a tolerant self-image. The invasion of Iraq and draconian solution to problems in Northern Territory Indigenous communities were increasingly resisted. Yet Howard's 2007 defeat was attributed, not to any defusing of the racist message, but mainly to the fact that long-sought

Senate dominance tempted it into introducing deeply unpopular industrial relations laws.

I suspect there is more to the successful substitution of religion for race than a need to show voters, in the manner of Mendelberg's analysis, how they are being primed. One reason why we have seen a fairly straightforward translation of (relatively unsayable) racist sentiment into (comparatively acceptable) religious terms, both in Australia and elsewhere, has to do with the ways religion is understood in western political thought. For the reviling of Islam depends on its political portrayal as 'fundamentalist,' 'extremist,' 'pre-enlightenment' and 'irrational'. Earnest appeals for a 'Muslim reformation' and endless calls for 'moderates' to disown and denounce (once again! and again! and again!) the extremist actions—as though failure to be heard doing so somehow implicated them in violence—both reflect and contribute to a general depiction of Islam as intrinsically backward or benighted.

The self-congratulatory western story of the glorious path from intolerance to tolerance has its own particular history. The version of religious tolerance forged in seventeenth and eighteenth century Europe arose not from any burst of spontaneous enlightenment or eureka moment in some ivory tower. It grew out of the blood and suffering of the wars of religion which had periodically torn post-Reformation Europe apart. The solution to disastrous and potentially endless religious strife involved a very particular move: recasting 'religion' from something whose meaning was largely social to something whose significance was largely internal, individual and private. From being an external force which makes demands on individuals, religion came to be understood as an internal resource, about which individuals make personal, largely intellectual decisions—to believe or not to believe certain propositions; to hold some beliefs to be orthodox and others heresy; to engage in or refrain from particular religious practices. This reconceptualisation of religion, as a matter of individual choice, facilitated the western version of religious tolerance, in that it became possible to agree to differ over questions of faith, because they were, after all, ultimately to do with an individual's own private, internal world and able to be stripped of social or political significance (see Maddox 2007).

Yet, paradoxically, this move has also facilitated the latest western manifestation of religious intolerance. If religion is understood as fundamentally a matter of individual choice, it is also fundamentally contingent. One's religious choices may be a matter of chance, or misguided. Where 'race' is represented in popular discourse as immutable, an innate and unchosen, quasi-bilogical attribute, 'religion,' stripped of its social, political and communal significances, is portrayed as able to be adopted or disavowed at will. Consequently, denigrating people or discriminating against them on the basis of their religion is able to be represented as 'reasonable,' or at least forgiveable, where comparable racial practices would be rendered problematic by the almost universal acceptance of at least the forms of multicultural, anti-racist discourse. This comparative acceptability of religious vilification is even more the case when others' religion is perceived as collective irrationality, awaiting the western gift of enlightenment.

This comparison is suggestively developed by Shakira Hussein, discussing the admission by Tony Blair's Home Secretary, Jack Straw, that he found some female Muslim constituents' face covering to be a barrier to communication. "Such a visible statement of separation and difference," he said, would hinder positive relations between Muslims and non-Muslims. Straw addressed this perceived problem by asking veiled women to remove their niqab when meeting him. Hussein explains:

> As Straw and Blair conceded, it is perfectly legal to wear niqab ... and only a small minority of Muslim women do so. Many dress codes signal (or once signalled) a separation from 'mainstream society': goth, punk, facial tattoos. So why choose to confront this particular mode of dress as 'hindering integration,' if not to indulge in a spot of polite Paki-bashing? (Hussein 2006)

In this latest version of the Enlightenment compact, religion, no less than religious dress, is understood as something that can theoretically be put on and taken off at will (or even on request). Moreover, the cause of social harmony which once mandated the privatizing of religion now suggests that some, whose circumstances have positioned them as the 'Them' of fearful societies, have an obligation either to take it off altogether or to wear it only in the privacy of their own home. Tolerance's triumphant march has led in a strange direction.

References

Asia Pacific Human Rights Network and Human Rights Documentation Centre, 2003, 'Australia: Religious Minorities—Down and Under,' *Human Rights Feature* 6(2) 24-31 March.

Australian Broadcasting Corporation, 2002, *7.30 Report* 30 October.

Fear, Josh, 2006, *Under the Radar: Dog-Whistle Politics in Australia,* Canberra: The Australia Institute.

Human Rights and Equal Opportunity Commission 2003 'Listen: National consultations on eliminating prejudice against Arab and Muslim Australians,' Lakemba, 10 September 2003.

Hussein, Shakira, 2006, 'Why Do Some Muslim Women 'Choose' to Wear the Niqab?,' *New Matilda* 25 October.

Kintz, Linda, 1997, *Between Jesus and the Market: The Emotions that Matter in Right Wing America,* Duke University Press.

Mackay, Hugh, 2001, *The Mackay Report,* 'Mind and Mood,' July.

Maddox, Marion, 2007 ',Accommodating Religious Diversity: Beyond Liberal Dilemmas' presented at the 2007 International Conference of CESNUR Centre for Studies on New Religions, Bordeaux, France, 7-9 June, http://www.cesnur.org/2007/bord_maddox.htm.

Marr, David and Marian Wilkinson, 2003, *Dark Victory,* Sydney: Allen and Unwin.

Mendelberg, Tali, 2001, *The Race Card: Campaign Strategy, Implicit Messages and the Norm of Equality,* Princeton University Press.

Pitcher, Ben, 2006, '"Are You Thinking What We're Thinking?" Immigration, Multiculturalism and the Disavowal of Racism in the Run-up to the 2005 British General Election,' *Social Semiotics* 16(4): 535-551.

Riley, Mark Matthew Moore and Paul Daley, 2002, 'ASIO Raids Justified, Claims PM,' *Sydney Morning Herald,* 2 November.

Shine, Katherine, 2001, 'PM Outraged as Arson Destroys Mosque,' *Sun Herald,* 23 September.

Tavan, Gwenda, 2005, *The Long, Slow Death of White Australia,* Melbourne: Scribe.

Williams, Pamela, 1997, *The Victory: The Inside Story of the Takeover of Australia,* Sydney: Allen and Unwin.

Wilson, Ronald, 1998, 'Reconciliation and Human Rights,' Fulbright Symposium, University of Adelaide, 14-16 April.

Chapter 6

THE SUFFERING AND SURVIVAL OF AFRICAN REFUGEES: A SOCIOLOGICAL PERSPECTIVE

By Fantaye A Keshebo

First things first! When I was asked to write a contribution on refugee issues, I didn't have any specific topic to write on the subject. However, when I thought about it the contribution was about refugees. It's something about millions of people who endure daily hardships in remote corners of the globe, often out of sight. Whenever I thought about refugees, the first thing that popped to mind was always the hardship of refugee life—the sufferings and the struggle for survival. Suffering and survival in a refugee setting is two sides of the same coin. But also two coins with different sides. In this regard, I decided to shed light on the refugee perspective of suffering and survival. I decided to write briefly about the difficulties surrounding the lives of refugees, and their daily struggle to overcome the adverse conditions they face in foreign lands.

Throughout the writing I focused on highlighting the significance of sociological aspects of refugee life, which is often marginalized and overlooked by many when reporting on refugees and refugee camps. I tried to explore the role of group support and social relationships in minimizing the suffering and/or maximizing the survival endeavors among refugee populations at large.

This contribution is based on the writer's first-hand accounts of the refugee camps in Kenya, and it roughly covers a decade from the 1990's through to 2000. At times I used a participant observer's approach. I also employed both deductive and inductive methods as needed.

REFUGEE SUFFERING

The Oxford Advanced Learner's Dictionary defines suffering as "*physical or mental pain*." But suffering is sometimes a loaded word, a different thing to different people. A person may suffer when his leg is bruised or bled, when he has gone without sleep for two nights, when his romantic relationship ends, when he cannot eat the food he craves, ice cream in affluent societies, for instance, when he has lost a loved one, when he is involved in an accident, and so on. Yes, all of the above scenarios could cause suffering in one form or another. In my opinion, however, the refugee sufferings I will discuss here are different in their scope and intensity in three major ways.

First, the duration of suffering, or what the renowned Psychiatrist Dr Viktor Frankl called a "*time-experience*," is unknown. Unlike people in normal settings, refugee suffering could last much longer and, in most cases, it's indefinite. It is not uncommon to see people living in refugee camps for ten, fifteen, or twenty years, and even for a generation, in the same situation with no end in sight.

Second, people in refugee camps do not have control over their situations. This is perhaps one of the main characteristics of refugee life. Their movement is basically confined to refugee camps only, which are often remote and isolated areas of host nations. From food supply to where they live, location of refugee camps, to their safety and their future prospects refugees are literally dependent upon others: United Nations High Commission for Refugees (UNHCR), Non-Governmental Organizations (NGO's), the host country, etc.

The third factor that distinguishes refugee suffering is the sense of helplessness and hopelessness that surrounds a refugee's life. As far as refugees are concerned, I think, hopelessness and helplessness are by-products of the above two conditions. Lack of control over ones destiny and the constant challenges of adverse living conditions paint gloomy circumstances which, in some instances, lead some refugees to consider their lives as miserable and meaningless, resulting in them taking their own lives.

THE 'STIGMA' OF BEING A REFUGEE

The entire concept of suffering and survival, in this context, boils down to a word 'refugee.' It may be ironic to suggest that refugees are uncomfortable with the word 'refugee,' because of its connotations, but it is true. The word 'refugee' is widely considered among refugees as a labeling, belittling, and stigmatizing word. I remember some aid workers and non-refugee persons, who used the word 'refugee' interchangeably with proper names when addressing individual refugees. It was sometimes used in such a way that it implied the role and status of a lesser person in comparison to other non-refugee persons—receiver vs. giver, dependent vs. independent, follower vs. leader.

In the words of Jaarso Hagaloo (aka Gidi Abamegal), "the stigma associated with the word refugee runs so deep that at times you think you have not become a refugee out of circumstances but born to a cast called 'Refugee.'"

Yilma Tafere Tasew considers the ambiguous nature of the word refugee in his poem titled *Agonizing Wound*.

> **R**-fugee! Mysterious word
> **E**-ven hard to define
> **F**-rom any point of view
> **U**-nique either for philosophy or
> **G**-enerally for psychology
> **E**-ndless cycle of
> **E**-vil progress

Although he was a refugee and living in a refugee camp at the time he wrote this poem, Yilma found the word 'refugee' "hard to define." This was the case with many other refugees as well.

I remember once I woke up after midnight, lit a lamp in the darkness of my shack and struggled for hours to re-define the word 'refugee.' I did not have any illusions that my definition would go further than my own doorstep. Besides, I was then well aware of the grand definition of the 1951 Geneva Convention. But I wanted to respond to the real life experience of the thousands of people I had been interacting with. I thought the existing definition did not tell the whole story. As far as I was concerned, the definition was insufficient because it explained only the first chapter of the refugee story. It stated only the conditions/

reasons that forced someone to leave his/her country of origin to seek asylum, to become a refugee, in a host country.

So, I thought, the existing definition fell short of mirroring the real-life conditions that a person experiences daily once he/she crosses the border: dispossession, separation, alienation, loss, dependence, rejection, nostalgia, and dwelling in two distinct worlds; hope and despair, past and present, learning and unlearning, relief and apprehension, safety and insecurity, being self and other. I believed these conditions, by and large, could cause immense suffering, often unrecognized by others, to the refugees psyche. They are conditions only a refugee understands because he lives them, he breathes them, he smells them, he meditates on them, he wrestles with them, and he laments about them constantly.

Many refugees were disillusioned by what it meant to be a 'refugee' and they expressed their opinions in writing. One such writing was Yissac Mulatu's article entitled Refugee, which appeared on September- November 1994 issue of Kakuma News Bulletin (13), a news bulletin run and produced by the refugees themselves. "I decided to look up the meaning of a refugee in my Oxford Dictionary of current English [edition] but found the meaning [is] limited to a few facts of what a refugee is," he wrote. Yissac stated that, the reason why he wrote the article was, "to clarify," and "to help those who have never been refugees and have that dictionary meaning of a refugee in [their] mind." He went on to say that "no one knows what refugee means unless he becomes one. Leaving your lovely homeland implies leaving comfort, respect, dignity and all the status which you had in that homeland."

Andrew Mayak, a Sudanese refugee, asked a question and answered it in his poem, *What is a refugee?*

> To answer such a question
> needs you first to take refuge,
> otherwise your answer will be simple and meaningless.

And he goes further to describe how it feels being a refugee.

> But as a refugee,
> you are always simple in front of anybody.
> You are subject to prejudice and mistaken always.
> You are a human being without any value.

You can pass through any disaster
and nobody will care about you.
Oh, what is lovely like our homeland?
In your own country, you are free,
free like a butterfly when it flies from flower to
flower,
Homeland is a second heaven.
Without your home
you are like a dog without a tail.

Barbara Harrell-Bond in her report, *Can Humanitarian Work with Refugees be Humane?* put it as follows:

> Given the increasing use of negative adjectives such as
> 'bogus,' 'scroungers,' 'fortune seekers,' even 'sores,' to
> modify 'refugee,' it is not surprising that many of them
> believe their very identity and status has been degraded.
> However, the image of the 'good,' deserving refugee also
> can have its degrading dimensions.

Barbara quoted from Mamdani's (a Ugandan Asian refugee) book—
From Citizen to Refugee—to further explain what it means to be a
refugee.

> Contrary to what I believed in Uganda, before being
> expelled, a refugee is not just a person who has been dis-
> placed and has lost all or most of his possessions. A refugee
> is in fact more akin to a child: helpless, devoid of initiative,
> somebody on whom any kind of charity can be practiced,
> in short, a totally malleable creature.

One of my earliest memories, perhaps the first real experience of
the refugee camp, occurred on my first day of arrival to Walda Refugee
Camp in Kenya. The fact that I met acquaintances, by mere coinci-
dence, upon my arrival had eased my trouble a lot. They took me to
their 'house,' a shack made up of plastic sheeting wrapped over and
around a few wood poles; obviously the poles were cut from the forest
surrounding the camp. One of them had a very thin used mattress laid
on leveled ground for his bed. Another one had no mattress, but made
his bed by spreading the blanket over raised ground. Their bags, stuffed

with few belongings, were in the left corner while a few utensils and a bucket occupied the corner by the door. They asked me to stay with them. It was an offer I didn't hesitate to accept. In fact, abiding to the hospitality and culture of their home country, they insisted I should sleep on the 'mattress bed.'

Shortly afterwards, they grabbed a bucket and I accompanied them to the only tap water distribution center. Buckets, jerrycans, pots, and containers of all sorts were queued in long lines. The owners—men, women, boys, girls, and children—guarded their containers, moving them an inch forward at a time. The noise was deafening. Nobody seemed to be paying attention to anyone. After all, who understands all those languages anyway?

Some refugees did not have the patience to wait for their turn and went straight to the first spot to fetch some water. Some, flexing their muscles, went straight to the first spot disregarding all those patiently waiting folks. They acted as if no one was around them. Attempting to remind those muscle men to queue and to wait for their turn would obviously mean inviting trouble upon oneself. I believe those guys were deliberately seeking a target to vent their frustration, whatever their frustration might be. The manner in which they acted and behaved was simply provocative. But what can be done to stop them? No one wishes to be a punching bag, in a place where the law of the jungle prevails!

I observed some refugees politely asking permission to go first because their container was 'too small to wait' for hours in the line, or they had a 'very sick' person who needed a cup of water to quench their thirst, or else they needed 'some water for the meal' they were cooking. Still others wanted to go first because they 'left a baby crying' at home, or they were 'too weak to wait' for their turn. Even though every one there had a problem, I was amazed to see them letting those refugees with more pressing problems fetch water first.

As I waited for my friend's turn, my eyes were busy looking around all kinds of cinematic activities happening in the vicinities of the water pump. So many people, so many activities, in so little space! Only a few days ago, seeing such unrehearsed theatre was unimaginable.

Some men were 'taking a shower' in the open areas not far away from the crowd. They did not seem to be bothered much about exposing themselves to passers by; except for private parts, it reminded me of one of the paintings of Adam and Eve. Some men were taking a shower using trees and dense bushes as their shower curtains. I saw some girls and women, carrying buckets of water and clothes, going further into the bush than men so as to make sure they were out of sight. Unlike men, girls and women, were going for showers in groups of two, three, or four so that at least one of them would serve as a guard watching the surroundings to make sure the others could take a shower safely. The circumstances necessitated not only an individual refugee's struggle to survive, but the support of a fellow refugee.

"What is happening here?" "What is a refugee?" "Who is in charge of these people?" "Are they left alone in the midst of nowhere?" To me everything was happening so fast I did not have time to process the information. The young men and women swarming around the tap water and taking a shower in the bush used to be university students, civil servants, professionals, ranking military officers, high school students, city kids, farmers, pasturalists, etc. Not long ago they used to live in the comfort of their homes and apartments. Now here they are! Refugees!

In his book, *On Immigration and Refugees: Thinking In Action*, Professor Michael Dummett, noted rightly that "*refugees arrive bewildered, traumatized, nervous, and confused.*" If I may add to it, refugees remain bewildered, traumatized, nervous, and confused even after their arrival.

RISKS AND HARDSHIPS

In the days, months, and years that followed I witnessed lots of tensions, violence, deaths, and burials taking their toll on refugees due to diseases, inter-communal conflicts, slayings, arson, malnutrition, disappearances, and armed attacks by unknown groups. Unsanitary living conditions, coupled with various other conditions that characterize refugee camps, had created a fertile ground for diseases to easily attack refugees. In the Walda and Kakuma Refugee camps, there were hosts of diseases which competed with each other to attack their easily yielding and vulnerable prey.

> The list of diseases in Kakuma is as long as the variety of dishes in a menu you get in a good restaurant. We hear that people out there are worried to death by the contagious computer bugs and computer viruses. There goes the

> trouble with ICs. Here in our world malaria with all its
> variants wipe out many of our comrades and drive others
> mad. I have been attacked more than nine times but so far
> have refused to call it a day and throw in my ration card. I
> told you I am an IC.[1] TB, typhoid, yellow fever, diarrhea,
> jaundice, amoeba, bilharzias, trachoma, malnutrition,
> anemia, scurvy, depression, paranoia, STDs, and HIV-
> AIDS are some of the main maladies that 'permanently
> resettle' each day a significant number of us in the fields set
> aside as graveyards. Hastily dumping them there, we plant
> a small sign...on their graves and trickle back to our cages...

For a refugee the news of someone's death in the neighborhood or
in the community is not just news of a death. It is a shockwave that
rattles one's inner-self because it brings death one step closer to one's
own doorstep. Whether one knows the dead person personally or not,
often the news of the dead refugee is a reminder to a living refugee
of one's own fate, of one's 'eternal' separation from his/her roots, of
being lost in foreign lands, of being buried in unmarked graves, and
of being forgotten forever. When refugees farewell the dead, they
wail and weep—a lot. Their tears flow like a winter stream. When a
refugee sheds tears, he/she is partly crying for himself/herself. Besides,
sicknesses and deaths would bring individual refugees and their community members closer to each other as they struggle against common
fear and constant loss of lives. Out of such a sad situation develops a
sense of belonging to a group or community.

In the early 1990's thousands of refugees, mainly women and children, perished in Walda Refugee Camp due to a disease outbreak and
malnutrition. The daily death rate was so alarming that the UNHCR
had to hire a refugee, whose job description included, among other
things, counting the number of refugees that die every day and every
hour. The only way he could get accurate information on dead refugees was by going to the scattered graveyards, throughout the day, and
counting the dead as they were buried or shortly after their burials. Even
that became overwhelming for him, because many were being buried
during his meal break hours or in the evenings, making it hard to dif-
ferentiate those graves he had already counted from the fresh ones. So
he came up with a creative idea of using white wash paint to mark the
graves he had already counted. Any grave without white wash paint

was a new grave to be counted. While writing this article I contacted him, in the country where he lives now, and asked him if he remembers how many refugees died during that tragic period. The figure he told me was *"more than three thousand three hundred."*[2] Humanitarian aid had begun trickling to Walda Refugee Camp only after the news of the epidemic and malnutrition had reached major western media sources and it finally averted a total catastrophe.

In the refugee camps the very system of distribution of basic necessities was liable to create painful experiences. Waiting in lines is part and parcel of a refugee's life. It's one thing to queue under the fiercest sun for hours to get food stuffs; it's another thing when the lines end up in chaos and conflict, and you return home hungry and empty handed.

"All of them (refugees) had been for much of their lives forced to wait and wait and wait in endless lines- in the camps, in the UN offices, in government offices, in jails, in hospitals," wrote James Martin, a Jesuit missionary, describing the situations he observed while working with refugees in Kenya. The conditions I witnessed at the Care Distribution Center in Walda Refugee Camp often flashed back several years later, as though I had suffered post traumatic stress disorder. During bi-weekly ration distribution periods tens of thousands of refugees, of diverse backgrounds, had to collect their most prized commodity (ration) from one location and they had to collect it on specific days only. Due to the sheer number of refugees converging at the gate of one distribution center, chaos and conflict arose constantly, which in turn produced chain reactions.

First, in order to restore order, the *askaris* would unleash attacks indiscriminately with clubs, batons, and sticks. This, in turn, triggered a stampede of refugees who trampled upon one another causing deafening noises—some trying to escape from beatings, some trying to form new lines, some wailing and crying for help, some cursing police and calling names and/or throwing objects toward them. Not surprisingly some refugees watched the chaos from a distance with resignation. Seemingly too proud to fight for grains or beans, a few kilograms of wheat/corn flour, and a half cup of oil, or they were scared of hurting themselves if they joined the crowd. In these chaotic scenes, it makes one assume that Darwin's *Struggle for Existence* theory was, at least partially, at work.

All those who could not overcome the heat, shoving and waiting hours in the lines—such as the elderly, sick, physically frail, and some unlucky ones—had to try their luck the next day. If they could face the chaos again, then they had to try the day after because, however frail their physical condition might be, their ration could not be collected by friends or volunteers. This was because the people in charge of the distribution center wanted to control 'recycling refugees.'

As Barbara Harrell-Bond summed up, "Refugee populations are heterogeneous in every respect (age, education, gender, social class and so on), but the per capita method of distribution of aid is the 'leveler,' it emphasizes their 'equality.'" Food distribution centers are primary school grounds for refugees to learn the meaning of dispossession.

In Walda Refugee Camp, refugees had to go into the forest to gather firewood. I heard first hand reports of those refugees who lost direction in the jungle and wandered around for hours, probably gripped with the fear of coming face to face with a wild animal such as a lion. In Dadaab Camp in north-eastern Kenya, where mainly Somali refugees were housed, local media and NGO's had reported that refugee women were often subjected to rape while collecting fire-wood. In this regard, the UNCHR and Lutheran World Federation deserve appreciation for providing fire-wood when refugees were relocated to Kakuma Camp, which ensured not only the safety of refugees but it also prevented environmental degradation.

PROBLEMS OF REFUGEE WOMEN

Refugee camps are much harsher on female refugees than males. The arduous nature of refugee camps forces most refugee women to end up in cohabitation. Only a handful of strong willed refugee women can live as single women in the camps. In such cases, they have to persevere through constant stalking and harassments. The sexual and physical abuse, unwanted pregnancies, and abortion complications of such relationships put the lives of many women at risk. Living and working among various refugee communities in Kakuma, I had the unique opportunity to witness several physical abuse cases against female refugees.

Chronic sex-ratio imbalance was also a contributing factor to some of the problems both refugee women and men faced in the camps. In most refugee communities males, by far, outnumber females. The high demand for women increases conflict among couples and exacerbates instability of 'marriages' as some men tried to tighten their grip upon their 'wives' while others successfully persuade the women to switch partners. Moreover, due to there being fewer women in the camps, more men are forced to prolong or forgo marriage. This writer has heard several refugee men expressing their frustrations as they saw themselves aging and growing grey hair while still remaining single persons. For thousands of refugees it was one of the highest stress factors.

According to one Kakuma Sub Office report, as of the end of February 1999, there were 70 920 refugees in Kakuma Refugee Camp, of which 42,348 (60%) were men and 28,572 (40%) were women. The problem of sex ratio imbalance is more telling if we look at each refugee community. According to the above report, for instance, in Sudanese communities males constituted 60.8% and women 39.2%; in Ethiopian communities the ratio of males to females was 71.2% and 28.8% respectively, among Somalis 55% and 45% respectively, and all other communities 62% and 38% respectively.

The problem of sex-ratio imbalance was not limited to one refugee camp. It was a chronic problem in several refugee camps. The title of a brief article that appeared in the East African Standard[3] summed up the problem: Men too many but not enough women. The article stated that "out of the over 300 Sudanese refugees in Dadaab (Refugee Camp), there are only three single women—hardly enough to go around. All the young men eye these women." In the same article a 28 year old Sudanese guy, Abacha Meluk, addressed his own and his peers concerns: "Are we not men enough to be allowed to exercise our manhood? Must we suffer for our sanity? We have grown too old to stay without wives. We are ripe for marriage. We want to start families and watch our offspring grow."

Women in the refugee camps were subjected to more cultural and religious dictates of their countries of origin than men. In some communities refugee wives would toil daily in the burning sun while their husbands engaged in day long informal group visitations and discussions, and sweetened their conversations with coffee, tea, and music.

In Kakuma and Dadaab Camps, among the hottest places on earth, one would see veiled women draped from head to toe with multi-layered heat-absorbing clothing, making them what Jaarso Hagaloo called "*a walking heater.*" In those same places, male refugees of all communities stroll around wearing T-shirts, shorts, sandals, and non-wool clothing; some almost half-naked. Jarsoo went on to ask why refugee men "try to get their wives, sisters, and daughters, to cover up from head to toe [...] by turning them into a walking heater. With no offense to religion and with much respect to their tastes of clothing, the climate in Kakuma compels one to walk naked, not draped."[4]

In my attempt to address some of the problems of female refugees I scribbled the following poem in 1998 for publication in *KANEBU: Kakuma News Bulletin.*

Lily in the Wilderness

> Compelled by circumstances, cohabited
> Her movements confined and regulated.
> By the authority of beliefs and traditions, veiled
> Behold in the wilderness, Lily rooted
> Wretched, discolored, and deserted.
> In the queue to fetch the water
> In a long queue at distribution center
> Lily spends hours,
> Fixed like statues.
> She overcomes adversities and endures
> She stands firm and perseveres.
> Under the scorching sun
> That burns like a frying pan,
> She toils from dawn to dusk.
> She labors to accomplish her routine task
> She lives in uncertainty and fear
> Death and despair always near
> Her eyes often full of tears.
> Notwithstanding,
> Lily looks ahead for a day
> Holds on a hope of ray
> That makes her become somebody
> Out of nobody
> Out of nobody!
> Hostile Climatic Conditions

It goes without saying that the location of refugee camps compounded the hardships of refugees and caused greater discomfort to them. Refugees had to endure scorching sun on a daily basis, owing to the locations of refugee camps. As if there was a universal (unwritten) law, refugee camps in most countries, if not all, are relegated to the remotest areas of the host nations. One of the reasons for this may be the host nations concerns that 'foreigners' would cause 'insecurity' and 'overburden' their limited resources. While such concerns may be understandable, the 'fear' is sometimes unrealistic and overly exaggerated. Such unfounded fear was used as grounds to throw 'unwanted guests' into semi-arid and inhospitable lands where refugees would be easily checked and would become less threatening.

During informal conversations one would hear refugees causally mentioning Kakuma as a 'tenth planet,' (now Pluto is demoted, the camp communities might have promoted Kakuma to the ninth planet). Unlike Pluto, however, Kakuma remains 'the nearest planet' to sun.

In my poem, *Rise Kakuma,* I personified Kakuma in order to relate the climate of the camp with the refugees' sufferings; the following is a portion of the poem.

> Kakuma, a desolate wilderness
> A blazing fire, an earthly furnace,
> Venue of day darkness
> Don't shut your eyes blind!
> Speak the truth loudly!
> Disclose yourself thoroughly!
> You are a storehouse of whirlwinds,
> Abominable dust and a heap of sand
> Home of the undernourished,
> A graveyard never satisfied.

Several refugee writings reflected the concerns of refugees regarding climatic conditions of the refugee camps. I think, no pen was sharper than Jaarso Hagaloo's pen in offering readers a graphic and interactive tour of Kakuma Camp:

> ...particularly in Kakuma Refugee Camp where the sweltering heat saps much of the liquid in your body, the hunger squeezes all but the last drop of energy from your system, despair gnaws at your heart, and the furious wind storms fill your mouth and eyes with hot sandy dusts...the hot red orb called the sun hanging right over your head.

The sun you think is high up in the sky, isn't it? But the one in Kakuma is not. Or is it our lonely planet in Kakuma that is orbiting closer to the sun?

In the refugee camps physiological problems, such as skin discoloration, sun burns, pimples, wrinkles, untimely aging; and psychological problems, such as memory lapses and various other mental illnesses, were common among refugee populations. Did I assume that their causes may be attributed to the refugees' long-term exposure to harsh climatic conditions? Yes, I did.

UNSPOKEN, UNNOTICED ILLNESSES

The physical and mental health conditions of some refugee's deteriorates drastically for reasons unknown to their peers, to their friends, or even to themselves. The deterioration is often sudden. A person stops his association with peers. He breaks all contacts with others. All attempts to reestablish his 'routine' become fruitless because the person exhibits 'strange' behaviors: being verbally aggressive to those who attempt to help him, and/or being delusional, rigid, despondent, and uncooperative. Some quit taking care of themselves, which leaves them with very poor personal hygiene. Some hear voices and hallucinate. Sadly all such symptoms are not considered to be mental illness, but 'weird behavior.'

Among several such cases, I'll briefly mention two that I closely observed.

The first was Mr. Kassa. According to his account, prior to becoming a refugee he was an engineer by profession and had traveled abroad for specialized training. Kassa was perhaps one of the first refugees I met suffering with unexplained illness. Sometimes his speech and stories were incomprehensible and even laughable. So much so that many refugees dismissed him as "*crazy*," because of his "*weird*" stories, like pointing to the sky and saying: "*Look, the Prime Minster* [of his native country]! *I know him. We used to be together* [they weren't]." "*Look at the American satellite!*" "*That is an Israeli satellite!*" "*Those are Germans. I know Nazis!*" Often, he would be seen writing, sketching figures and doodling images throughout the day, every day. He would fill a fifty to hundred page exercise book within a day or two (I wish I had asked him to keep his note books).

Within a short interval, however, one would see a calm, cool, and 'normal' person appreciating Americans, or Israelis. Those who dismissed him as crazy had also respected him for the depth of knowledge he possessed. At times he was busy writing applications and petitions for refugees who desperately needed his help—his flawless and fluent English language skills and beautiful hand writing were highly demanded commodities.

While Kassa was suffering his illness, the NGO in charge of Kakuma Refugee Camp administration posted advertisements for an 'energy consultant.' Among many applicants, including the citizens, Kassa won the position. He was hired despite the fact that he was visibly ill. Besides his knowledge, the NGO that hired him had benefited by saving lots of money because, as a rule, all 'refugee workers' are paid 'incentives'- only a tiny fraction of other employees salaries- for the same position and same skill.

For a while the job kept him busy and the incentives helped him cover his routine expenses: cigarettes, coffee, notebooks, pens, and sometimes meals in the camp restaurants. A few months before his employment, he asked me how he could "*get into the Compound*" (of the camp administration center). He told me that he wanted to talk to the officers about his "*hallucinations*" (I must admit that that was the first time I ever heard the word 'hallucination'). Unfortunately, his job did not last long. As years passed his illness progressed. Kassa could be seen frequently walking around the camp streets regardless of the stifling heat. His friends had pushed him hard to return to his homeland and he finally agreed to repatriate. The last time I saw him was in Eastleigh 9th Street, in Nairobi city. He was wearing a used black suit and a tie, but barefoot. By then he had been in Nairobi for a few weeks waiting for his flight home. We hugged and said goodbye for the last time.

Teshome was another example. He was approximately in his midforties. He had a well-built, almost athlete, physique and he was often described as a 'handsome guy.' His smile was infectious to everyone around him and he had a charming personality. Whenever discussion of family matters arose Teshome never missed the opportunity to mention his "*two kids and beautiful wife*" whom he had left behind in Ethiopia. But his smile used to switch instantly to sadness when someone asked him if he had contact with his family. In fact, he hadn't had any communication with them for several years.

Any one who knew Teshome understood that he was suffering from separation anxiety, but what could they do? Almost every refugee has a similar story and each bleeds internally with his/her own wound. Alienation and a sense of loss is a cureless, refugee viral infection that kills in a piecemeal way. He used to tell us, with nostalgia and a sense of pride, that he used to be *a very successful businessman* who used to donate to local charities.

Then one morning I heard that Teshome had locked himself up in his 'home.' At first it seemed to be a joke to me and to others. It was an unbelievable story that could not be easily related to Teshome's personality. I later learned that he gave away all of his clothes (except one shirt and a pair of trousers he wore) to local Turkana children. He also refused to talk to anyone. After several attempts, he agreed to talk to me and a few others. I visited him several times as he kept himself a prisoner for months. Anyone who listened to his speeches and claims could easily understand that he was delusional and hearing voices. The sad thing about his story was that no one, including aid workers, even suggested his symptoms were related to serious mental illnesses. Or perhaps, honestly, no one knew such illnesses existed.

How could such an outgoing, seemingly strong person end up like that? It was a talking point in his community for a while. It was 'unbelievable.'

All attempts to get him out of his self-imposed quarantine had failed time and again. His one shirt and one pair of trousers had literally worn out on his body as he wore them day and night. He refused used, or new, clothes donations from fellow refugees. He lost his connection to everything: his life, his friends, his hobbies, his future, and his surroundings. His shacks plastic sheeting roof was torn apart and mud-brick walls were disintegrated, creating holes as he lived inside it. As a result of starvation, malnutrition, and life rejection within a few months his majestic body had shrunk down into a frail centenarian's body. Toward the end of his life, he reached the stage where he could not stand up or walk independently, without the support of a cane. He refused to go to a hospital. His friends, afraid to see him die before their eyes, took him to the hospital against his will but he became uncooperative to routine treatment. He preferred dieing to living, and he died in Kakuma Refugee Camp.

I read Viktor Frankl's book, *Man's Search for Reason*, shortly before Teshome got 'sick.' I was surprised to find striking similarities between the behavior of prisoners in German concentration camps, described in the book, and some of the refugees who gave up the will to live (However, I must add that a refugee camp, per se, cannot be compared to a concentration camp by any means because there are major differences between them, as far as I am concerned the similarities are purely behavioral.)

> The prisoner who had lost faith in the future—his future—was doomed. With his loss of belief in the future, he also lost his spiritual hold; he let himself decline and became subject to mental and physical decay. Usually this happened quite suddenly, in the form of a crisis, the symptoms of which were familiar to the experienced camp inmate. We all feared this moment- not for ourselves, which would have been pointless, but for our friends. Usually it began with the prisoner refusing one morning to get dressed and wash or to go on the parade grounds. No entreaties, no blows, no threats had any effect. He just lay there, hardly moving. If this crisis was brought on by an illness, he refused to be taken to the sick-bay or to do anything to help himself. He simply gave up. There he remained, lying in his own excreta, and nothing bothered him any more.

THE ROAD TO SURVIVAL

Kakuma Refugee Camp was established in June 1992 to accommodate about 20,000 South Sudanese refugees. Shortly afterwards, in March 1993, the UNHCR and Kenyan Government relocated thousands of refugees, of different nationalities, from Walda Refugee Camp to Kakuma, after the former was closed following widespread security problems caused by unknown armed groups. Kakuma Camp finally became not only the home for various groups of Sudanese refugees, but also for Ethiopians, Ugandans, Burundians, Rwandese, Congolese, Somalis, Eritreans, Liberians, 'Stateless,' and so on.

In March 1993 refugees and their luggage from Walda Camp arrived in Kakuma, after 3-4 days journey on the backs of trucks. But when refugees arrived there was no housing. There were no shelters. There were no tents. There was nothing except for a few slab latrines which were erected by wrapping plastic sheets around three or four poles. Refugees and their luggage were offloaded onto dry and dusty grounds, they had to live in an open field for three weeks before any kind of construction materials were brought in. Because of the gusty wind and dust showers, that welcomed these guests, some refugees quickly claimed ownership of the latrines and used them to shield their babies and wives from dust and sand rain. Nobody held a grudge against those who possessed the latrines because they did the only right thing they could do to protect their families and themselves. After that not a single toilet was left to use. Thus thousands had to resort to using the nearby bushes, dry riverbeds, and a rock hill as their latrines, in what was later known as Zone Five area. Of course they had to go there during poor visibility hours—late evenings, early mornings, or at noon (when the heat locks up everyone)—to avoid embarrassing themselves.

Such unexpected and unimaginable conditions made many think harder than ever before in search of a means of survival. Whoever said 'necessity is the mother of invention' was one hundred percent right. The over-all conditions of camp life necessitated refugees to do something—something different.

SELF SUPPORT

For the first time in years refugees clearly understood that they had to depend upon themselves and their fellow refugees rather than on the UNHCR. Up until that time many considered the UN agency as their sole provider, though its provisions were limited in scope from the beginning. Many refugees, especially Ethiopians, ended their UNHCR dependency to alleviate their problems. They had to look into themselves as Kakuma became drier, financially, than its dry grounds. Individuals began taking initiatives on their own. They undoubtedly understood that they couldn't change the circumstances they were in. So they started to take action to change themselves.

Refugees taught themselves the art of making mud-bricks to build relatively permanent shelters which lessened the infiltration of sand, dust, and heat. The scorching sun of Kakuma provided the ideal environment for drying the bricks within a day or two. Mud-brick making brought together individuals as one helped another in this cumbersome task. Besides forging group sentiment, mud-brick making gave independence to refugees from depending upon the NGOs unreliable and insufficient provisions for building shelters. It also freed them from complying with the UNHCR standard of building a 3 by 4 meter hut for three persons. Thanks to their innovation and improvisation some refugees built a larger sized mud-brick 'home' for themselves, which enabled them to free themselves from unwanted 'house' mates. They also built their own churches, mosques, tea shops, and kiosks, which served as community centers.

The business ventures pioneered by a handful of guys created job opportunities for fellow refugees and paved the way for many more to learn business skills and to start their own. They raised initial capital from ground zero: selling one or two of their belongings, borrowing a few shillings from friends, bartering items and so on. These business ventures enhanced self-perception among refugees. It enabled them to control some aspects of their lives, such as buying clothes and having transportation money to sneak out to the cities in order to satisfy their hunger for past lives- the nearest commercial town, Kitale, was located 400 kilometers away from Kakuma.

The introduction of business was an important step in the struggle for survival. It enabled most refugees to buy what they couldn't get from the UNHCR. Refugees may get a cup of sugar, a few tablespoons of salt, a few grams of beans, a few kilograms of wheat flour or maize grains in a typical biweekly distribution period but they never got tea, coffee, fruits, vegetables, meat, milk, pepper, or other ingredients necessary to make staple foods. Those few daring refugees, enduring the hurdles of dealing with police stationed at 'checkpoints' throughout the roads leading to and from refugee camp, had brought, from the mainland, commodities unavailable in the camp district. Thanks to the pass word of TKK (*Toa kitu kidogo*) they quickly became master players of police games and positioned themselves as go-betweens for novice businessmen. Camp business also alleviated boredom for most refugees. It brought together diverse refugee communities. It minimized conflicts as it created more inter-communal understanding as a result of daily interactions during transactions among buyers and sellers. Moreover, it brought citizens and refugees' closer as they bought and sold and as some of them engaged in indirect joint business ventures.

Refugee tea shops, coffee houses, restaurants, and kiosks offered informal forums for information exchanges about national and international current affairs and their ramifications for refugees. They became venues for informal social gatherings and for maintaining social contacts.

As a matter of fact, refugee camps were basically cut off from the world at large, there were no newspapers and no television broadcasts. Besides, refugees are not allowed, by law, to move outside the camp perimeters, which effectively cut off outside contact. Refugees filled this void with their radios. Short wave transistor radios were the only means to hear what was happening in the outside world. It was not uncommon to see refugees clustered together at news hours listening to the BBC, VOA, *Deutchwelle,* and, in some instances, radio broadcasts from their homelands.

Interestingly enough, elections in the countries which offered more resettlement quotas, such as the United States, Canada, and Australia, were closely monitored in the refugee camps. The US presidential campaigns and election results, in particular, were by far the most hotly debated among refugees than any other country's presidential elections. Just as the US electorate would like to know thier presidential candidates' stance on certain policy issues, refugees also discussed whether the victory of one or the other candidate would open up or close down humanitarian assistance or refugee resettlement programs. Refugees worried daily about their future. Resettlement to a third country is a refugees' ultimate hope of rescue from uncertainty, fear, and the hardship of camp life; and of becoming a 'somebody' once again.

James Martin SJ, who worked at the Jesuit Refugee Service in Nairobi, Kenya, from 1992-1994, with East African refugees, described in his book, *This Our Exile: A Spiritual Journey with the Refugees of East Africa*, that "resettlement concerns" are one of the "severe problems" facing refugees.

> In the entire camp there was one social worker to cope with an enormous caseload of thousands of people, all with severe problems- hunger, sickness, family worries, resettlement concerns, and fear.

REFUGEE INTERACTIONS: ARE THEY HELPFUL FOR THEIR SURVIVAL?

Obviously, the subject of most refugees interactions revolved around issues that affected their daily lives most often: the camp life (rations, weather, safety, diseases, death, burials, 'chances'), host government's attitudes towards refugees including its relationship with the government of their country of origin, the UNHCR, the arrival and/or departure of officials associated with refugee protection and resettlement programs, the current affairs of their countries of origin, and the United States' policy toward the government of their country of origin. When it comes to refugees expressing their opinions, I observed over the years that there were at least four categories of refugees' in the camps: analysts, optimists, alarmists, and rumor disseminators. My observations included opinions expressed in group settings during formal and informal discussions, for instance, in religious places, community meetings, coffee shops, kiosks, and in-group settings.

The opinions of analysts (there are many educated refugees in the camps) were grounded on realistic assessments and evaluations. In effect, their views were seen as gloomy by many refugees who desperately sought 'to escape' from refugee life sooner. Analysts' were guarded from offering promises and they hardly ever saw a light at the end of the tunnel. The message of the optimists, on the other hand, was centered around reassuring others that deliverance would come sooner rather than later. They 'saw' light on the horizon. "United States, Australia, Canada, New Zealand, etc...are going to increase their resettlement quotas." "A shipment of wheat floor, oil, and other materials has arrived in Mombassa Port, and the convoy carrying such items is en route to Kakuma." They delivered messages that encouraged refugees to persevere 'for a while.' Their message was focused on giving hope and on encouraging refugees to persevere through difficulties. Alarmists talked about the 'trouble' refugees could face soon, and the 'conspiracy' against refugees. "The Kenyan government is going to shut down the camp." "There won't be rations next month because..." "Bandits are going to attack the camp..., watch out!" Although their information was often unfounded and highly exaggerated it created concern among refugees who had previously witnessed other refugee camps being closed by the government, or who lacked rations for various reasons, or who had experienced armed attacks against refugees. The topics of choice for rumor disseminators included everything from home countries to host nations, from The United States to The UNHCR. The people associated with being the sources of rumors were known to many refugees because of their humor and feel-good talks. They often frequented coffee shops, public places, and kiosk windows. Places where laughter is the scarcest of commodities, who cared whether their stories were true or not when they lightened heavy hearts a little bit?

In my opinion all four, or even more types of people, were important in enhancing (unknowingly) refugees' survival. Being frequently exposed to optimistic, pessimistic, confusing, and/or alarming information (all at the same time or in short intervals) would make, I think, refugees neither excited, nor depressed as one counteracts the other. I think they offer some sort of Exposure Therapy that desensitizes refugees.

Even though the circumstances in the camps are more depressing than exciting, I thought such (conflicting) information flow was important in maintaining the status quo of the refugees' mental health. It's even more important when we consider refugees have no, or very little, means of updating themselves on what's going on in their lives, in particular, and in the outside world in general. Whether it's factual or fiction, they get a variety of 'news;' and getting the 'news' is more important than its content.

GROUP SUPPORT

In places like refugee camps groups are more important than an individual for survival, in terms of sharing meager resources, supporting each other, and counseling and comforting during a crisis. Refugees utilise various coping mechanisms to ward off "physical and mental decay." One of the surest methods was maintaining a social support system. Among various Sudanese and Somalis refugee groups I observed strong social bonds and group support systems. In these communities, most families and kin members fled their countries of origin together. This had helped them to maintain their culture, norms, and cohesiveness. I witnessed the same cohesiveness among some Ugandan refugee groups. For obvious reasons, the Sudanese community was by far the most organized in delivering services to its members. Sudanese community leaders and elders did a wonderful job of organizing and overseeing the "Lost Boys," about ten thousand Sudanese children who were orphaned as a result of war; and they successfully advocated for a permanent resettlement solution for them.

When it comes to the Ethiopian communities, their demographic and social composition was different than most communities. Almost all Ethiopian refugees were young individuals and predominantly male. They mainly originated from urban centers. They did not flee with their families or relatives. In the refugee camps, however, they created alternative support systems that filled the void and enabled them to reach out to individual refugees during a social crisis such as illnesses, hospitalization, death, and burials; and even during festivities such as weddings and holiday celebrations. Among Ethiopians, like most refugee communities, refugee churches, mosques, community leaders, volunteers, and in-groups were at the forefront of administering and running the services needed to support needy persons among them.

The hardship of overall camp life necessitated smaller communities, such as Bantus, Rwandese, Burundians, Congolese, Liberians, Eritreans etc, to come together as a group to help their communities and to advance their causes, especially in seeking durable solutions. I remember one Rwandese community leader who walked miles every day, Monday through Friday, from his home to the UNHCR compound to advocate for his community and, of course, for himself. One day he told me that he was "*making real progress.*" Likewise, Oromo community leaders had shown similar conviction and persistence in advocating for their members.

Refugee communities, at large, provided a sense of belonging and protection for their members. They created an environment of social bonding where friends, churches, mosques, and persons living in the immediate neighborhoods, formed strong social support systems. 'In-groups' and refugee faith organizations played near-similar roles, like those of families and communities back in their homelands. Most refugee communities commemorated the New Year and national holidays of their country of origin in the camps. Their community leaders played an important role in organising ceremonies that helped refugees to maintain connections to their national heritages, to their cultures and norms. For instance, Sudanese youth parades during Christmas and special occasions, and the Ethiopian New Year celebrations were among the colorful events to watch. Besides, refugee leaders played a crucial role in maintaining the rule of law in the camp by being bridges between their community members on one hand, and the camp management and Kenyan law enforcement bodies on the other hand. As representatives, they often advocated on behalf of their community members. In so doing they offered hope and optimism. These were important tools of survival for refugees.

Belonging to a group, whether it's a large community group or a few friends, is important for individuals to cope with adverse camp situations. Maybe this was why Darwin widened the definition of the term, "Struggle for Survival," to include "dependence of one being on another, and including...the life of the individual."

One major problem of refugee group support, however, is that the group is unstable and fluid. There were plenty of situations where refugees lost their friends and acquaintances, and hence they would be drift away to the world of loneliness. Repatriation, resettlement, death, a refugee's own decision to move to another location are some of the ways refugees lose their close friends and group members. Those who were left behind in the camp would not only face separation anxiety but also would worry about their fate. When they looked around at their surroundings, it only added pessimism and visions of a bleak future, to the extent that hopelessness would creep into their mind. This would lead some refugees to a mental meltdown.

HOPE

If there is one thing that defines a refugees' life, it is the uncertainty of the future. For them the future is bleak and life is stagnant. In the words of Misganaw Workneh, "All tomorrows are the same." Refugees live in the past and the present but they talk little about the future because they have no control over it. For good reason, their present circumstances breed fear and uncertainty. The camp life often makes it hard for refugees to be hopeful. However, they get hope from current and former refugees, from their religions, their beliefs, their values, their inner strength, and from their conviction to persevere through hardship 'imposed' on them by circumstance. An Ethiopian saying sums up such this conviction to persevere: "Yehim ken yalfal" (Even this day could pass). In other words, one should look forward to a better tomorrow and should not give in to hardship.

A Ugandan refugee, Jimmy Bosco Oryema, recounted in his poem, *The Day I Will Never Forget*, the significance of hope and the reason for his living. Part of the poem reads:

> Because of hope I still live
> Because of hope I can sing and dance
> It is because of hope that I laugh
> It is because of hope that I love.

I had heard Oryema—he was known as Bosco—reading the whole poem in a 'Refugee Writers Workshop' in Kakuma Camp. Hearing him explaining the significance of hope in his life and what the poem meant to him was a moving experience.

Sometimes little things would make a difference in unexpected ways. Such was the case when I read *Man's Search for Reason,* which changed my perspective of living in difficult circumstances. It enhanced my appreciation for 'hope' and the role it plays in promoting the chances of human survival. The images of the prisoners, Dr Frankl described in the book, who became vulnerable to simple illnesses because they "lost hope" stuck in my mind. Some of the phrases I read in the book were also unforgettable: "future goal," "man's inner strength," "getting through suffering," "giving up hope," "to find a meaning in one's life," and so on. In particular one sentence, which Dr. Viktor quoted from the late 19th century German philosopher, Nietzsche, had stuck in my mind: "He who has a why to live can bear with almost any how." After all, he wrote this book after surviving the most horrendous experience in human history. His "why" to live was finishing the book he had started before he ended up in the concentration camp and reuniting with his family. Regardless of situational differences the readers of the book could easily relate to his story and his philosophy of life.

Besides, I anchored my thoughts on one verse from the Book of Proverbs: "If you falter in times of trouble, how small is your strength!" I equated faltering to lack of strength and weakness from within. So in order not to falter one has to refuse to be weak within. In other words, one has to build up inner strength, a hope to live and a hope for a better tomorrow. Back then I talked to some friends about that verse—about building inner strength. Several years later, I had a phone conversation with a former refugee who now lives in Canada. He asked me: "Do you still remember that verse?" I said, "Yes, I do, but I don't remember the chapter." He laughed and said: "Proverbs 24:10." He told me that he never forgot it. I was glad to hear that he had been meditating on it.

REFUGEE WRITINGS

If inspirations were motivations for writers elsewhere, refugees were inspired to write by the circumstances of their living. Refugee writings are mediums to compare and contrast circumstances of self—a refugee—with others—the outside world. They are channels for venting anger and frustration against real or imagined forces of unfairness. Refugee writings are vehicles of soul-searching, of finding courage and determination, of describing the "sense of double dislocation," and of rallying fellow refugees to endure hardships for the sake of their beliefs and life principles that made them flee their homelands in the first place. Refugee writers would feel they had 'spoken' their minds and advocated on behalf of their peers.

In a sense refugee writings are therapeutic. For the writer, they offer therapy. They are cathartic—they are channels for "relieving emotional tensions." For refugees, they give a sense of being heard by others and a sense of having an advocate to voice their concerns. Refugee writings, as Gedi had summed up, are "a means of survival."

Refugees, particularly those in Kakuma camp, had widely expressed their feelings, frustrations, opinions, dismay, hope, protests, and life lessons via poetry, short stories, essays, and prose. I recommend any one interested in specializing in refugee issues to examine refugee writings, especially *KANEBU: Kakuma News Bulletin* issues from 1994 to date; anthologies of refugee writings such as *Tilting Cages* (1995), Japanese translation of *Tilting Cages* (1998), and *Mama Kakuma* (2002). *Diasporic Ghosts: A Discourse on Refugee & Exile Issues* (2005) not only illuminated refugee issues to a wider audience; but also brought together various perspectives on advocating and understanding refugee issues.

INTERVENTIONS

The establishment of schools in Kakuma Camp for Sudanese children and the "Lost Boys;" the introduction of a degree program in collaboration with a South African University, the limited scholarships offered to refugees by some agencies to join Kenyan colleges and universities, and the implementation of vocational and capacity building programs are some of the examples of what I call positive interventions by humanitarian organizations.

Such interventions not only help some refugees in meaningful ways but they can also serve as lessons for any future endeavors to assist refugees.

The first lesson would be realising the willingness of refugees to learn and to improve themselves even in difficult circumstances, if given the opportunity. This was demonstrated by Sudanese children who attended classes (some of them at outdoor classrooms) overcoming hunger, dust, and heat. The willingness and determination of refugees was also demonstrated by refugees of various nationalities who showed persistence while studying extension degree programs in the camp regardless of shortages of textbooks, reference materials, and difficult circumstances. It was also demonstrated by those few refugees who got the chance to compete with citizens and who graduated with distinction from Kenyan higher education institutions.

The second lesson, which I think is often neglected, was the resourcefulness of the refugee population. Almost all teachers from about 20 refugee schools in Greater Kakuma area, the tutors of various degree programs of distance education classes, and the trainers of vocational programs (e.g. tailoring, soap making, agro-forestry, massages, carpentry, masonry, handcrafts, and typing) were refugees. This proved that refugees are not only the people who crossed borders carrying their bags but they also constituted people from all walks of life who are productive citizens eager to overcome adverse situations in their lives.

CONCLUSION

Life in a refugee camp is a journey of trial and tribulation. Besides the difficult living conditions of the camps refugees had to wrestle daily with mighty forces within themselves: alienation (from their families, friends, lands, cultures); dispossession and loss of respect (somebody becoming nobody); fear (of diseases, death, attacks); uncertainty (of tomorrow, of their life direction); and lack of control over their situation. These forces often eat at the body and soul of a refugee in a piecemeal way, although the degree in which they affect refugees varies from one refugee to another. While there were several severe cases of mental health issues in the camps, I think this problem remained unrecognized or overlooked.

Refugees overcome the hardship of camp life partly by re-creating their previous environment, as was witnessed in transforming the wilderness of Kakuma to a somehow livable and 'normal' place. It was a transformation from within. Such transformation involved refugees self-enabling and improvising, such as self-initiated small business schemes, and fostering social bonds and group support mechanisms, which substituted the roles of families back home, with fellow refugees and refugee communities.

Notes

1. IC stands for Individual Case. The acronym is used almost exclusively by UNHCR officers to refer to a refugee or a case submitted by a refugee.

2. Yilma Tafere, telephone conversation, December, 2007.

3. "Men too many but not enough women," *East African Standard*, May 12, 1999.

4. Hagaloo, Jaarso, 29

Chapter 7

EXILE IN EARLY NIGERIAN LITERATURE: A COMPARATIVE STUDY OF NWANA'S *OMENUKO* AND ACHEBE'S *THINGS FALL APART*

By Francoise Ugochukwu

THE TWO PANELS OF A DIPTYCH

"Where is exile? [...] Is there a state of exile? For surely even an exile must exist in some space—physical or mental," Soyinka (2000:62) once asked. It is significant that the first lines of the very first novel in Igbo should start with a definition of exile, not the exile abroad already experienced by the first Nigerian scholars at the time as they travelled to Britain or the USA for further studies, but an exile within. There, as in Achebe's first novel, the exile retains the use of his first language but experiences the meaning of the Nigerian Igbo word 'abroad' still in use today, more than fifty years later, with the road fulfilling its role of "meeting place of space and time" (Everett 2004:23). In the introduction to his only novel, Nwana both announces the storyline and reveals a rather positive and optimistic view of that experience:

> Around our town in Africa, this belief is accepted as law:
> if anyone goes to another town and lives there as a guest,

even if things are good, or he is a merciful person, or a gracious one, or a fair judge, he will always be reminded that he is a guest in that land and he will be preparing himself for his inevitable return to the town of his birth. At any time he may be told, proverbially or directly, that he is a guest and must not fail to return home.

This belief is strong. That is why anyone who has bad luck that causes him to be shamed in any way will pack up his things and go home. When he reaches the town of his birth, the joy he encounters will repay him more than everything he experienced in the other town where he lived as a guest. His people will welcome his return with rejoicing and happiness. In good time, he will teach his people about the interesting things he learned on his expedition, and he will have a chance to apply what he learned to work in his own town. All these things will contribute to his joy and he says, 'Good town, good town,' as the story in this book will demonstrate.

These lines carefully placed at the onset of the story do present exile, whatever the circumstances that led to it, as a positive learning experience that eventually turns out to be for the common good—a picture similar to that later presented in a good number of African novels, that of immigrants "essentially portrayed as expatriates destined to return to their homeland and 'true' country" (Albert 2005:45). It is a journey within the limits of a known territory by a well-behaved character that finds himself as a guest in his newfound land, an experience crafted like a two-sided coin, with the guest first enjoying a warm welcome, before being told in no uncertain terms, after a while, that he has exceeded his welcome. Nwana presents exile as meant to be temporary, his length hinging on the person's ability to discern the 'signs of the time' and take the expected decision soon enough to avoid undue embarrassment and shame. This implies that the sojourner is both discerning and willing to turn back. It predicts a stable, warm and forgiving home group that keeps the sojourner's place in his absence, awaiting his return with great anticipation. It describes a rapturous return heralding the recognition of the returnee as a local hero as he shares the gained wisdom and knowledge with his fellow villagers, proving exile as a journey towards both knowledge of self and others and confirming the truth of the Igbo proverb -- "the traveller is wiser than the white-haired man."

Both Nwana and Achebe take their main protagonists through the same experience: that of successful self-made men, respected in their community and entrusted with the care of wards, suddenly found to have violated the laws of the land and consequently forced into years of exile, within their linguistic and cultural area but away from their home-town. Both come from a poor, obscure background: in *Things Fall Apart*, Okonkwo is the son of Unoka, a lazy farmer who preferred wine and merriment to hard work; Omenuko's parents on the other hand, though hardworking, only had tiny yam barns. Both men grow up to become mature, highly successful community leaders, whose words are respected and who are entrusted with young ones to train. Both are family men: Omenuko has four children and Okonkwo eight in the opening pages of the novels. They are both successful at work, Omenuko as a businessman and the other as a farmer. Both of them adhere to the ancestral religion, even though this is clearer in Okonkwo's case. They both commit a major crime against the land: and although Okonkwo's killing of a young man during a funeral as his gun explodes (Achebe 1958:87) is accidental, it places him in the same situation as Omenuko who, faced with a major business setback and imminent bankruptcy after losing all his goods in a freak accident while crossing a bridge, sells his young cousin and some of his trainees into slavery.

They both are then forced to flee and go into exile during the night, a move that keeps them just a walking distance away from their clan, in an age-long pre-agreed, traditional place of refuge with people they know. Both are made to feel welcome by their hosts and given substantive support to start life anew. Both stay a number of years in exile—some twenty years for Omenuko, seven for Okonkwo. While there, they both greatly prosper and rise to take on leadership roles within their host communities. They both struggle to come to terms with their fate, bemoan their exile and do experience some form of homesickness, especially Okonkwo, whereas Omenuko suffers more from a guilty conscience. They both receive the regular visits of a trusted friend who acts as confident and adviser and eventually helps them to negotiate their return to the ancestral home. The end alone is strikingly different: while Omenuko, though violently pushed away by envious fellow warrant chiefs, returns as a hero and revels in his now peaceful prosperity and well-earned reputation, Okonkwo fails to succeed in making the grand come back he had envisaged and ends up committing suicide after a time in prison and the murder of a court messenger. Exile acts as a catalyst, revealing two very different men.

The way those two men handle their exile is shaped by their character: both are focused, ambitious, risk-oriented, hard-working, born leaders, impulsive, faithful in friendship. Yet in some respects, Omenuko and Okonkwo are quite different: the first is a manoeuvring, calculating, shrewd character who embodies the famous Igbo tortoise's ancestral wisdom; the latter displays a violent temper triggered by a constant fear of losing the reputation acquired at great cost, and proves both obstinate and set in his ways. This double story of exile is set in two different yet complementary moments of Igbo history, with Achebe's novel rooted at the onset of the colonial penetration whereas Nwana shows Omenuko negotiating with an ever-present colonial power.

RESETTLEMENT AND CONTRASTING FEELINGS

Being a wealthy businessman buying and selling along the market towns of the land, Omenuko was used to travelling and enjoyed a network of business partners. But what happens to him in the novel triggers a different kind of journey. Once told by Omenuko about his brisk business with the slave dealers, the businessman's brothers at once realise the seriousness of his action: "what you did will be remembered forever. This is what our grandfathers described as something grandchildren grow up to deal with. This means that our children will suffer because of it; and our children's children will also suffer as well" (Chapter 2). They thus encourage him to run away—a decision which spares the family the need to explain the sale of the young boys and avoids the villagers' angry reaction and ensuing public shame. Omenuko's family joins him in his flight, deserting the town in the dead of the night in a carefully staged plan to seek refuge in Mgborogwu, a nearby town that recorded a shared history with theirs in a culture where sanctuaries were always provided:

> If anyone found that he had done something bad that made it impossible for him to live in our village, that person would run away to another village called [...] Mgborogwu. Also, if a person coming from [...] Mgborogwu did something very bad, he would be sure to run away to our village.

> This is something that began so long ago that I cannot say
> what caused it or brought it on. A thing like this is what
> the people of our village call "reciprocity." That is why the
> people of our village and the Mgborogwu people still
> honour the reciprocity arrangement (Chapter 2).

As announced in the introduction to the novel, the family's arrival in Mgborogwu is the signal of a celebration, because they make up a large number of young able-bodied men and women who will add to the town's workforce—a feeling the author explains at great length. *Things Fall Apart* (1958:87) tells a similar story: after his accidental killing of a young townsman during a funeral, "the only course open to Okonkwo was to flee from the clan. It was a crime against the earth goddess to kill a clansman and a man who committed it must flee from the land." The misfortune that befalls the two characters follows a well rehearsed pattern rooted in tradition as confirmed by Basden: in the case of accidental killing, "the manslayer is notified and given opportunity to flee the town. He must remain in exile for three years. After that interval, he may return, if he so desires, and will be received on payment of compensation to the relatives of the man slain, at a rate to be fixed." As the culprit leaves the town, "[his] huts are burnt, [his] walls broken down and trees felled" (Basden 1938:259-260).

On arrival, both men are fully supported and given land to build on. The two books complement themselves in offering the full picture of the communities' expectations on the exiles: the host community expects them to integrate, show appreciation for the welcome and support given, and function as useful members of the group. The home community on the other hand, in spite of its having ostracised them, secretly hopes they will keep them in remembrance, make amends for their wrong doing and eventually return with something to show for the years spent 'abroad'. Conscious of these expectations, and keen to display manly qualities, both men thus try their utmost to integrate with their host communities, trying to recreate home by building houses and farming, and boosting their ego through leadership affirmation and gifts: "Okonkwo and his family worked very hard to plant a new farm" (Achebe 1958: 92). Okonkwo equally takes part in local politics, albeit half-heartedly—when things did not go his way, "this is a womanly clan, he thought. Such a thing would never happen in his fatherland Umuofia" (Achebe 1958:113). As days go by, his thoughts teach him the art "to exist in a kind of paradox, a state of tension where the mind simultaneously embraces an anchor in alien territory, yet ensures that it stays at one removed from that alien milieu"(Soyinka 2000:63). This attitude, triggered by his forced displacement and fed by his sense of loss, is made worse by his having to live by himself—as Achebe put it himself in an interview, "man is [not] strong enough on his own to counter these forces that he might come up against. He stands a better chance if he is operating from within his society. This is the value of a society like our traditional society where you were part of a bigger unit" (Emenyonu 1997:42). Tradition meant that Okonkwo's maternal community could not offer their in-law the same support he enjoyed in his hometown.

Omenuko's case proves very different from that of Okonkwo's manslaughter—he decided to commit a crime. The boys' sale barely signed, he is consumed with guilt, and upon his return home that night, looses no time in confessing his crime to his immediate family and to seek their advice. In exile,

> he was constantly thinking about what he had done. His conscience bothered him greatly, and even though Omenuko was no longer in our town, his heart could not rest and he had no peace of mind on account of what he had done" (Chapter 3).

Another difference between Okonkwo and Omenuko is the latter's eagerness, probably facilitated by his household's backing and no doubt by his temperament, to engage in local politics while in exile. His good advice and worthy behaviour win the heart of the local chief who makes him his spokesman and, on his death bed, gives Omenuko his warrant to manage until his son grows up. Omenuko then leads the Chief's burial rites to the town's satisfaction and starts directing their affairs, having had his leadership recognised by the colonial authorities.

> Because of Omenuko's good deeds toward his fellow men, no one remembered that he was a stranger in the land he was governing, nor did anyone remember that it was Obiefula's warrant that Omenuko was using to govern the land. Neither did they call him a stranger, because Omenuko and his brothers married women from there and from surrounding towns (Chapter 6).

This is a remarkable statement that wholly differs from Okonkwo's despair, expressed in his dull summary of his life in Mbanta:

> It was like beginning life anew without the vigour and enthusiasm of youth, like learning to become left-handed in old age. Work no longer had for him the pleasure it used to have, and when there was no work to do he sat in a silent half-sleep. His life had been ruled by a great passion—to become one of the lords of the clan. That has been his life-spring. And he had all but achieved it. Then everything had been broken. He has been cast out of his clan like a fish on to a dry, sandy beach, panting (Achebe 1958:92).

Nwana's Omenuko loses no time and takes more wives from his host community, produces more children and settles his brothers as well—a sign he has a long term vision to prosper in his new environment. Yet whenever he remembers the past and his flight, he feels sad.

LOST IN BOTH TIME AND SPACE

The fact is that both men, after a rather promising resettlement, end up finding out that "exile is about pain, about physical and psychical pain" (Everett 2004:112). While Omenuko's days, behind the façade of his assertive behaviour, are consumed by guilt and worrying about the fate of those he sold, Okonkwo cries over the loss of his compound and fame. For him, exile is indeed "generalised spiritual or existential state of incompletion. [...] A melancholy and solitary state" (Everett 2004:4) triggered by his spatial and temporal estrangement from the community that sustained his life. Conscious of the potential danger this attitude to life represents for both Okonkwo and his household, Uchendu, the oldest man in the host community, calls his people to shake the warrior out of despondency—this he does by first bluntly defining Okonkwo's present condition: "Why is Okonkwo with us today? This is not his clan. We are only his mother's kinsmen. He does not belong here. He is an exile, condemned for seven years to live in a strange land. And so he is bowed with grief" (Achebe 1958:93-4). Having dealt the blow and faced his in-law with the facts, he then encourages Okonkwo to comfort his household to ensure they eventually all go back after the seven years without losing any of their number to death, since "if you allow sorrow to weigh you down and kill you, they will all die in exile." In his talk, Uchendu presents exile as an unavoidable yet great loss comparable to that of children, a loss people cannot comprehend, yet need to accept as a part of life. Okonkwo still tries to make sense of his fate and resorts to traditional beliefs: "he saw clearly in it the finger of his personal God or Chi. For how else could he explain this great misfortune and exile [...]?" (Achebe 1958:108).

All through his exiled years, Okonkwo's mind will remain focused on his return, in a sort of 'back to the future' mental frame. He never really invests in Mbanta's affairs, refuses to marry his daughters there and only works to survive. His life hangs on the news brought from home and he keeps trading his yams at home and getting money from their sale, as someone torn between two worlds and constantly feeding on past memories to take his past into his future. There is no sign of reflection or change on his part: he just feels cheated and stays frozen in time. His despair translates into the naming of his children and will still show in his later evaluation of his years in exile

> the seven wasted and weary years were at last dragging to a close. Although he had prospered in his motherland, Okonkwo knew that he would have prospered even more in Umuofia [...]. In these seven years, he would have climbed to the utmost heights. And so he regretted every day of his exile. His mother's kinsmen had been very kind to him and he was grateful. But that did not alter the facts. He had called the first child born to him in exile Nneka— 'Mother is supreme'—out of politeness to his mother's kinsmen. But two years later when a son was born, he called him Nwofia—'Begotten in the wilderness' (Achebe 1958:115).

Home support is indeed of peculiar importance to the two exiles. Obierika visits Okonkwo after one year and brings money from the sale of his yams and news from home and the region. Nearly two years later, he returns with bad news about the arrival of Europeans and the conversion of Okonkwo's son to Christianity. These conversations were meant to help Okonkwo keep abreast of developments in his home town. Omenuko too receives support from home in the person of his wealthy friend Igwe. "As the years of exile passed one by one, Okonkwo's dreams of going back home are fuelled by his friend's visits: it seemed to him that his chi might now be making amends for the past disaster. His yams grew abundantly, not only in his motherland but also in Umuofia, where his friend gave them out year by year to share-croppers." (Achebe 1958:121). Yet he will eventually discover that a successful return is now impossible, as home is not only a place but also a time that has now elapsed—he will come back home as one from the past into a present that has no place for him. His exile was into both time and place: it stopped time for him while his village moved on. Deep down, Okonkwo, whose wisdom was rooted in oral tradition, had known that from the start: "seven years was a long time to be away from one's clan. A man's place was not always there, waiting for him. As soon as he left, someone else rose and filled it. The clan was like a lizard; if it lost its tail, it soon grew another" (Achebe 1958:121).

FIGHTING OVER A PIECE OF LAND

If he had ever completed the dream of erasing his past and enjoying the rights and privileges of a son of the soil in his new community, the penny soon dropped for Omenuko. The 'honeymoon' period of initial resettlement over, he discovers that "the recognition of frontiers can be overwhelming, and [that] the condition of exile is the daily knowledge, indeed the palpable experience of such frontiers" (Soyinka 2000: 64). Hearing that the people of Mgborogwu remain bent on forcing him to hand over his father's warrant to the now adult son of the late chief, considering his political career threatened and seeing no other alterna-tive as he does not want to return home yet, he prepares to move to the only available land, the evil forest on the confines of their town (Chapter 6). This is a foul-smelling wilderness, a cursed place—the only way for Omenuko to escape his hosts' murderous envy. Deciding to build in that place went against Igbo tradition, as Achebe explains: "every clan and village had its 'evil forest'. In it were buried all those who died of the really evil diseases, like leprosy and smallpox. It was also the dumping ground for the potent fetishes of great medicine men when they died. An 'evil forest' was, therefore, alive with sinister forces and powers of darkness" (1958:105)—in *Things Fall Apart*, that place was given to the Christians to build their church in the hope that they would not survive. This move is painted by Nwana as a huge victory over the odds, with a whole Chapter devoted to the colourful descrip-tion of the stylish traditional houses that spring in the forest and attract the attention of both surrounding towns and the colonial authorities.

In reality, this desperate and futile attempt to take root only leaves Omenuko tired and homesick, the sign of "the anguish of a lost past, [...] sense of uncertainty, aimless wandering, lack of direction, nowhere to go" (Everett 2004:52). His speech to his former hosts explains his decision while revealing his disappointment and bitterness:

> this [Mgborogwu] is no longer a place of refuge or rest for me, since you forgot that I am one who saved land that was being lost--that is, this our land, as you know very well. But now you have forgotten these things and treat me as if I were your enemy. I shall call you my masters even if you have forgotten me; I myself shall not forget you, so that the land will not kill me because you are my brothers. But since you plotted secretly behind my back, you have counted me out from among you and set me apart as a stranger. Because of this it will be better for me if I remain indeed a stranger (Chapter 6).

He then builds a whole new village in the 'Cold Bush', manages to attract a number of people to his new abode and obtains a new warrant for himself. Yet, in the midst of his now secured wealth and prosperity, his mind is still divided as he asks his brothers for advice on how to trace and buy back the boys he sold—a constant worry that robs him of his peace. He eventually buys most of them back and at that point, as the title of Chapter 9 implies, "Omenuko longs to return to his native land." He explains:

> I came to live in this forest, and because of that I was not one of the Mgborogwu, nor did I belong to the people of our land. Now, what I have in mind is to find a way that I and the men and the spirits whom I offended in our land can be reconciled (Chapter 9).

He then asks his friend to negotiate his return for him. Later on, presenting the items traditionally required for the banquet and public sacrifice of reconciliation to his people, Omenuko reminds them:

> Please, everyone who sees me, let him remember that I belong to you and you belong to me. From today on, if there is anything I did wrong in the past, tell me how I

can remedy it; I will not fail to do as you want. There is no law in our land that I do not remember, even in the place where I live now; it is the law of our land that I am following (Chapter 10).

The reconciliation is then sealed by the chief in a short discourse. The second ceremony, in the sanctuary, seals Omenuko's reconciliation with the ancestral spirits of the land. The way is now reopened for the entire family to freely return and for Omenuko's brothers to take wives from their home town. Omenuko concludes:

> Since that time when I left my village, it is true that the place where I live and my life did not please me as they should, but now I am happier, and if death should come to me now, I will not be afraid of it, because I will not feel remorse before I draw my last breath. That is all I wanted to tell you (Chapter 10).

At that point in the novel, one expects him to move back to his home town and take the full benefit of the costly celebrations just performed. Instead, the author shows his main character building more houses where he lives (Chapter 11) and rising to the enviable position of a top warrant chief, unleashing added resentment and envy among the forty-five other less successful chiefs who are now his subordinates. The chiefs' ominous statement is a reminder of Omenuko's status in the land he tried to claim: "No, this will not happen in our land -a stranger being the head over all of us. If he is going to be the government, let him go to his own village—he will not stay in our village." (Chapter 12). After trying all kinds of tricks to remove him from his position, twenty-six of the villages conspire against him and decide to engage him in a bloody battle. While realising the implications of his fighting them, Omenuko decides to prepare, knowing that this will lead to his having to leave the place permanently and encourages his people, saying: "It is better that we go home alive than go home dead" (Chapter 13).

HOME AT LAST

The moment eventually comes for the two exiles to move back home at long last.

Okonkwo knew [...] that he had lost his place among the
nine masked spirits who administered justice in the clan.
He had lost the chance to lead his warlike clan against the
new religion [...]. He had lost the years in which he might
have taken the highest titles in the clan. But some of these
losses were not irreparable. He was determined that his
return should be marked by his people. He would return
with a flourish, and regain the seven wasted years. Even in
his first year in exile he had begun to plan for his return
(Achebe 1958:121).

These plans included rebuilding his compound on a more magnifi-
cent scale, with a bigger barn, building huts for two more new wives,
showing his wealth by initiating his sons into Ozo society and taking
for himself the highest title in the land. He then sent money to Obierika
to build two huts in his old compound—he would himself build more
huts and the outside wall on his return. At the end of his last harvest
in Mbanta, Okonkwo throws a big feast to thank his hosts before he
goes—"my mother's people have been good to me and I must show
my gratitude" (Achebe 1958:117). He then departs with his in-laws'
blessings. But Okonkwo's hopes regarding his return to his native town
will not materialise: apart from the appearance of his two marriageable
daughters causing a stir, Umuofia takes no special notice of the warrior's return. The clan has changed too much for that and Okonkwo's
failure to realise that the time for war had passed leads him to murder
and to suicide.

Omenuko's return could not be more radically different: his whole
town gives him a hand in transporting his goods back home, and

from the year 1918 on when they returned to our village,
no year passed when you would not have seen one or two of
his children in primary six. Neither was there a year when
you would not see one of his children going for a white
collar job. Several of his children worked for the Railway
Corporation, and some were traders (Chapter 15).

His wealth does not only help him train all the children in his
extended family: his town brands him "a man of the people" for his
generosity—he contributes to the betterment of his clan and helps the

local judge in his spare time on a voluntary basis. For him at least, exile came to an end for good.

References

Achebe C., *Things Fall Apart*, London, Heinemann 1958, 158p. (1982 ed.)

Afigbo A.E., *The Warrant Chiefs—Indirect rule in SouthEastern Nigeria 1891-1929*, Longman 1972, 338p.

Albert C., *L'immigration dans le roman francophone contemporain*, Paris, Karthala 2005, 220p.

Basden G.T., *Niger Ibos*, London, F. Cass 1938, reprint 1966, 456p.

Emenyonu Ernest & Pat, "Achebe: Accountable to Our society," in B. Lindfors (ed), *Conversations with Chinua Achebe*, Jackson, University Press of Mississippi 1997 pp.35-44.

Everett W. & Wagstaff P. (eds), *Cultures of Exile. Images of Displacement*, New York, Berghahn Books 2004, 192p.

Igboanusi H., *A Dictionary of Nigerian English Usage*, Ibadan, Enicrownfit Publishers 2002, 307p.

Lindfors B. (ed), *Conversations with Chinua Achebe*, Jackson, University Press of Mississippi 1997, 199p.

Nwana P., *Omenuko*, Ikeja, Longmans of Nigeria, 1964 ed. (1933, Igbo text).

Nwana P., *Omenuko, the first Igbo novel*, translated from the Igbo by Pritchett Frances W., http://www.columbia.edu/itc/mealac/pritchett/00fwp/igbo/omenuko/index.html#index

Soyinka Wole, "Exile: Thresholds of Loss and Identity" in *Seuils/Thresholds. Les literatures africaines anglophones, Anglophonia* 7, 2000, pp.61-70

Chapter 8

REFUGEES IN LITERATURE: HUMANIZING THE STRANGE

Andrea Useem

Lilly Abdal is not your average Ethiopian refugee. For one thing, she's a white European by birth, and she grew up in Morocco. If that combination sounds improbable, that may be because it is fictional: Lilly is the protagonist of a 2005 novel by anthropologist Camilla Gibb entitled *Sweetness in the Belly*.

Lilly is an Ethiopian refugee not by birthright, but because political violence forced her to flee the home she knew and loved. Born to hippie British parents, she was adopted by an Ethiopian Sufi leader in Morocco at age five, after her own parents were murdered in a Tangiers alleyway. She grew up in a nurturing but cloistered Sufi shrine, memorizing Qur'an and learning the lore of her *Sheikh*, or Sufi master, who was born in the ancient walled city of Harar in Ethiopia. Culturally and religiously an African, Lilly's adult life began at 16, when she made a trans-Africa trek to the shrine city of Harar. There she lived with a poor family, teaching the children to memorize the Qur'an while performing the everyday tasks of poverty and tradition: hauling water, visiting neighbors and honoring the saints.

Lilly's world expanded when she fell in love with a handsome Harari doctor at the nearby hospital. Just as she was struggling to reconcile her deepest longings with her conservative religious devotion, politics intervened, and she suddenly found herself uprooted and dropped, a stranger, into London. Emperor Haile Selassie had been deposed by Marxists in a far-away city she had never visited, and her life was changed forever.

In London Lilly struggled to hold onto her sense of home, offering prayers through incense, helping fellow Ethiopians, even setting up a bureau where other refugees could contact one another. She learned to weave a life in London, sharing hardships with the other refugees who lived in her dreary, cement-walled, public apartment block. Said Lilly of refugee life:

> You grapple with language, navigate your way on the Underground, stretch your meager allowance, adapt unfamiliar provisions to make familiar food and find people from back home in queues at government offices, which at once invests you with a new sense of possibility and devastates you with the reminder of all the people you have left.

But if Lilly's story is not real, does it matter? With so many real-life refugees in need of assistance, isn't a fictional refugee simply taking up precious attention resources that could be better spent elsewhere?

In fact, Gibb's book plays a vital role, providing a spoonful of well-written fiction to help the medicine of refugee realities go down. The book is a far cry from a dry Amnesty International report; rather, it is a book that is given as a gift, passed along to a friend, read on an airplane. In short, it is a piece of art that turns strangers into humans.

Gibb's book is not alone. Other works of fiction and quasi-fiction have recently called attention to the plight of refugees in a way that any number of United Nations or other humanitarian research reports may not. In *What is the What*, bestselling American author Dave Eggers related the real-life story of Valentino Achak Deng, a Southern Sudanese "Lost Boy" who was violently separated from his family and village as a child and forced to trek to a series of refugee camps in Ethiopia and Kenya before being resettled in the United States, where he struggled to make a life for himself in a new and sometimes hostile society.

Through his expert retelling of Achak's tale, Eggers' book shone a compassionate but honest light on the life of refugees, showing how the trauma of exile does not end when the refugee reaches safety in a foreign country. While the 'Lost Boys of Sudan' received significant media attention in the United States and elsewhere, Eggers' high profile as a writer brought their story to a large audience of readers who might otherwise have seen it as just another media report of atrocities overseas.

But perhaps the highest impact, on American and Western consciousness, of refugee realities has come in the form of Khalid Hosseini's mega bestseller, *The Kite Runner*, the fictional story of Amir, an upper-class Afghani boy who flees Kabul with his father after the Russians invade in 1979; the pair are forced to cross the border into Pakistan while hiding in a suffocating empty fuel tank before eventually arriving in America. Some passages of the book are set at a California flea market, where once prominent Afghani professionals—doctors, military officers, lawyers—now earn a marginal living selling used clothes and knick-knacks. But the story, which is filled with emotional twists and turns, is not bleak. Amir finds love in the very flea market that represents the humiliation of Afghani refugees, and he creates a new family out of the ruins of war-torn Afghanistan. Amir is a refugee but he is also a dreamer and a writer. It is obvious to anyone reading the book, or watching the yet-to-be-released Hollywood movie, that Amir has much to offer the world in spite of, or perhaps because of, the terrible hardship he has both endured and inflicted on himself.

These three books, and many others like them, come at a crucial time, for Americans in particular. The security restrictions following the terrorist attacks of September 11, 2001, have resulted in drastically fewer refugees being resettled in the United States, according to Seyoum Berhe, director of Catholic Diocese of Arlington's Office of Migration and Refugee Services, a regional office outside of Washington D.C. Even the most tangential or involuntary association with a group or individual deemed suspicious by the U.S. government has resulted in refugees being denied resettlement, says Berhe. The solution, he says, lies in changing policies so that more refugees are welcomed into the United States.

Average Americans have an important role to play in pressing their lawmakers to make refugees a priority. And refugees only seem like a priority when people realize that refugees are not statistics, or humanitarian burdens, but rather people struggling to make their way in a harsh and sometimes violent world.

Authors like Gibb, Eggers and Hosseini are important emissaries of the refugee message, even if they do not write their books with a humanitarian agenda. Below, Camilla Gibb answers questions about what motivated her to write her novel, how exile gives birth to new identities, and how literature can help overcome stereotypes about refugees.

Q. You began your professional life as an academic. Can you tell us a bit about yourself and how you came to write *Sweetness in the Belly*?

I was born in England, grew up in Canada, and went to university in Canada, Egypt and England. After finishing my PhD I returned to Toronto from England and did two years of post-doctoral research amongst Ethiopians living in Toronto.

I was on course for an academic career, but beneath the academic exterior lay a secret. I wanted, above all, to write fiction. It's an emotional, intellectual and physical compulsion, it's what keeps me sane and it's how I relate to the world. When my first novel, *Mouthing the Words*, was published in 1999, the secret was out. And that was it for me and academia. I've been writing full time ever since.

My first two novels were dark-humoured stories about growing up in dysfunctional families. *Sweetness in the Belly* is a book set against a much bigger backdrop than the first two, but the same concerns of identity, belonging, how we make meaning in our lives, how we situate ourselves in the context of relationships, and how we understand our world are there. These are the issues that concern me and they are evident in all my work.

Q. *Sweetness in the Belly* included a lot of rich detail about every-day life in Harar. How did you come to know so much about life in north-east Ethiopia?

I did a year of archival research about Harar and then went to live there in 1994 and 1995. I was conducting research about religious practices in the city, particularly the role of saints' shrines in the life of the community, but it was the 'lived' experience that really taught me about Harar. I lived with a Harari family, in their walled compound in the heart of the city, immersed in the lives of their nine children, two of whom were very close to me in age. I was a student of Harari religion, language and culture, a 'farenji' daughter in this household. I wore a veil, learned to pray, developed a wonderful circle of friends and behaved much as a daughter would.

The household in which I lived was, relatively speaking, much more affluent than the households where Lilly lived. Part of this had to do with the fact that I lived in Harar two decades after Lilly did, and part of it to do with the fact that I lived with Hararis, who are generally wealthier than Oromos in Harar. We had four rooms, an intermittent supply of water and electricity, and meat in our diet, for instance. But it's an area where things like drought, political violence, lack of clean water, disease and lack of access to medicine remain common struggles in everyday life.

Q. Why did you choose to write about your experiences in Ethiopia in the form of a novel? Why not write a non-fiction book of anthropology?

I wanted to tell a story about this place and its people in a much more intimate, sensory, vivid, and experiential way than academic language would afford. Intellectualizing issues, placing them in theoretical context, doesn't necessarily elicit empathy and compassion. I wanted to be able to transport a reader and have them 'feel' what it might be like to live there. A novel can allow you to walk in the shoes of another, see the world through the eyes of someone else, empathize with the experience of someone who has lived an entirely different life, and recognize our common humanity.

Q. *Sweetness*' historical background is the 1974 overthrow of Emperor Haile Selassie. Why did you choose this time period and not more recent history? How did you research that time period? For example, how did you learn what life was like in Harar in the early 1970s?

From 1974 to 1991, Ethiopia was largely hidden from the rest of the world—concealed behind an iron curtain, where the Dergue, the brutal socialist dictatorship in power, perpetrated gross crimes against humanity. I lived in Ethiopia during a period of transition, the immediate post-Dergue era, which was a time of introspection and promise. People were reflecting, comparatively, upon the differences in their lives under the Dergue and under Haile Sellasie and exploring the mistakes of the past in the hopes of creating a better future. In some cases they were looking to restore what had been lost under the Dergue, a very practical example of which were the attempts to reinstate claims to land and property that had been confiscated with collectivization and the abolishing of private ownership.

Life pre-Dergue seemed to be a critical point of reference for people, and I was privy to a lot of conversation in Harar that reflected this. To some extent it helped create a picture for me of what life in Harar must have looked like in the early 1970s. I supplemented what I learned through conversation by reading everything about the era that I could and, where information about Harar was limited, I used my imagination. The totality of it then—the book that resulted—was a product of equal parts friendship, research and imagination.

Q. The novel is also partially set among the Ethiopian refugee community in London. Did you spend time yourself with Ethiopian refugees in London?

I conducted two years of academic research amongst Hararis and members of other Ethiopian groups in Toronto in the mid 1990s. Much of what I know about how life changes when one becomes a part of, or grows up in, a Diaspora comes from this research.

However, when it came to writing the novel, I wanted a more dynamic backdrop against which to explore issues of race and racism than Toronto in the late 1990s offered. I looked to Thatcher's Britain, where there was considerable tension around issues of race—i.e. rioting and police brutality.

In order to research what life might have been like for Ethiopian refugees in London during the Thatcher years, I turned to very good friends who had lived there at the time and were willing to share their experiences with me. A very good friend of mine, the Oromo historian Mohammed Hassen Ali, who is a professor in Atlanta, was tremendously helpful and through him I came to meet members of a community association in London who really educated me.

Q. In the book, Lilly and a fellow Ethiopian refugee, Amina, start a voluntary agency where they attempt to match up refugees with their lost family members. Was simply finding information about family members a major problem for refugees then?

During the Dergue years there was no free flow of information between Ethiopia and the Diaspora. Simply receiving a letter from abroad could indict one as counterrevolutionary. Relatives were scattered without knowledge of each others' whereabouts. Many friends of mine did not have information about their relatives for years. But the internet has been revolutionary in this regard. It is a vital tool for rebuilding communities in the Diaspora.

Q. In your real life research, how did you find Ethiopian refugees adapting to life in the West? Lilly wraps herself in a protective shield of rituals, while her friend Amina is more embracing of her new English life. Is there a natural progression of adaptation and assimilation for refugees?

Most of the Ethiopians I know in London have been there for some time and time is, perhaps, the greatest determinant of someone's level of adaptation. But it differs from country to country. I live in a fiercely multicultural country, where everyone is immigrant—myself included—and diversity is celebrated. That is not the case in Britain. The pressure to assimilate in Britain is more acute, though the possibility of ever achieving that, given the class structure and history of the country, is all the more remote.

Most of all I wanted to avoid applying a 'template' to refugee experience, whatever the country. While there are commonalities in people's experiences, we each have unique resources we draw upon to manage a situation. We each react differently based on any number of different factors. I wanted each of my characters to have a complex personality of their own.

Q. Your book describes a refugee/immigrant culture in London, where boundaries of tribe and even nation are blurred. In Harar, for example, tribal identity mattered very much. In the subsidized London flats where your characters live, however, just being Ethiopian, or Muslim, or even just non-English seemed to bring people together. Do you see this blurring of boundaries as a positive aspect of refugee life?

In a country where there are longstanding historical differences between ethnic groups these divisions are not simply erased in the Diaspora—particularly where one ethnic group has dominated another. In fact, in the Diaspora, people can choose not to interact with those who might have dominated them at home. So divisions between ethnic groups may actually become more forcefully entrenched in the Diaspora, while connections with people of other nationalities who share things in common may be forged.

Amongst Hararis in Toronto, I noticed that religious identity—being Muslim—tended to trump cultural identity—being Harari—in the next generation, i.e. those born outside Ethiopia. There is strength and solidarity in numbers—being part of the Canadian Muslim community gives one more influence in the social and political landscape than being part of a small ethnic minority from Ethiopia.

Q. Does this same phenomenon have a darker side? Lilly disdains the homogenized, Saudi-flavored Islam she finds at the mosques in Britain, where imams rail against 'cultural Islam' and hold up an ideal of a unifying, universal religious identity. Is there a danger in shedding your particular cultural identity and assuming a more global identity?

My characters feel differently about this issue. I wanted to explore both sides of that debate. I don't think there's a right and wrong in this, except in so far as cultural diversity makes the world an interesting and lively place and the more diverse we are the more freedom we have in that we are not all forced to subscribe to one standard. But as I said above, there is something empowering and strengthening in numbers. I think we all simply seek to belong somewhere and better a place that affords us some influence.

Q. What, in your mind, is the most difficult aspect of refugee life?

We all struggle with the same issue of how to build a meaningful life. How to do that though with the memory of trauma, with the weight of loss—loss of people, of status, of family, of connections to one's place or origin, of ownership and financial resources—in a new language, in a new land.

Why did you choose a Westerner—albeit a Westerner with an African pedigree—as your main character? Why not make an African a main character?

I wanted both to draw a portrait of this place that would be meaningful to people who called it home, and to lead a Western audience there through the eyes of a character who was not so unlike them that they would treat her as foreign or exotic.

Q. You've noted before that immigrant literature is popular right now in the West, and any number of recent novels come to mind, such as Jhumpa Lahiri's *The Namesake* or Monica Ali's *Brick Lane*. Do you see the concerns of immigrants as being very different from those of refugees?

Immigrants have largely chosen to move. Refugees have not. Immigrant stories tend to use a lot of humour, of the see-the-mistakes-the-funny-foreigner-makes-in-a-new-land variety. I didn't want to belittle the seriousness of refugee stories by telling anecdotes that would amuse a Western reader. I wanted to do something real. To write something my Ethiopian friends would recognize. *Sweetness* is ultimately a very hopeful story, but it doesn't flinch away from the hard stuff. And I didn't want to patronize Western readers by dusting the hard stuff with sugar, as Hollywood is wont to do.

Q. Did you have any humanitarian objectives in writing this book? Were you hoping to call attention to the lives of refugees in the West?

I wanted to expose Western readers to a part of the world we know so little about beyond stereotypes of famine and refugees.

I wanted to undermine stereotypes about, and humanize portraits of, refugees by giving people names and personalities and complex lives.

And I wanted to speak about Islam. I wanted to complicate the damaging and demonizing picture of Islam, that is so predominant in the Western media, by looking at its diversity, and at the peaceful and positive role it plays in the lives of the vast majority of Muslims.

Q. In the United States, the "Lost Boys of Sudan" received lots of positive press attention, while the much larger community of Somali refugees in the U.S. did not. Do you feel refugee groups receive different treatment in the West according to how they are portrayed in the media and through literature? Should the media and literary elite have a special responsibility when it comes to refugees?

Big question. Certainly, stereotypes about different groups are propagated by the media. The media is not particularly kind to Muslims right now, for instance. At the risk of oversimplifying—Somalis are Muslim while Southern Sudanese are largely Christians and animists persecuted by the Muslim government in the north. The media has a tendency to dumb it down for us and label people as enemies or friends. And the victim of your enemy is by definition your friend. But that has everything to do with government. Our sensitivity, or receptiveness, to certain refugee groups has everything to do with our own foreign policies. And we have enough recent examples that illustrate how often media is cowered or complicit with government, to doubt there is true independence.

Q. The average Westerner probably knows little about refugees, even the ones resettled in their own countries. What do you hope such a person would gain from reading your book?

I suppose I would hope that people might look more kindly upon someone they might dismiss as 'other' as a consequence of reading the book. That they might throw out their assumptions about refugees and simply encounter people as people. But ultimately the story has to work as a story, not as a political statement. Or that political statement has to be so truly integrated into the work that it doesn't come across as didactic. One has painlessly absorbed something during the course of reading the story—in this case a story about love and belonging.

Chapter 9

HIV/AIDS FEAR AND AFRICAN IMMIGRANTS

By L. E. Scott

In the early part of 2006 I was asked to contribute to an anthology entitled *Fingernails Across The Chalkboard: An Anthology of Poetry and Prose on HIV/AIDS from the Black Diaspora* being published by Third World Press, which is based in Chicago and is the oldest African American publishing house in the United States of America. The co-editors of the anthology are Randall Horton, who is a poet, former editor of *Warpland: A Journal of Black Literature and Ideas*, and presently completing his doctorate in creative writing at SUNY (Albany), Mr. M. L. Hunter, an administrator with the Chicago Public Health Department's programme on STD/HIV/AIDS who is completing his MFA in creative writing at Chicago State University, and Dr Becky Thompson, author of several books on social justice and currently teaching African American Studies and Sociology at Simmons College in Boston.

The world is told, with sickening regularity, about the high rates of HIV infection and AIDS-related death in Africa and how the HIV/AIDS rate for African Americans (particularly for Black women) is growing faster than for white Americans. *Fingernails Across The Chalkboard*, which shines a light on the truth behind the headlines, is long overdue. Firstly, it challenges the silence and fear that lives in the Black communities and reminds them that their silence and fear are nothing less than a deadly roadmap by which this disease continues to travel amongst them. Secondly, it confronts the homophobic in the Black communities and urges dialogue and discussion as opposed to resentment and condemnation. Thirdly, it reveals the influence of poverty, racism and lack of political will from governments as the unseen allies of HIV/AIDS.

The essays, poems and personal testimonies in this anthology deal with all these issues and a message that emerges with profound clarity is that if Africans, African Americans and people of colour around the world, are to survive this HIV/AIDS epidemic we must act as a world community to fight the governments who don't give a damn about our lives. The lives in this anthology are not comfortable, but the voices that tell their stories are compelling. Voices like that of a 34 year old woman finding the courage to tell her 10 year old son that she is HIV-positive and that he is not and of families, friends, and lovers bearing witness to their loved one wasting away. Death, life and hope walk its pages for, while the anthology doesn't look away from the wretchedness of this killing virus, it is about life and hope as much as it is about death. Black people and people of colour around the world don't have time 'not' to confront this crisis with every ounce of their energy. Yesterday is today, this disease is here right now!

The piece I wrote for the anthology was entitled *The Vilification of Peter Mwai: A Story of Fear and Racism*. Peter was a young African man who in 1993 was charged under the Crimes Act with "knowingly spreading an infectious disease," in this case the HIV virus. This was the first such case in Aotearoa/New Zealand and long before Peter Mwai was found guilty in a court of law he had been judged guilty by much of the media and the general public.

My essay dealt with the media and public treatment of the Mwai case, with the lurid headlines and articles that fuelled the fear and ignorance of many about HIV/AIDS and coupled it with the racism and prejudice that lies close to the surface in many parts of Aotearoa/New Zealand to produce a casual disregard for the human lives bound up in this story.

It was a bad time and many in the African community felt they were being judged by the wider community simply by the association of race. The cloak of prejudice did indeed cast its ugly shadow wide.

Peter Mwai was convicted in 1994 and sentenced to prison for seven years. In early 1998, after nearly five years in prison and near death (he then had full-blown AIDS), newspapers carried the story that Mwai was about to be released and deported to Africa and also that he had asked to be allowed to stay here for whatever time he had left to live. It was known that Mwai had, had a child with his New Zealand partner and that she was prepared to care for him. Again the media waded in with headlines such as "Evil Peter Mwai—should this beast be let loose?"

In June 1998 he was released from prison. His request on compassionate grounds to be allowed to stay in this country was refused and he was deported to Kenya. A few months later he died of AIDS-related illness.

I have provided this backdrop to bring into focus a recent development regarding HIV and African immigrants in Aotearoa/New Zealand. Between 2000 and 2004 more that 1300 Zimbabwean refugees were allowed to enter the country without the normal health checks because they were fleeing the violent regime of President Robert Mugabe. The Immigration Service has confirmed that the predominantly middle-class refugees were given entry on visitors' visas, which do not require health checks.

As of November 2005, all permanent migrants to Aotearoa/New Zealand must take an HIV test and if the test is positive, will only be allowed to stay under "exceptional circumstances." The government announced in August 2006 that they wanted the 1300 Zimbabweans who had not been tested as part of their entry process to present themselves for HIV testing, with the assurance that regardless of their HIV status, they would be able to remain in the country. The amnesty was offered until February 2007. So far about 500 Zimbabweans have come forward, with 42 testing positive.

On August 31, 2006 the front page of The Dominion Post, the capital city's daily paper, led with the headline "$3m AIDS error on refugees—Taxpayers must foot the bill for treatment of up to 200 HIV positive Africans." The article carried on to say that the cost of treatment, including antiretroviral drugs, could be as much as $18,000 a year per patient. It also stated that the Health Minister, Peter Hodgson, and Immigration Minister, David Cunliffe, conceded that "the Government erred in allowing Zimbabweans in in the first place without testing for HIV—despite knowing the country's deadly infection rates." The article further stated: "Zimbabwe has one of the world's highest HIV/AIDS rates with two million confirmed cases—a quarter of the population, the United Nations says. The disease has slashed life expectancy there from 57 in 1990 to 34 in 2002."

Politics can be a dirty game with few rules and fewer scruples, so it is not a surprise that this issue quickly became grist to the political mill. When the government went public with the 'problem' of the 1300 untested migrants, the National and NZ First parties, in particular, went in for the kill. They pointed out that not only were the Zimbabweans not tested the government were not even sure of their current whereabouts. They criticized the amnesty offer emphasizing its cost on the basis of estimates that at least 200 of the 1300 would test HIV-positive. These two parties also said that they had grave fears regarding the social impact of these untested refugees. Of course the media came to that party, producing such headlines as: "HIV cases rise in NZ," "Government offers HIV amnesty for Zimbabweans," and "Refugees could pose many more health risks." There has also been speculation as to why, given the amnesty offer with its guarantee of residency, more than half of the 1300 Zimbabweans have not come forward.

I believe there are a number of reasons why so many have not presented themselves for HIV testing. The main reason is fear. I don't mean fear of what the test may reveal, though that fear is certainly real as well, but fear of what might happen with the information gathered. Yes, the amnesty is in place and their residency is guaranteed, but refugees as a rule come out of countries where there is good reason not to put much faith or trust in the government.

In addition, Black Zimbabweans cannot fail to know that they are very visible here and that there is a quite widely held perception, in their host country, that every African is HIV-positive. Equally, in the African community itself there is still a strong stigma attached to HIV/AIDS, so there is concern in the Zimbabwean community about the effect this scrutiny may have on their relationship with the wider African community.

When all is said and done, it is for the government to handle the situation with sensitivity and for those who have played political games with it to desist with their foolishness. The Zimbabweans who fled to Aotearoa/New Zealand, between 2000—2004, need to feel safe in the knowledge that, whatever the outcome of the testing process, they will not be judged or scorned as a threat to the community that has offered them sanctuary.

Chapter 10

LIBERALISM AND THE REFUGEE: EXPLORING THE CONTRADICTIONS

By Christopher LaMonica

Nota bene: Throughout this chapter, the term 'liberalism' refers to the classical understanding of the term, i.e. to mean 'freedom.'

The New Colossus

Not like the brazen giant of Greek fame,
With conquering limbs astride from land to land;
Here at our sea-washed, sunset gates shall stand
A mighty woman with a torch, whose flame
Is the imprisoned lightning, and her name
Mother of Exiles. From her beacon-hand
Glows world-wide welcome; her mild eyes command
The air-bridged harbor that twin cities frame.
"Keep ancient lands, your storied pomp!" cries she
With silent lips. "Give me your tired, your poor,
Your huddled masses yearning to breathe free,
The wretched refuse of your teeming shore.
Send these, the homeless, tempest-tost to me,
I lift my lamp beside the golden door!"

—*Emma Lazarus, 1883*

INTRODUCTION

The above poem, written by the famous American poet, Emma Lazarus, is now displayed on a bronze plaque placed at the base of the Statue of Liberty in New York Harbour. Increasingly, Lazarus' poem is being cited in discussions of US immigration policy. As is the case in other developed states of the world, Americans are now paying closer attention to immigration policy than ever before. In those discussions, the message of Lazarus still rings true but for many others the free movement of peoples is now perceived as a growing threat to their own livelihoods. These real or alleged threats include: job loss, loss of physical space (housing), new difficulties maintaining social welfare programmes, and the introduction of different/adverse cultural norms. Without doubt, as we enter the twenty-first century, more people in crisis can move with greater ability than ever before. The resulting encounter of peoples and their cultures has been interpreted in a variety of ways: 1) as a "clash" with "zero-sum" threats (where one will prevail at the expense of another); 2) as a renewed need to respect diverse cultures (policies that support multiculturalism); or 3) as a synergistic blending of cultures with "positive-sum" gains. As discussed in this chapter, today's debates over migration policy are full of controversies and contradictions; today's proponents of one or another view routinely make seemingly desperate references to statistical data and/ or hearken back to some of the founding principles of liberalism. And, more than ever, it seems clear that the prevailing norm is to use policy statements or data that support one's point of view, while ignoring inconvenient or contradictory 'evidence.'

What is also clear is that all three interpretations of the ongoing (and unstoppable) influx of peoples to "liberal" worlds are now a seemingly permanent feature of the political landscape of Western industrial states. Today, however, the positions of political parties and political candidates are generally not as clear as those of yesteryear; certainly the traditional Cold War categories of 'left' versus 'right' seem not to apply to this renewed twenty-first century challenge. For instance, during much of Western industrial history a sizable portion of labor unions were made up of first and second generation immigrants. Today, however, many of these same labor groups argue that immigration is a threat to their jobs. Similarly, traditional minority groups in the US, such as African-American and Hispanic communities, are often adamantly anti-immigration, arguing that immigration "hurts the poor." Often, leftists and conservatives are now in agreement over restrictive immigration, albeit for different reasons. For example, political conservatives such as Samuel P. Huntington have emphasized immigrants' challenges to mainstream American culture, while leftist politicians such as MA Rep. Barney Frank, argue that the arrival of additional immigrant workers is "bad for blue-collars." In the 1990s, the popular (Independent) US presidential candidate, Ross Perot, campaigned largely on the growing threats to US jobs and in 2007 he was made the Reform Party candidate—an indication that his anti-immigrant views remain popular. Indeed, in recent years, many of the anti-immigration arguments have become increasingly desperate in tone. Consider, for example, the recent titles of books by conservative populist Pat Buchanan which leave little room for misunderstanding: *State of Emergency: Third World Invasion and Conquest of America* (2007) and *The Death of the West: How Dying Populations and Immigrant Invasions Imperil Our Country and Civilization* (2002). Even within political parties and advocacy groups there is disagreement. This has been heard, for example, in the 2008 US presidential debates, where Republicans are seemingly split between pro-immigration business leaders and anti-immigration "law-and-order" conservatives. As discussed above, US Democrats are similarly split on the matter. But they have resisted the increasingly popular reference to "illegal immigration" and now call for a more "humane" approach to those "simply trying to work." According to the Democrats.org web-page, for example, "We have to protect our borders, but scapegoating immigrants is not the way to do it."

In the post-Cold War era many of the arguments *against* the free movement of peoples are based on heightened "security" concerns. In *Global Migrants Global Refugees*, published just months prior to 9-11, Aristide Zolberg comments for example:

> The massive movement of human beings across international borders has come to be regarded as one of the most intractable problems the United States and the other affluent democracies face in the strange new post-Communist world. Long a marginal subject even for demographers and social scientists, international migration quickly ascended

to the status of a security issue, imperatively requiring attention in the highest places.

Since 9-11 there has been increased scrutiny of all immigrants into liberal states. Concerned citizens have suddenly become quite vocal and politically active; some going as far as to advocate a new "zero immigration" policy, while others are seemingly more concerned with the legality of having "several hundreds or thousands of men who were detained for months or longer without being charged with crimes..." in the post 9-11 environment. In other words, how to truly interpret liberal philosophy always enters into the debates, pro or con.

While some of these concerns may be well-founded, the primary aim of this chapter is to identify some of the contradictions that underlie liberal state policies, particularly as they relate to the issue of migration and economic liberalization. In doing so, I reconsider some of the 'classic' or founding arguments on political and economic liberalization. I also consider the use of statistics in the ongoing policy debates; as we will see many of these arguments are analogous to the original rift between the liberals (e.g. Smith) and historical materialists (e.g. Marx).

USING STATISTICS

Policymakers and policy advocates everywhere tend to find statistics that support their own point of view and then talk right past each other, hoping their own view will prevail. Of course the pretense in both policymaking and the social sciences is that the data is objective, as if to say: "We had no agenda here; the data speaks for itself." However, the framing of policy questions is generally a normative affair. That is—understandably—the types of questions we ask are based on personal values or concerns; we generally do not 'objectively' pick policy questions out of a proverbial hat, absent any kind of personal judgment or concern. For this simple reason I submit that questions over immigration policy are rarely motivated by objective analysis. Moreover, one should think critically about the increased use of statistical data to support policy claims. In today's "brave new world" of statistical regression, "testing for statistical significance" has become the trump phrase among those who allege to be simply providing us with 'the facts' of the matter. Today the interpreters of such data are aided by high-powered statistical software such as SPSS, Stata or even Microsoft Excel that is becoming more and more "user friendly" with each new market version. If one is to follow the recent direction of many social science journals, such as *The American Political Science Review*, it is hard not to be left with the impression that an older generation is being challenged, if not replaced, by a younger generation of statistical "whiz kids." If the use of statistics led us to more objective understandings and policy, there would be no reason to question statistical methodology and the corresponding claims to objective analysis. But the results of such "objective analysis" are more often used as statistical support for one or another point of view; that is, there are glaring contradictions between the ideal of objectivity and the practical use of statistical data in policy and social science debates. Particularly when it comes to 'emotional' matters such as immigration, this needs to be said.

What also needs to be said is that debates over immigration are often intertwined with discussions regarding the prospects for economic growth. Consider how remarkable it is that, to this day, we have ongoing academic and political debates that use statistical data to 'prove' entirely opposite points of view. As any student of economics will understand, this is not unusual; it is the norm. When it comes to the history of economic growth, for example, two seemingly opposite views emerge. On the one hand, it is said that liberal economists are right: over the past several hundred years of human history the free movement of scarce economic resources has led to remarkable levels of production; that is, the material results of free commerce and trade are, as many liberal economists noted in the eighteenth and nineteenth-centuries, quite miraculous! But critics of free commerce and trade have also proven to be right: over the past several hundred years of global capitalist development, the rich have gotten richer and world's poor poorer. Comments on these seemingly opposite points of view, using statistics, can be quite provocative. Joshua Goldstein writes, for example:

> Globalization in the 1990s increased the gap between the world's richest and poorest countries. The number of people living on less than $1 per day—about 1.2 billion— has grown since the mid-1980s. The greatest setbacks have been in Africa, where 29 of the 34 lowest ranked countries are located...

Publications such as the *Human Development Report* similarly continue to dutifully report that "Dozens of countries are worse off than 20 years ago, even while other countries in the South rise gradually out of poverty." The statistical evidence for these kinds of arguments is clearly available.

What is potentially confusing is that, simultaneously, global wealth is increasing; in fact, the *global average income* has been steadily increasing since around 1500, even when population growth is taken into account. In his 2007 book, *Contours of the World Economy, 1-2030 A.D.*, liberal economist Angus Madison provides historical data to demonstrate that the rise of "world average" per capita GDP income (in 1990 $) has been as follows:

Table 10.1: The Liberal Argument

"World Average" per capita GDP

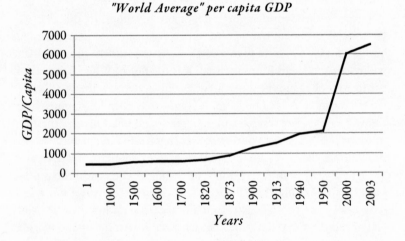

These seemingly opposite points of view often result in glaring policy inconsistencies. The fundamental rift, it seems, is between those who view liberalism as a righteous and "miraculous" force and those who interpret liberalism as an agenda-driven and often exploitative force. Both, I will argue here, are true: liberalism, in its many forms, has proven to be both a blessing and a curse.

THE REFUGEE

There is nothing new about populations moving from one geographical region to another in search of a safer, more secure, or generally 'better' life. Human beings have been doing so as a matter of course for at least 50,000 years, starting from our common place of origin in northeastern Africa. In recent human history, the exact reasons for seeking safety, security, "asylum" or a "sanctuary" have been codified, using religious or political "justification." The right to seek asylum in a church or other "holy place" has been an established norm since at least the "Axial Age," starting around 500 B.C., although even this practice has come into question given recent conflicts in, for example, Rwanda and Iraq. During the 1994 Rwandan genocide, crowded churches were often targeted and, in the ongoing war in Iraq, mosques have been destroyed amidst great consternation.

Conflicts in Europe during the Middle Ages supported the view that members of one religion or "nation" could reside, in peace, within one's own sovereign territory—the ideal being that individuals would therefore be subject only to the laws of one national sovereign. The authors of Article CXXIII of the oft-mentioned 1648 Treaty of Westphalia (that forever established "state sovereignty" as a norm in international relations) wrote:

> the concluded Peace shall remain in force, and all Partys
> in this Transaction shall be oblig'd to defend and protect
> all and every Article of this Peace against any one, without
> distinction of Religion...

This, of course, is the romantic ideal of nations of people coming together to form their own sovereign state, a principle that remains fundamental to the conduct of international politics. US President Woodrow Wilson is generally portrayed as history's fiercest advocate of this liberal principle, which became known as the "right to self-determination." At an April 1941 meeting off the coast of Newfoundland with the British Prime Minister Winston Churchill, US President Franklin D. Roosevelt pushed for this very view (some say to the annoyance of Churchill who, after all, was head of the world's most powerful colonial power) which later influenced the wording of the 1945 United Nations Charter which reads that the purposes of the U.N. are, in part:

> To develop friendly relations among nations based on respect of the principle of equal rights and self-determination of peoples.... Encourage respect for human rights and for fundamental freedoms for all without distinction as to race, sex, language, or religion.

Well before these principles were applied to the entire world, however, challenges to the liberal ideal of a world of "nation-states" were already emerging. Wilson, it is said, suffered from a stroke in his attempts to convince weary American and European publics of the merit of a League of Nations, precursor to the United Nations. At the 1919 Treaty of Versailles, Wilson's vision won the day. Political resistance in the US was largely based on the difficulties of having a new international organization (the League) mandate US state action. As the Massachusetts State Senator, Henry Cabot Lodge, argued:

> No doubt many excellent and patriotic people see a coming fulfillment of noble ideals in the words 'league for peace.' We all respect and share these aspirations and desires, but some of us see no hope, but rather defeat, for them in this murky covenant....Our first ideal is our country, and we see her in the future, as in the past, giving service to all her people and to the world. Our ideal of the future is that she should continue to render that service of her own free will.

What is generally not acknowledged today is that there was, similarly, political resistance on the European continent. Many asked: How could the dramatic ethnic and other cleavages that had marked so much of European history be tamed within existing national borders? Desperate for financial and other assistance, European state leaders were nevertheless inclined to agree with Wilson's liberal principles; in fact, the desperate circumstances of post-WWI were very much repeated in the aftermath of the aforementioned 1941 Atlantic Charter. Several months after the clandestine meeting between Churchill and FDR, at an Inter-Allied Meeting in London, General de Gaulle, as leader of the "Free French," along with leaders from Belgium, Luxembourg, Greece, Czechoslovakia, the Netherlands, Yugoslavia, the Soviet Union,

Norway and Poland, unanimously approved the principles outlined in the Charter. To many, the very fact that the Axis powers unanimously rejected these same "liberal" principles could only serve to demonstrate the righteousness of the Allied cause. And, with the Japanese attack on Pearl Harbor on December 7, 1941, the Americans were "finally" (as far as Churchill was concerned) involved in the great allied battle for freedom.

As Oxford historian Niall Ferguson has convincingly argued in his recent book, *The War of the World* (2007), "applying the principle of self-determination proved far from easy." In a highly critical fashion, Ferguson describes Wilson's League and "biblical Covenant" as an ideal that was, in short, not very well thought through. He quotes Wilson as saying "every people has a right to choose the sovereignty under which they shall live" but suggests that the reordering the entire European map on the basis of national "self-determination" led to even more conflict on the European continent, and elsewhere in the world. In other words, far from helping to prevent conflict, Wilson's liberal ideals helped to create new ones. Political liberalism, according to this view, defined as the "self-determination of peoples," has led to nationalist strivings of diverse peoples within the confines of previously established sovereign states—what has been termed "balkanization." This has been particularly apparent, suggests Ferguson, in the multi-ethnic regions of Central and Eastern Europe where much twentieth-century conflict can be understood as ongoing challenges to the 19th-century liberal ideal of nationalism.

In her best-selling book, World on Fire (2004), Amy Chua similarly suggests that liberalism has ironically and tragically led to much ethnic conflict. And this is not simply what has occurred in history—it continues to this day. Given that much of history has been undemocratic, suggests Chua, the post-Cold War processes of "democratization" have led to the instability of previously dominant minorities throughout the world, who are now desperately trying to maintain one or another "order." According to Chua, "The bottom line is this. Democracy can be inimical to the interests of market-dominant minorities." To support this view, Chua surveys the market-domination of several ethnic minorities in history, including the Ibo in Cameroon, the Jews in Europe, the Indians in Kenya, religious fundamentalists in the Middle East and the whites in South Africa, to say that their status has now been challenged by liberalism and the forces of globalization.

As the twenty-first century marches on, the image we are getting is of an increasingly liberal world, but of one that is faced with a myriad of challenges and contradictions. Some of this, as we see in the writings of Ferguson and Chua, suggests that liberalism itself—the very ideal that so many have sought after for generations—may be a trickier affair than has been so commonly supposed. In fact, liberalism may underlie some of the most violent post-Cold War challenges that the world has experienced, from former Yugoslavia to fundamentalist violence. And it can no longer be assumed, by anyone, anywhere, that these problems are "over there." For a variety of reasons people now move with greater ease; without doubt, whatever bubble of exclusion that may have existed in the past, has now burst. Consider the words of Turkish writer, Orhan Pamuk:

> It is neither Islam nor even poverty itself that directly engenders support for terrorists whose ferocity and ingenuity are unprecedented in human history; it is, rather, the crushing humiliation that has infected the third-world countries. At no time in history has the gulf between rich and poor been so wide... at no time in history have the lives of the rich been so forcefully brought to the attention of the poor through television and Hollywood films.

More than ever, marginalized, impoverished, discriminated, humiliated, and desperate peoples of the world see hope in migration. For the lucky, this entails migration to a "liberal" society, where the reasons for their marginalization, impoverishment, discrimination, etc. can be, ideally, swept away. But we cannot assume that the transition to liberalism is always peaceful and righteous; the process has historically proven to be full of contradictions and, all too often, accompanied by violence. Proponents of liberal policy, from Wilson to those behind today's 'Washington Consensus' (e.g. the National Endowment for Democracy), need to keep this violent history, that has all too often resulted from well-intentioned "liberal policy," in mind.

If one is to venture through the increasingly restrictive language of immigration law, one inevitably finds a list of terms for these global migrants. Over the past century, pro and anti-immigration legislation has been passed as one or another view prevails, wherein the most extreme cases are often referred to as "refugees." One might think that the label of "refugee" would be an unwelcome one and, once established in a free society, this can certainly be the case. But, in many thousands of cases, it is a label that people can only hope to have; it is the prospect of freedom, of reaching a liberal, hopeful world. The formal definition varies, but since 1951 the United Nations has defined a "refugee" as:

> Every person who, owing to external aggression, occupation, foreign domination or events seriously disturbing public order in either part or the whole of his country of origin or nationality, is compelled to leave his place of habitual residence in order to seek refuge in another place outside his country of origin or nationality.

Imagine, now, the dramatic differences that might emerge in interpreting this definition. Those in positions of decision-making power would likely consider only the most extreme cases as being valid, with only the strictest interpretation as to what constitutes serious disturbance of "public order." Certainly, the history of colonial domination, imperialism, and/or under-development would not enter into the decision-making process. However, many of those in positions of desperation, striving to move and achieve refugee status, could easily describe (if they had the opportunity to do so) their circumstance in those terms. Of course, to do so would only be "shooting themselves in the foot" and, therefore, the more pragmatic concern is "what is appropriate to say" to achieve refugee status. Accordingly, arguments are made—falsely or otherwise—to "prove" that one's life is in jeopardy, etc. Those who have been through the process are well aware of the kinds of procedures and arguments that need to be made. But, again, it is very difficult to know the truth of the matter given what can and cannot be said before, during and after the process. Clear identification of the "rights" of one or another refugee applicant is a dramatic affair, and all involved are very aware that the stakes could not be higher.

Rarely acknowledged in the growing literature on the "rights" of refugees, is that the very quest for their protection is a very recent historical phenomenon. The "refugee problem" did not come on to the "policy radar" of Western industrial states until the early twentieth-century. In fact, it wasn't until the 1951 Convention (relating to the

Status of Refugees) that the issue was discussed within the halls of the U.N. The way that this sudden interest in the status of refugees is normally presented is in terms of humanitarian aims, i.e. those in positions of decision-making power now describe this event as a monumental step forward for the "rights" of people to move from desperate circumstances. What is odd, in retrospect, is that the issue came to the fore at all; previous decades of colonial and other forms of domination in the "third world" did not lead to any real discussion of refugee concerns. Certainly, in history, there was less of a need to frame the issue in these terms. One wonders, for example, how Smith or Locke might have adjusted their arguments!

What then changed by 1951? Taking a broader historical view on the matter, the post-World War II era was a dramatic moment for the aforementioned Wilsonian aims; that is, the former colonial powers were losing their grip on their colonial holdings throughout the world. In the decade that followed, virtually all of the colonized world took that dramatic step toward "freedom." Practically speaking this translated to a tremendous growth in the number of "sovereign states" within the U.N. General Assembly, from 51 members in 1945 to over double that number by the 1960s. What had originally started as an organization clearly dominated by Western powers quickly became one of "third-world" domination. In fact, many would argue that this is exactly what happened within the U.N. General Assembly, starting in the 1960s. And so, by 1951, there was a growing sense that this was about to happen, i.e. there was a growing concern that newly independent sovereign states were likely to make demands on the powerful minority of the world. The question for today is: Was the sudden 'concern' for refugees based on the potential threat or self-interest of Western industrial states, fearing a sudden surge of migrants from former colonies? We can never really know for certain. What has become institutional procedure, however, is for potential "refugees" to be hand-picked by field staff of the U.N. High Commissioner for Refugees (UNHCR), which then appeals to the world community.

The mandate of the UNHCR is to "coordinate international action to protect refugees and resolve refugee problems worldwide." According to its official web-site:

> Its primary purpose is to safeguard the rights and well-being of refugees. It strives to ensure that everyone can

exercise the right to seek asylum and find safe refuge in
another State, with the option to return home voluntarily,
integrate locally or to resettle in a third country.

While this sounds wonderful on the surface, the reality of transferring
thousands of people each year across the globe is that it requires many
administrative steps and the political support of "host" countries.
In other words, even if someone is miraculously deemed worthy of
refugee status, there remains the challenge of finding welcoming hosts.
And this, it just so happens, remains voluntary; that is, there is no
international mandate of any kind to accept migrants of any status into
one's sovereign territory. As discussed elsewhere in this book, many of
the administrative hurdles to deeming someone worthy are suspect, if
not outright corruption—certainly the power of UNHCR adminis-
trators to identify people as refugees or not is very one-sided. Locally
and globally, these discussions do not take place amongst "equals."

All the while, within the "liberal" states of the world, tremendous
efforts and resources are put into the proper categorization of peoples
for immigration purposes, bureaucratic state barriers systematically put
in place, sometimes walls are built. All the while, within those same
liberal states, think tanks, such as the Bonn-based Institute for the
Study of Labour (IZA), continue to provide studies to demonstrate
that migration has not been harmful to local economies. Similarly,
well-known academics, such as Howard Zinn, continue to argue, for
example, that "no human being is illegal." Zinn, an historian, suggests that anti-immigration sentiment is far from new in free societies; through US history, a variety of anti-immigration legislation was
passed, often in the name of "public safety." He suggests that, more
often than not, these were populist responses to ethnic hatred or fear
of the new "other." Slogans such as "No Irish Need Apply" and "The
Chinese Must Go," etc. came and went, suggests Zinn, and these did
little more than to satisfy the political ambitions of those who are now
long gone.

Today, once again, "illegal immigration" is becoming the catch-all
phrase for many. What is particularly ironic is that many of these same
groups had historically viewed freedom as a generally welcome concept
but are now turning to restrictions. In these debates, the "free citizen"
is heard to say, in one way or another "we earned this and we're not
going to give it up." Some are even heard to say: "Zero immigration is

the only answer." What Mark Lowry, the author of the aforementioned quote, had to do with the creation of the circumstances he now lives in is not described in his article to the conservative *American Chronicle*. But that is not typically the concern of such writers. Rather than consider the liberal circumstances that allowed his desperate (European?) relatives to leave for America, so that he and others like him could have more opportunities in their lives, Lowry finds it appropriate and within his "rights" as a "citizen" to restrict the free movement of others. To quote Lowry's article:

> America you must recognize that we are at war. WE are invaded for a reason. It is not about economics for poor peasants who don't have ability to support their families. It is about destruction of America, its sovereignty, its liberty and the creation of communist one world order under economic rule of international corporations.
>
> Wake up before it is too, late. Stop apologizing for defending America. WE as a nation cannot take another immigrant into our country until we recover our sovereignty and our liberty. Stop this crap of saying you are for "legal" immigration. That is another code phrase for I am for legal Marxist invasion.
>
> How dumb can Americans be? Are you so stupid as to limit defense of your nation your family with the "I love legal immigrants" sign? Get over it.

This is the level of vindictive language that one typically finds in debates over immigration policy: If you are not with "us" on this one, you must be a communist.

The authors of the editorial page of *The Wall Street Journal*, who are traditionally conservative (and probably not communist), as well as many libertarians, believe in what George Borjas terms "unrestricted immigration." In other words, freedom of movement of economic resources—to include labour—has historically led to increases in the general welfare: today's anti-immigrant descendants of free-moving migrants, who are now beneficiaries of such liberal policies in history (or, perhaps, "illegal" free movement of our forefathers and foremothers), may want to take careful note of this fact. In other words, restrictions on the free movement of all economic resources have historically tended to restrict our potential for economic growth.

Setting aside these bitter debates, there remains the irrefutable fact: today, people from all over the world, of whatever migrant statuses we provide to them, seek to fulfill the liberal creed; in other words, they yearn to be 'free.' Today, the increased ease with which people, in search of a better life, can travel has resulted in dramatic pressures on the conduct of domestic and international politics: the historical proponents of liberalism are now being asked by the world to show their cards. Has it been a bluff? Did the world's proponents of freedom, from the Enlightenment onwards, really mean what they said? In truth, as we shall see, the history of liberalism has not meant "liberty for all" but "liberty for the few." Even for those liberals who truly meant what they said—perhaps Wilson?—it is becoming abundantly clear that the realization of liberalism, on a global scale, is a daunting challenge.

LIBERALISM AND ECONOMIC GROWTH: EXPLORING THE ARGUMENTS

Economic historians of all views generally agree that during most of human history there was little to no economic growth. Periodically, wealth would be accumulated by one kingdom or civilization, only to be lost through battle and other historical and environmental reasons for civilizational decline. For example, as the historian Basil Davidson explains, the historical expansion of the Sahara permanently threatened and doomed a great many ancient civilizations across the region. In the "ancient world"—a geographic region that spans across the northeast of Africa, the Mediterranean, and into the "Fertile Crescent" of the Middle East (the flood plains surrounding the Tigris and Euphrates rivers)—human populations first grew alongside rivers. Anthropologists tell us that, from a common hunting and gathering population in northeast Africa, the prospects for human sustenance were greatly improved with the advent and subsequent spread of subsistence agriculture circa 20,000—10,000 B.C.E. A great many economic historians now tell us that wealth, generated by trade, is a relatively recent historical phenomenon. This again, all would tend to agree, changed dramatically post-1500: a year, or era, that is commonly cited as being of pivotal importance to global economic history. Immanuel Wallerstein comments that the "modern world-system originated in the sixteenth century [or during the] long sixteenth-century as Fernand Braudel has called it, that is, from 1450 to 1640."

To be certain, the endeavours of the earliest mercantilist states, such as those of Spain and Portugal, were not motivated by "positive-sum" gains that could be had through trade; rather they were, as countless economic texts now tell us, interested in acquiring and stockpiling as much gold (and other forms of wealth) as they could in what they perceived as a global "zero-sum" race with other states of the world. In the literature these sixteenth-century mercantilist states are often portrayed as war-mongering nation-states. In a somewhat romanticized view of history it is the European monarchs of the time that are described as most interested in acquiring the means to finance wars against other European monarchs. David Balaam and Michael Veseth suggest, for example:

> Soon after Venice and other Italian city-states... Portugal, Spain, the Netherlands, France [and] England... formed a system of states and fought long wars with one another. To help pay for their wars, these states tried to accumulate trade surpluses by promoting exports and limiting imports. Currency earned from trade helped them to purchase gold and silver bullion... which was added to the monarch's treasury.

In Adam Smith's seminal book, *The Wealth of Nations* (1776), the mercantilist policies of European powers (notably Britain) were among his greatest concerns. Although Smith's writing is often contradictory and, at times, downright bigoted, he does strongly suggest that when an individual is left to his own devices, pursuing his own self-interest, this has a tendency to promote the general welfare:

> ...he intends only his own gain, and he is in this, as in many other cases, led by an invisible hand to promote an end which was no part of his intention... By pursuing his own interest he frequently promotes that of the society more effectually than when he really intends to promote it. I have never known much good done by those who affected trade for the public good.

The liberal project, which Smith and his adherents promote, is wholly Lockean and, from the onset, openly biased in favour of the interests of the European powers. "Among the savage and barbarous nations,"

Smith suggests, "the nature progress of law and government is still slower." "Waste lands of the greatest natural fertility," he continues, "are to be had for a trifle." Smith's vision, therefore, is one that promotes the free movement of those with more relative power in society who, in much of the literature (from Marx onwards), are sometimes referred to as "the capitalists." Certainly, where the global movement of peoples was concerned, Smith advocated the free movement of European peoples. But to refer to all Europeans who did move to what Smith terms "the savage and barbarous nations"—the "waste lands"— as "capitalists" would not be accurate. On this point, Marx & Engels would likely agree. In *The Communist Manifesto* (1848) they state: "To be a capitalist is to have not only a purely personal product but a social status in production.... Capital is... not personal, it is a social power."

Like many philosophers of the time, Smith was likely inspired by the arguments of the English philosopher John Locke who, when making his argument for "every man" in his seminal *Second Treatise on Civil Government* (1690), was more likely thinking in terms of the European man:

> The *labour* of his body and the *work* of his hands, we may say, are properly his. Whatsoever, then, he removes out of the state that nature hath mixed his labour with it, and joined to it something that is his own, and thereby make it his property. It being by him removed from the common state of nature placed it in, it hath by his labour something annexed to it that excludes the common right of other men.

Locke's statement, of course, was made in an era of "exploration" and wild speculation; it is the logic of the colonizer who sees no need to consider the welfare of the "barbarous" or "uncivilized" people in his plan. If anything the colonizer, inspired by the words of Smith and Locke, is determined that his liberal cause is right: "waste lands" beckon, suggests Smith, and, suggests Locke, your 'labour' can help to separate what exists in a "state of nature" to make it your own private property.

To be clear, the 'miracle' of economic and political liberalism, as it is expressed by Smith and Locke, involves: 1) the privatization of property and 2) the pursuit of self-interest. These remain founding principles of all liberal societies. Of course, these ideas are packaged along-side others of the Enlightenment era—as above—all deemed righteous but often, again, individualistic. It is during the French and American revolutions, we are told, that the inherent worth of the individual is stressed, an individual who is often described as having "inalienable rights"—that is, rights that are God given and unquestionable. And this is where tricky matters of philosophy enter into the equation.

Within the study of political philosophy, one might well encounter a presentation of one of the "fundamental rifts" of the Enlightenment Age, as it is called, between the "Anglo/American" and "Continental" European philosophers. While much of this tends to be exaggerated, this "rift" remains thought-provoking. If we consider, on the one hand, that there exists an Anglo/American version of liberalism, as it is described by Smith and Locke that is quite individualistic, we are then presented with another "Continental" European philosophy that is seemingly more burdened with individual 'responsibilities' tied to the notion of 'citizenship'. Jean-Jacques Rousseau classically states, for example: "Man is born free, and everywhere he is in chains." To Rousseau and others 'freedom' in any society necessarily requires a consideration of the limitations on individual freedoms; to some, such as Immanuel Kant, individual conduct required some consideration of what 'morality' entailed—what Kant termed the "categorical imperative." Moral behaviour requires restrictions on individual liberty of some kind, socially determined codes of behaviour of some kind, and this has forever concerned the study of liberal philosophy. Today, many libertarians will have none of it—arguing, for example, "my freedom ends where your nose begins"—while some consider the global expansion of liberalism to be a real threat to local norms and culture that support a different view on ethics. Elements of this debate, or concern, can be heard in the words of religious prophets during the "Axial Age" (as Karl Jaspers has called it); it is therefore far from new.

To some, the "testing ground" for the limits of freedom is the United States and there have been clear responses to this view of liberalization. One has come from the first Prime Minister of Singapore, Lee Kuan Yew, who has become adamantly opposed to many 'Western' understandings of freedom, including that of the US. Lee is apparently not alone in holding this view. In 1994 an American teenager, Michael P. Fay, was sentenced to four months in jail, a S$3,500 fine, and six lashes with a cane, for a wild night of vandalism that included the stealing of street signs and spray painting of cars in the streets of Singapore. Following a flurry of US critique of this "harsh" punishment, Fay's sentence was reduced to four lashes, instead of six, as a gesture of respect to President Clinton. This incident and other seemingly 'restrictive' policies on individual behaviour (such as a chewing gum ban) have led to a debate as to whether another version of freedom might be developing on the Asian continent. But there are those who argue that these debates have existed for thousands of years. Former South Korean President Kim Dae Jung, for example, has suggested that philosophical debates over the issue of liberalism existed in Asia "well before Locke" and can be found in many of the Ancient Asian classics. So again, we see that the issue of liberalism is not viewed as something 'new.'

Increasingly, however, it is the "American" version of liberalism that is coming under attack. For example, concerns regarding what renowned Egyptian scholar Samir Amin terms the "Americanization of the world" are expressed in his best-selling book *The Liberal Virus* (2004). His view is that, in the American understanding of liberalism, political and economic liberalization are generally regarded as "complementary to one another." Certainly this is how the aforementioned works of Smith and Locke are generally presented, as liberal classics that have led to a brilliant "synergy" of some kind, with nothing but the best results. Amin continues:

> Apparently the most 'developed' country, the one in which
> the political is actually conceived and practiced entirely in
> the exclusive service of the economy (of capital, in fact)—
> obviously the United States—is held to be the best model
> for 'all.'

It should be recalled that Amin's tone is comparatively mild to that of some, including the "terrorist" who has been quoted as saying that pop stars like Madonna and Britney Spears should be beheaded as they are promoters of (an overly liberal) American culture that is adversely impacting global youth. Amin's decidedly more tempered view—one that is similarly expressed in Edward Said's writings—is that the debates over limits on individual freedoms have been seemingly forgotten in favour of a more radicalized and ideological view of liberalism that is tied to the priorities of capitalists. He argues that today "Capitalist economics in fact governs the political, whose creative potential it eliminates."

Today, one of the areas where state policymakers have been "losing their creative way" is with immigration policy. Given the seemingly overwhelming evidence that wealth is generated by the free movement of scarce economic resources, including labour, one might expect policymakers to be a bit more lax when it comes to the free movement of peoples. Our careful consideration of the words of Locke and Smith above can only lead us to the conclusion that they were "a product of their own time," a 'time' when many referred to other peoples as "barbarous" and "uncivilized," a 'context' within which European colonization was a policy priority.

In fact, John Locke is generally considered to be a founding Enlightenment Era philosopher: with important caveats that might also be applicable to the writings of Smith and others, Locke did believe in the "equality of man." Certainly, this is how the Spirit of the Enlightenment is generally portrayed in the Western literature: as a dramatic step forward for the freedom of 'all mankind', not just European colonists. One popular text suggests: "the Enlightenment was, in fact, an intellectual movement that knew no national boundaries." To quote Locke himself: "No man has natural authority over his fellows and since Might can produce no Right, the only foundation left for legitimate authority in human societies is agreement." One can only wonder what the migrant, deemed refugee, would say to this? As for the Enlightenment writers, their views remain clear, if one is consider them today. In 1784, Kant wrote, for example: "Have courage to use your own reason—that is the motto of the Enlightenment."

ECONOMIC LIBERALISM: 'MIRACLE' OR 'EXPLOITATION'?

Readers of this book will, upon reflection, understand what a remarkable achievement it is: a clean bound book with a well designed cover, in this instance with contributors from all over the globe. Readers will also recognize—and it may require a moment of reflection—other remarkable material achievements that they can see and/or enjoy every day: the automobile, electricity, running water, a computer, a portable (cell) phone, and so on. These are remarkable achievements of material production and, when regularly surrounded by them on a regular basis, we can all too easily forget just how remarkable they are! I will often suggest to students that, when standing alone in a field, a forest, or desert (if they have the opportunity to do so), they should reflect back on these consumer products, to remind themselves just how remarkable they are. Many of these products are, let us be clear, the 'efficient' results of markets; others have historically required some involvement of the state.

A standard description of the fundamental requirements for markets will include (Lockean) privatization of property and government institutions that hold title to property (to authenticate private ownership). Entrepreneurs, striving for profit, have invested in the development of a consumer good that they hope we will later purchase. "Free-market" arguments made by liberal economists, from Adam Smith to Milton Friedman, suggest that the increased ease with which economic resources are shifted in an economy will lead to a more "efficient" use of those scarce resources. Friedman, whose works strongly influenced the Reagan and Thatcher era of the 1980s, was such a strong believer in the "free market" that he described it as "a necessary condition for political freedom." Free markets should not, as Samir Amin argues, take-over the processes that support political freedoms and even Friedman acknowledges that "economic freedom is not an end in itself." To better understand this, I often ask my students to think of the differences between STATE and MARKET goals, as follows:

Table 10.2: Recalling Liberal State vs. Market Goals

STATE	MARKET
Equity	Efficiency
Fairness	
Justice	
Security	

The goal—or virtue—of a free market is, as liberal economists have long argued, 'efficiency.' Concretely, what this means is the oft-quoted phrase, in the study of economics: "the efficient allocation of a society's scarce resources." But even this phrase can be somewhat confusing. I would therefore suggest taking the logic one step further. By 'efficiency' in a market we mean, specifically, the efficient use of the resources available to society and they are (as is classically presented in economics):

land, labour, and capital (wealth). The economist Edwin Mansfield, for example, bemoans the inefficiency of monopoly as follows:

> [A] factor that can reduce our economic growth rate is the increased strength of the monopolistic forces that prevent resources from being allocated efficiently.

That said one must not conclude, as some do, that the study of economics is simply concerned with "the efficient use of scarce resources in a society." Again, even the leading free-market guru, Milton Friedman, from the leading university on free-market economics, the University of Chicago, recognizes this fact. While the results of efficiently allocating resources are amazing (!), and all around us in an industrial society, we must not lose sight of 'other virtues' that we also care about, such as: 'equity', 'fairness', 'justice', and 'security', to name a few.

In short, the material output of an industrial society can blind many to other values—other than efficiency—that we all care about. In democratic societies, it is generally through the mechanisms of the state that these other values are pursued, albeit inefficiently in many cases. These values are generally not provided (or protected) through free-market mechanisms, although many have tried to push the 'miracle' of private sector efficiency into the often inefficient public sector. Sometimes, efficient market mechanisms can help improve the service of what is traditionally a public sector task. Infrastructure, utilities, mail services have been privatized—in whole or in part—and, at times, with great results for the consumer. But it is often forgotten that these public services were started where there was nothing prior. Sadly, free-market mechanisms do not always have solutions to society's desires or needs. Consider what it takes to start the construction of a light house or a public park, for these are not necessarily the kinds of things that the private sector would provide. The building of roads into rural regions is another classic example of the kinds of projects a state can undertake in the name of the "greater good." Fundamentally, this requires a redistribution of a community's wealth and this is where 'politics' comes into play.

Obviously, not everyone will agree as to what 'equity', 'fairness', or 'justice' will entail. For this reason, in pluralistic democratic states, we debate these matters—ideally, again, freely and openly—with the hope that a compromised position or policy on these matters can be reached. In pluralistic states we understand that not everyone will agree with policy decisions that result but we also allow—ideally—for some hope for flexibility and change in the system. In other words, state policies, laws, even state constitutions, can always be changed. The hope is that, on balance, a sense that these virtues have been realized, or are being realized, will prevail. Upon reflection it should be clear that we would not want to privatize legal or political systems, for efficiency is not the ultimate aim in those areas. Of course, we can always push for more efficient courts, elections, and the like! Another important area of state service is security: police and fire departments, a state's military and the like. Again, these can be privatized, and people do have privately owned security services, but when speaking of society as a whole, we generally view this as an important public service. The goals, then, of the state are more complicated than those of the free-market. State bureaucracies will always be inherently less 'efficient' than the private sector; it is "the nature of the beast." What motivates individuals to be involved in state politics and policy-making tends to be different from our motivations in the market place.

The free-market is generally motivated by self-interest, profit, and competition and results in better efficiency but the policy focus, since at least the time of the Industrial Revolution, has been on the free movement of capital (wealth) for investors and 'not' the free movement of another important resource, that more of us have readily available: labor. Consider again the scarce resources mentioned above. Today's dominant "development" logic is that if capital is moved around freely, with little state intrusion or "red tape," that resource will be used more efficiently, to where it is most needed on this earth. This is, in fact, the very logic behind the Multilateral Agreement on Investment (MAI), a policy that has been advocated within the halls of the Organisation for Economic Cooperation and Development (OECD). Exact reasons as to why the MAI has been stalled vary within the literature; of importance here is the primary aim of the MAI, namely, the free-movement of 'one' of the aforementioned resources: capital. The argument can be thought of as a "trickle-down" or "supply-side" argument for the world: poverty and economic stagnation exist, argue the OECD's liberal economists, the best path out of this circumstance is to free-up the movement of investment capital by, for example, streamlining business regulations and, generally, removing red-tape that might be in the way of an interested entrepreneur.

There has been ongoing resistance to the MAI and similar initiatives; something which leaves many liberal economists incredulous: How could this be? One reason, I would suggest, is that the history of capitalism has been interpreted by many as a process that has disproportionately benefited the capitalists, to the detriment of the rest. Another is that, when one considers the potential benefits of the free movement of 'all' resources, not just capital, the policy goals of the wealthy do seem odd indeed. To understand the latter concern, one can simply consider the historical "reaction" of the followers of Smith, and the followers of Marx, to the proverbial "factory." On the one hand, Smith interpreted the free movement of resources and the specialization of labour (in a pin factory) as a "miracle." Certainly, the impact on material production in the world has been remarkable, as liberal economists would attest.

Later industrial age liberals, such as Emile Durkheim, went as far as to describe this process as "moral." While there are those who would still agree with Durkheim's view, the dramatic opposite reaction was that of, classically, Marx & Engels who view the same processes in factories as "exploitation."

Table 10.3: Classic 'Reactions' to the Industrial Age

SMITH	MARX
(Liberals)	(Historical Materialists)
'Miracle'	'Exploitation'

In fact, as we all know, Marx proposes the creation of an entirely different non-capitalist (Communist) society—something he terms an "enlightened political economy" and which he obviously considers to be more "moral." Communism was a dismal moral failure; the reasons for that are beyond the scope of this chapter. What is notable is that, in his writings, Marx cites the works of the French physiocrats, who inspired Adam Smith's views—on, for example, *laissez-faire*—to suggest that some state regulation is required in a private ownership market-oriented society. For example, Marx cites Jean-Baptiste Say, who states: "Even supposing that capital is not simply the fruit of robbery... it still needs the help of legislation..." This logic, again, echoes that of the modern liberal economist Milton Friedman: "economic freedom is not an end in itself."

CONCLUSION: GETTING PAST THE CONTRADICTIONS

What if state leaders everywhere agreed on a policy that would support the free movement of peoples throughout the world? Based on what has been discussed in this chapter, such a policy would be: 1) 'Liberal;' 2) Most 'consistent' with the economic liberalization logic that has been long advocated by Western industrial leaders; 3) Most 'equitable,' fair and just, given the disproportionate capital benefits accrued in core capitalist states since the fifteenth-century; and 4) Most 'efficient' in terms of a reallocation of scarce economic resources that would lead to even higher levels of economic growth across the globe and the alleviation of seemingly intractable poverty problems. Given the dynamics of power, wealth and policy in the world this is not likely to happen; we don't, yet, live in a truly liberal world.

But as leaders of the powerful states of the world continue to push for liberalization, contradictions in their policies are emerging. Several have been addressed in this chapter. Some of this begins with the social sciences, where there exists a pretense of objectivity; as discussed, similar patterns are to be found in the political debates over immigration policy. Beyond this, there exist a great many anomalies with regard to the history and processes that surround today's 'refugee' status—what might be thought of as 'challenges' to today's liberal societies. These are summarized below:

1. The free movement of the colonizer was justified in the founding documents on liberalization (e.g. Smith and Locke); yet today the same logic does not apply to the aspiring migrant;

2. "Humanitarian" interest in protecting the rights of refugees (e.g. 1951 Convention) coincided with the seemingly sudden wave of independence movements throughout the formerly colonized world, i.e. since the formation of the UNHCR, procedures for the identification of "refugees" and the "placement" of peoples, has led to increased red-tape hurdles to the free movement of peoples;

3. The political leftist, traditionally made-up of many immigrant workers (and their descendants), has now deemed liberal immigration policies as harmful to "blue collar" workers;

4. The political conservative (often, also, a descendant of immigrants!), traditionally supportive of the free-movement of resources, has now turned to "socially conservative" arguments such as threats to local culture;

5. Leaders of "capital rich" Western (OECD) industrial states are seemingly more interested in the free-movement of capital (e.g. MAI) than in the free-movement of other economic resources (e.g. labor);

6. Staff of the UNHCR, charged with the determination of "refugee" status, have a disproportionate level of power, which opens doors to 'corruption' in the process, i.e. this is not a dialogue amongst equals;

7. The determination as to which states accept refugees is entirely determined by the powerful state citizens of potential "host" countries (based on numbers of potential refugees provided by the UNHCR)—a process that is entirely voluntary, i.e. there exists no international mandate;

8. Taken to their logical conclusion, it is doubtful that the liberal Wilsonian aims of "self-determination" are rarely practicable and can lead to new conflict (e.g. former Yugoslavia);

9. Neo-liberal/"Washington Consensus" policies aimed at liberalization have often resulted in the creation of regions with greater disparities between the rich and the poor (statistics to prove this), ironically through policies aimed at what has been termed "poverty production" and increased ethnic conflict (e.g. argument by Amy Chua).

10. The process of determining whether someone is a refugee, or not, tends to reject the impacts of colonial history, i.e. if someone is poor, so the argument goes, it is the result of circumstances in their home state and not of a history of economic exploitation, etc.

Those involved in the process are well aware of many of these anomalies; for example, many refugees could tell us the 'truth' of the processes that ultimately lead to 'refugee' status. Hopefully this book will help to reveal some of this truth. But the imbalances of power amongst those involved, and a pragmatic consideration of what is at stake, now and in the future, all act as barriers to true understanding.

Chapter 11 Photos

KAKUMA CAMP

Refugee Writers Group in the camp 1996. Photo by Yilma

Ethiopian New Year Celebration September 11, 1996, Photo by Yilma

Refugee Shelters in Kakuma Refugee Camp

International Women's Day Celebration in Kakuma Refugee Camp, refugee & local Tuekana Women. Photo by Yilma

Photograph Exhibition in the camp 'African Refugee Day' June 20th, 1996

Flood in Kakuma Refugee Camp. Photo by Yilma

Kakuma Refugee Library, Photo by Yilma

Ladies laying maize in equatorial community. Photo by Kanyinda Louis

At Water tap, people fetching water in Congolese community. Photo by
Kanyinda Louis

Dry River called in Kakuma Camp. Photo by Kanyinda Louis

Dinka boy (Sudanese) refection his hut. Photo by Kanyinda Louis

Mother and Chidren in equatorial community. Photo by Kanyinda Louis

Fabrication of mud bricks for shelter. Photo by Kanyinda Louis

Refugee working at home. Photo by Kanyinda Louis

Flood in kakuma after heavy rain. Photo by Kanyinda Louis

173

Gathering in Kakuma Camp. Photo by Kanyinda Louis

Storm devastates refugee shelter in Congolese community. Photo by
Kanyinda Louis

Storm devastates refugee shelter in Congolese community. Photo by
Kanyinda Louis

View of Kakuma 4. Photo by Kanyinda Louis

Fabrication of mud bricks. Photo by Kanyinda Louis

Disabled sport in Kakuma refugee camp. Photo by Kanyinda Louis

Ethiopian Orthodox Church at Kakuma Camp. Photo by Andrea Useem

Graves at Kakuma Camp. Photo by Kenyinda Louis

Graves at Kakuma Camp. Photo by Fantaye Keshebo

Refugees within camp. Photo by Fantaye Keshebo

Chapter 11

OUTCAST: THE PLIGHT OF BLACK AFRICAN REFUGEES
Part I: Pre-Resettlement

Yilma Tafere Tasew

Refugees, the human waste of the global frontier-land, are 'the outsider incarnate,' the absolute outsiders, outsiders everywhere and out of place everywhere, except in places that are themselves out of place—the 'nowhere places' that appear on no maps used by ordinary humans on their travels. Once outside, indefinitely outside, a secure fence with watching towers is the only contraption needed to re-enforce the 'indefiniteness,' the out of place hold forever.

I dreaded those public moments that highlighted the fact that I was a foreigner. Sometimes I sat at my desk plotting my revenge. I would master the English language. I would infiltrate the gringo culture without letting on that I was a traitor. I would battle in their tongue and make them stumble. I would cut out their soul and leave them on the shore to be pecked at by vultures. Winged words would be my weapon.

INTRODUCTION

The choice to leave one's country, to seek safe haven in a different place is never an easy one, yet it can sometimes, for a few people, be simple and at the same time the hardest and most complex decision of their lives—to stay in a hostile environment is to court death and torture, whereas, to leave will also have repercussions, where to flee to, how best to go about it? It may be as simple a decision as whether to live or die?

Most refugees seek sanctuary because of war, others because they belong to a subculture within a larger state culture—be it religious, tribal, political or any one of the myriads of reasons why people are singled out for persecution, torture, rape, 'marked for death' or other cruel, life threatening conditions.

As suggested by Matsuoka and Sorenson

> The typical image of 'uprooting' suggests that the process of displacement, of becoming a refugee or an exile, constitutes a complete break with one's past, culture, and identity. Many experience exile as a separation from their true place, which provides rootedness, continuity and meaning. Yet the break is not always complete, the past is not always the past, and not all exiles are powerless. Those who undergo this experience are not simply passive inhabitants of a dead zone, of loss and estrangement. Exile is also a fecund space for new ways of organizing experience—for creating new affiliations, associations, and communities and developing new identities. Transnationalism is an experience not a constant 'travel' and multiple returns but of separation, exile and longing rendered inescapable by global and local structural violence.

When African refugees arrive at a refugee camp they are in a state of limbo, gradually becoming shadows of their former selves, stripped of dignity and their basic human rights by the very people and agencies, such as the UNHCR (United Nations High Commission for Refugees), who are supposed to advocate for and protect the rights of refugees. In this kind of situation they cannot know what to expect but often see their families, friends, and fellow African refugees suffer and die avoidable deaths.

Revealing the truth about the ugly face of the UNHCR, an African Refugee situation was pointed out by Harrell-Bond:

Walk-up cites examples of institutional attempts to elimi-
nate the refugees, that is, the "organizational problem."
These include increasing attempts to repatriate refugees
prematurely, introducing efforts to prevent them from
fleeing violence by establishing 'safe havens' and the
practice of illegal, forced repatriations –all under taken
"simply because proper care for them became difficult
and they become a threatening budgetary problem for
the UNHCR." As we have seen, other strategies include
defining refugees as undeserving opportunists, ("recyclers",
"irregular movers") refusing them medical treatment and
cutting off support to refugees who were formerly defined
as 'in need of protection,' as in the case of the refugee who
the UNHCR attempted to 'starve' out of the Salvation
Army Hostel in Kampala. A case for 'understanding' or
the introduction of the rule of law?

The dilemma of refugee life, the puzzle of Black African refugees,
is unbearable. Particularly for Black African refugees in African refugee
camps and other concerned Africans in Diaspora-exile. The everyday
events and activities that are connecting and attaching themselves to
what happened to us, to our families, to our people and countries are
interrelated, interwoven with strands of complexity. Humankind, God,
the material universe, nature, civilization, the so-called international
community and everyone else, is turning against us. Even if we try to
assimilate and integrate; mix and change our legal and cultural identity
and make up, the machine of integration appears to be vomiting us
back out—ejecting us, thereby draining our pride and integrity. Every
one of the power barons seems to show us a cunning smile. Sometimes
our own people tread over us for leftovers here in the west, in exile, in a
manner similar to how they and their allies tread over our bones back
home in Africa.

People are not able to see the world, with its current structure and
projected image, as a better place. For a world to be a better place, not
just for a few but for all of us, all humanity must be included in human
discourse and action. Projecting one's own enclave as a representation
of the whole world and extolling the virtues of one's own segment of a
community as the way in which the whole of humanity should be, in
all frankness, amounts to delusions of grandeur and serves no positive
purpose. When a few racially challenged groups say that Africa should

be erased from the world map and be renamed "Continent X," and their opinion is indulged, I don't think there can be justice for refugees, save for a few nominal written documents.

Being a black African refugee who came from a refugee camp in Africa, was an urban refugee in Africa and now being a black African refugee living in the west, for the last eighteen years my life has been defined by the realities of refugee life and of the black African refugee regime. The main idea behind this paper was to tell the story of my refugee life during those years, which this paper details up to my arrival in New Zealand, essentially it is 'part one' of the journey. The second part, beginning with my arrival in New Zealand, will continue in another volume with the next book. In this part I detail people who travelled with me as well as places and conditions. It is the story of a ship unsure of its destination, floating for a life time.

Most black African refugees, before arriving in their country of asylum, have experienced torture and abuse in their home country. They have travelled for days and nights through the forests and deserts of Africa, witnessing the ugly face of war and genocide, being trauma-tised and decimated. On arrival at their country of asylum they also face a lot of problems, including the bureaucracy and corruption of the UNHCR and some other agencies and officers who demand bribes from refugees before determining their refugee status. The lucky ones, they are accepted, the rest will be sent to the refugee camps for an unspecified length of time to suffer or to die. The rich ones, "tourist refugees," who arrive by plane from their homeland, get accommo-dated in the cities and after a while get resettled in western countries using the money they have to 'buy' resettlement.

THE BEGINNING OF LONG LASTING AGONY: ODA AND WALDA REFUGEE CAMPS

I left my homeland, Ethiopia, in mid 1991 for Kenya. I hitchhiked on an Ethiopian military truck, which carried a few academics, stu-dents and civilians. The truck was loaded with machine guns, boxes of different ammunitions and explosives, which the military were selling all the way to the border with Kenya. They were also looting and robbing people by force in every village and city, beating people to death, shooting them directly in the leg or arm, on the way to Ethio-pian Moyale. We spent a night in the city of Hageremariam in a hotel, my food and accommodation was paid for by others in the group. I didn't have a penny with me and only possessed my jacket and trousers, which I carried in a plastic bag. Even though I had shown the others my teacher's union membership ID they were suspicious of me. All night they took shifts watching me.

The following night, after dark, we arrived at the border town of Moyale, Ethiopia, we spent the night there in a hotel. That night Moyale was a battle field. There was extensive gun fire throughout the night. I was scared; I couldn't sleep or lie on the bed. In the morning the people who I came with were in one of the hotel rooms, they were sharing out money, which they had looted and robbed the night before, openly. After they had finished each one of them had approximately twenty to thirty thousand Ethiopian Birr, which is equal to approximately four to six thousand American Dollars (USD.) A few of them gave me money as a gift, around five hundred Ethiopian Birr, which is equal to around one hundred USD, which was more than two months salary as a primary school teacher, a job I had done for ten years. After that I just walked over the border, which was approximately two hundred metres from the hotel, without anyone stopping or questioning me.

Once I was over the border I followed crowds of Ethiopians who were all moving in the same direction with their luggage. There was a name registration kiosk and I registered my name. I started asking people questions; I was confused having not been in this kind of situation before. I asked one young guy where the shops were and he offered to show me and I was able to buy a few things, like socks, underwear, a t-shirt and soap. We went back to the police station after having lunch in a small restaurant, where everyone was gathered to be transported to the transitional camp twelve kilometres away in a place called Oda.

My first night in Kenya I slept under a truck in an open field. I was exhausted, frightened, and lonely. When it got dark I started crying, sobbing, no one came to ask me why. I didn't know where to buy food; I could not find the guy who took me to the shops during the day again. Even though everyone in the crowd spoke the same language, Amharic, like me, from the same country, I had never met any of them before. I hated myself, the people who were gathered there acted as though they were at a picnic, eating, drinking, having sex in the open field drunk. I really felt that Ethiopia had no hope or future. I blamed the Mengistu Regime, who ruled the country by fear, terror and by killing innocent people, however, the rabble that overthrew him were just the opposite side of the same coin. While I was thinking these despairing thoughts it began to rain heavily. I decided not to move from under the truck but lay there using my belongings in the plastic bag as a pillow. I took in the rain. It was like a protest; that I would not give up hope in everything. For me it was an angry protest, of frustration against everything, my fate and the fate of my country, my people, my parents, siblings and Africa. I often transport myself back to that night under the truck, it was a turning point and the beginning of an unpredictable future that was out of my hands.

The following day I arranged a tent for shelter with around twelve young boys and girls. I had to buy my own food with the money left over from the previous day. After a few days people arrived from the UNHCR and they called everyone together using a loud speaker. They used one of the trucks as a stage to introduce themselves. I was listening and watching everything with uncertainty and confusion, using the shade of the truck far from the crowd. I was approached by Dr. Colleens, who, at the time, was the UNHCR Regional Medical Coordinator for East Africa; she asked me if I could speak English. I told her I might not be perfect but I could communicate, it was after this she asked me if I could pass on a message using the loud speaker in my own language. I said "yes, I can." She told me that pregnant women and mothers with children under five years old should gather where she was standing. I announced it and after a few minutes the pregnant women and women with children came. She produced a note book and asked me to register the women and the children by age and gender. Once I had done this she asked me to find a temporary shelter for them, she suggested one of the buses and asked the women to stay where they were. We went to one of the buses and talked to the people who were inside, after a short discussion they agreed to let the women use the bus as a temporary, overnight, shelter, so long as they kept it clean. After that she brought some cartons of milk for the children and we took them to the bus and explained the rules. She asked me if I was willing to look after them, I agreed and she handed me the notebook and introduced me to Ziff, who was a Kenyan of Indian origin. Ziff managed the logistics of emergency supplies and the store in Moyale, Kenya for the UNHCR. He explained to me what I was to do for the women and children. I had to record the children's weight every three days, supply them with emergency food of high nutritional value: biscuits, milk, as well as oats for the lactating mothers to make porridge. So I began to look after thirty eight mothers, forty seven children under five and twenty three pregnant women.

Ziff came to pick me up every morning to take me to the UNHCR store to collect food items needed for the women and children in my care. After a few days he began to use me as a distributor for food and non food items for the entire camp, which was divided into three groups: civilians, military and students. My duty became, on top of looking after the pregnant women and children, to distribute food, and non food items, all day to the representatives of each group. The food items included: wheat flour, rice, cooking oil, sugar and salt. The non food items included: Kitchen sets, gerry cans, blankets and tents. The only pay off for me, doing this job, was that I would get a feed. All day I would keep myself busy and learn how the emergency relief system operated. I was never given any payment for my work. I didn't know whether I should ask or not. After a few weeks the Civil Community Representatives, after collecting and selling most food and non food items instead of distributing them fairly, and selling fourteen cows, donated by President Moi, which were supposed to be slaughtered for their meat and distributed, disappeared with the supplies. It was after this incident that the Civilian Group decided to elect representatives. One morning they gathered and elected eight people to deal with the issues of the group and talk to any authorities who came to visit. I was elected as a chair person for the group, which was a huge task and experience for me. It required me to work sixteen hours a day, seven days a week. After I was elected I began having daily arguments with Ziff regarding the needs of the group I was representing. Finally I refused to do any more distribution work for him. I decided to work only with the Civilian Group and with the women and children whom I was still looking after.

Finally a permanent camp was established for us. The shifting of refugees from Oda camp to our new camp took about eight weeks. Throughout the move I remained behind with the women and children I had been looking after. We were the last group to move from Oda camp and it was finally closed.

We had been at Oda camp for about three months; it was a transitional camp for people who did not have the financial resources to find their own accommodation. The drinking water was from the ground and was full of algae and worms, which changed its colour from blue to green. Those who had the financial resources, especially high ranking military and civil officials of the overthrown military government, overthrown by Marxist guerrillas who still held power with an authoritarian regime, carried a lot of money with them on their way to the Kenyan border. They were robbing banks, shops and people, using their guns. These were the people who behaved as if they were at a picnic, slaughtered a cow, a lamb, drank wine, whiskey like water, attracting only the most helpless ladies who were, most of them, students, civil servants and prostitutes, a few of whom later became their wives.

After a while we were transported to an area called Walda where we cleared the desert of thorny trees and built our shelters with plastic sheets and tents supplied by a UNHCR man who dealt with the distribution of food and non food items. We had established the camp on our own. We had no medical assistance, no structure, anyone who had any money left Walda for the city of Nairobi. The new camp was divided into the same three groups, by the refugees themselves: civilian, military and students. The main reason for the split was that the students had submitted written applications to Daniel Areph Moi, the then Kenyan President, who came to visit us when we were at Oda transitional camp, with the American Ambassador to Kenya, who told me we should return to Ethiopia, that the government in power was adopting democracy, (I had a small argument with him). The students were expecting to be offered scholarships in Kenyan Universities. The military were expecting to return to Ethiopia to fight again so the students and the military didn't mix with the civilians, who were perceived by both groups to be criminals and murderers.

Knowing this we realised that it was not the best idea for the groups to remain separated. After a long discussion and negotiations we formed a combined committee who would manage the camp administration. I was elected as a chairperson for the refugees in the camp as well as for the civilian group committee. (I was re-elected as a civilian group chairman while I stayed behind in Oda camp). The civilian group had sub-committees that dealt with logistics, security and social services. Each sub-committee had five members with two overall supervisors of the leadership group. We didn't have any medical supplies or clinics so we centralised the medicine bought by the military and students from the Ethiopian Military camps to Kenya and we opened clinics in tents using the medical man power within the refugee camp, there were three doctors, four nurses and a few health assistants for about thirty five thousand Ethiopian refugees. We made contact with an independent District Catholic Mission Hospital, which was twenty kilometres from the camp. We sent daily referrals to Sololo Catholic Hospital and also got some medical supplies via a truck that travelled with members of the military group from Ethiopia when they crossed the border.

For the first nine months there was no water for refugees in the camp. There was some water, thanks to the Kenyan Government, who supplied water to the local nomads for themselves and their cattle but we were not allowed to drink the water first. First in line were the lions and other wild animals, so that they didn't attack the cattle while they drank, next in line were the cattle, then the locals, we were allowed to take whatever water remained. We spent most nights waiting in a queue, using our gerry cans as pillows, where dangerous snakes and scorpions attacked refugees every day. In December 2005 I observed an incident that reminded me of this nightmare in the camp. One weekend I saw people sleeping in a queue in front of a music shop, queuing to buy tickets to a *UB40* concert, who were touring New Zealand sometime later that year. The irony is that the desire to go to a concert, in the western world, makes people sleep outside. Africans regularly sleep outside to queue for such a basic item as water. Whether they are refugees or not they are living a nightmare that is sad and complicated.

The food we were given in the camp was not enough. We were not officially recognised as refugees for almost ten months. One supply drop of corn powder, one hundred and twenty three sacks, which is 12,300kgs, was completely contaminated and was full of worms. This situation made us decide to take action and voice our concerns to the Kenyan Government, officials and the world media. We called for a four day hunger strike and sent some refugees to Kenya, Moyale, one hundred and twenty five kilometres from Walda Camp, to share our message with the churches, NGO's (Non Government Organisations), media, and Embassies. Our message was that we had been left alone without any help in the middle of nowhere. We distributed the message via fax and phone from Kenya, Moyale and our efforts bore fruit. That evening everybody listened to the news about us on BBC, VOA, Voice of Germany and Kenyan Radio. The next day the District Officer and some other Kenyan Officials arrived at the camp from Marsabat. They promised us that the UNHCR officials and the WFP officials were on their way from Nairobi, Geneva and Rome and everything would be better. Later I found out that the contaminated corn, that was delivered to the camp, was collected from the Kenyan Cereal Board rubbish dump and was due to be burned in Marsabat. Ziff and his boss Ackbar Hussein sold the corn they were meant to have delivered and replaced it with the rotten corn, which was supplied to the UNHCR by the World Food Programme, on their way to Walda Camp. The UNHCR rewarded Ackbar Hussein by promoting him to Regional Programme Officer of the East Africa branch, based in Nairobi.

During the four-day hunger strike, around three hundred young refugees started a trip from Walda to Kampala, Uganda. The trip was intended, according to their belief, to bring them a better life. They believed that travelling across the desert, on foot, would enlighten them somehow and that in Uganda they would be better off. I tried to talk to them, as a community leader, and tell them of the danger they were facing and that they were putting their lives at risk. But they wouldn't listen. There were a few people whose mission was to disperse the refugees. The trip to Kampala was one plan to do this, they targeted the student group who were more impressionable and gullible and convinced them that the trip to Uganda would be easy. It was obvious that it was a plot of the Ethiopian Government. The rebel group who had taken power in Ethiopia had been refugees themselves some thirty years earlier and had fled from Ethiopia to Sudan and Somalia, including top officials such as Meles Zenawi. However, they underestimated the tenacity of the refugees and so did what they could to destroy them. As we had feared, about half of the students who embarked on the 'walk' were found scattered around the desert, collapsed and dispersed. Some of them managed to travel to Marsabat after hitchhiking. A few had been eaten by wild animals. Those who had survived were brought back to Walda by Kenyan police.

A few days later the representatives of the UNHCR, WFP (United Nations World Food Programme) and the Kenyan Government came to the camp and promised to head count all refugees and register us with the UNHCR. They promised that we would get better access to water and a hospital. True to their word, after a few days we were counted one by one by passing through a temporary fenced enclosure. The head count was only done because they needed to issue us all with ration cards to assist CARE Kenya with food distribution. Our medical needs were taken care of by the local NGO, called AMREF, and the water was taken care of by UNICEF, which established wells so we could get water.

Things became complicated from that day forward. The camp became a bloodless battlefield, filled with people with conflicting needs. It was especially hard if you were a committee member running refugee affairs day to day. People who had money were spending it on alcohol, gambling and adultery, in the desert having a 'good' time, some with money they had stolen. Some of the refugees were indeed criminals. When the rabble captured the Ethiopian capital, Addis Ababa, the prison gates were opened. With no system of government the criminals and political prisoners walked out. They began looting in groups, stealing vehicles and robbing banks all the way to their final destination. The army from south and central Ethiopia mostly ended up in Kenya. After the defeat the majority of the army went to Sudan, which was the nearest destination. The students were forced to sign up for National Military Service, which they were attending in southern Ethiopia in a remote semi desert called Bilatei. Walda camp became a centre of chaos, a city without structure, a city of strangers who bought to that desert land of Kenyan nomads a kind of 'dooms day.' On the other hand there were refugees who were genuinely good people who were afraid for their lives.

I didn't blame anyone who ran away from prison or committed a crime like theft. Nor did I judge the soldiers or civil servants who ran away when Mengistu left. The majority of them were the victims of a corrupt system who had no jobs and were taken from their homes at a young age to fight for a cause they didn't believe in. Who had been in a war zone for more than a decade without seeing their families and without enough food or shelter. The war, that they were forced to fight, was lost and their leader lied to them when he said "I will die for my country." He had taken refuge in Zimbabwe, to a pre-arranged sanctuary abandoning them, thanks to the CIA and a pre-negotiated arrangement. These were my people who were victims of generational corruption and military juntas. Even if I didn't agree with what they'd done during their refugee life I couldn't blame them for what they had done out of feelings of betrayal, despair and frustration.

In September 1991 I began a relationship with a young Ethiopian woman. For a few weeks we lived under a plastic sheet together. This relationship ended in disaster and caused me a lot of emotional distress. I embarrassed myself crying for her. When I love I love with all my heart, fully open. When I am cheated and betrayed I feel devastated. It took me a long time to recover from this emotional crisis.

One time of chaos was when we were told by the Kenyan Police District Chief that we had to return the vehicles to Ethiopia that the military and civilians had brought with them when they fled across the border. At the time this was a difficult issue for me to deal with. The Kenyans, as our hosts, didn't want their security threatened by this issue. The Ethiopian authorities had warned them that if they were not able to return the vehicles they would come and take them by force. On the other hand the refugees, especially the former military refugees, didn't want to hand them over. I was caught in the middle, after discussing the issue with the committee members, even though some of them didn't agree, we decided that it was wise to return the vehicles. I was chosen to be the one to inform the former military and civilian refugees in a meeting. This was a battle and I had to throw hard words, even though no-one was convinced or prepared to help me show that there was no other option. After a few days of confrontational meetings and name calling they were able to see that, in reality, even though the return of the vehicles created a sense of defeat for most, they needed to be returned peacefully and without confrontation.

At this time Ziff was in charge of Walda camp along with Ackbar Hussein, who was always drunk. In later years, when I was in Nairobi, he was the Regional Programme Officer of the UNHCR, in charge of agencies budgets. He gave me a hard time while I was working on refugee transport in and out of the camps, for this I had to deal with him directly.

Before becoming a refugee I was a primary school teacher who thought for more than ten years that life was no more than my teaching job, family and friends. I was happy, more or less, even if I only ate once a day. I was happy in my own way in my own tiny, small world. Before the teaching job I was arrested, tortured several times, accused of what not. I was fed up with my harsh life, the processes, the city prisons, red terror, white terror and the military regime, which withered away my youth, my hope, my dreams. My youth was gone, like a morning frost it melted in front of me and was gone. The teaching job was like going underground, disappearing from the view of the Government Officials, becoming a fugitive. By teaching in the most remote areas of the country I had no means of communication, unless I applied for a transfer after two years of service but I knew no-one would bother to transfer me. This remoteness of course helped to save my physical life; emotionally I had withered away a long time ago. I was dead.

By May 1991 the rebels, who to this day are still in power, defeated the military regime after seventeen years of dictatorship and communist rule. The rebels claimed they were much better communists than the military regime. They followed the extreme communist theories of Albania. I didn't want my life to fall into the hands of these young, power hungry hyenas taken over from the old weak hyena. So I decided to cross the border into Kenya.

For me it was a different experience. I can't explain it. Maybe it was the idea of feeling important; doing something useful for me and others or maybe it was fate that made me become a refugee community leader. In that complex composition of refugee population, from the lowest strata of Ethiopian society to the highest social status: intellectuals, doctors, military, officials, civil servants, for a person like me, who had no experience or knowledge of leadership, it came as a surprise. I am not sure what to call it. At that time the people who were not happy with my leadership would abuse, insult and intimidate me. I cried several times in front of all the refugees at gatherings. I also resigned from leadership several times only to be elected again. The experience and knowledge, especially that Walda refugee camp gave me, is a life time gift and achievement. It returned my self confidence, which had been stripped away from me by the military regime back home. I regained the ability to give and receive the love of humankind. I was rewarded by seeing the change I made in others lives, especially for people who were helpless, like me, I told them to hold hands with me no matter what came to pass.

For some refugees Walda camp became a place of transformation, from being a follower of communist ideology, some of them communist cadres, commissars, military and civil authorities, who in the past might have destroyed lives, tried to wash themselves clean and get redemption. For criminals, burglars, pickpockets and prostitutes it was a time to cleanse themselves. So the refugee camp became a centre of religious competition and conversion. To try and become idealists because the materialistic ways of communism had resulted in defeat. There was also a belief in the camp that the churches, NGO's, UNHCR and western countries preferred to take refugees for resettlement who were 'religious' as opposed to 'communist.' So they prepared themselves for 'the world of golden opportunity' as it is said in one of the African proverbs, 'The religion of rude is stronger than iron string.' Some of the people who became the leaders of camp churches were former communists from Mengistu's regime.

After the hunger strike and the head count Ziff left Walda camp. No-one knew his whereabouts so he was replaced by Dr. Lamine Camara. Dr. Camara was originally from Sierra Leone, he told us that he had worked for six years, during the time of Emperor Haile Silassie, with OAU, in Ethiopia. His wife was an Ethiopian from the eastern region. Dr. Camara was physically short and fat, which made day to day activities physically difficult for him in the heat and scorching sun of Walda. With him was a Kenyan guy from the coast who was assigned to the camp as a field officer, he was travelling to the border and giving money to local chiefs to bring to the border as many members of the Geri and Borena tribes as they could to become refugees, who, at the time, were highly affected by drought and tribal conflict in Ethiopia. The reason he did this was so he could get a lot of emergency funding that would not be audited. Dr. Camara's lazy and careless management created disaster in the camp and also gave more power to Mohammed, which he abused. One of the things Mohammed did was to gather all the young women together and put them in accommodation close to the UNHCR compound; calling them a vulnerable group he had sexual relations with each of them in the evenings, turn by turn. In return they expected a better future, through him. They were also given sanitary pads at the expense of some other women in the camp. This situation did not affect the young women in the student group because they were more conscious of what he was doing and the location of the student group was far from the locations of the other two groups. This practice of putting young women in separate accommodation and abusing them had an effect on relationships in the rest of the camp as well as relationships with the women who were separated from the groups, they became alienated and were looked at, by most refugees in the camp, as no better than prostitutes.

As a result of this situation a committee meeting was demanded by the refugees and it was decided to write a letter to the UNHCR in Nairobi. But no one gave the issue serious attention. Mohammed continued to do as he liked. Later, when the Deputy Representative of the UNHCR came to visit the camp for a few hours, I approached her and talked to her about our concerns. She listened carefully and told me that she would look into it and get back to me but she didn't.

With the situation remaining unchanged the rain started and the refugee shelters of plastic sheets collapsed. Only the refugees who had money were able to repair their shelters by buying new plastic sheets from the UNHCR. Expatriate refugees and local CARE staff were selling UNHCR issued plastic sheets and whatever else they could find in the refugee camp. This transgression had been discussed several times with Dr. Camara; the issue became worse when some of the refugee representatives from the civil and military groups got involved in the chain of theft. The situation exploded one rainy day. The refugees marched to the UNHCR compound demanding materials for shelters. When they reached the gate demanding to talk to Dr. Camara, one of the refugees, who was working as a distribution clerk and who lived in the compound, came out carrying a big chain and began beating his own people with the chain of iron. He attempted to force them from the gate, he wounded a few of them on the head and face, they began bleeding to death. Then the refugees got even angrier and became violent. They pushed themselves, by force, into the compound. They found themselves inside the compound dismantling and breaking anything they could lay their hands on. Some of them got hold of Dr. Camara and began to beat him round the head with their slippers. It was at this time that a refugee ran to the police station at the back of the compound and informed them of what was happening. The police came quickly and started firing their guns into the air to disperse the crowd. When I heard the first bullet I started running to the compound with other refugees from all groups. By the time we reached the compound the police had stopped firing.

After a while the situation calmed down again until, during a meeting, someone suggested that we were not truly living unless we could find a solution to this problem. The group became agitated, at the same time a group of visitors, who'd travelled from Nairobi, drove into the compound. The attention of the crowd shifted to the visitors and they started throwing stones at their land cruiser. A window was broken. A U.S Regional Program Officer and some other delegates were in the car. I decided to talk to them and explain the situation. We made an agreement that he would talk to the refugees once they vacated the compound. I spoke to the crowd, I told them that we had made our point and now we needed to be systematic; that one of the officials would come to speak to us in an hour's time if we all waited outside the compound. After a few noisy protests everyone left the compound. I remained behind with other community leaders to do some damage control and stabilise the situation. After an hour we gathered in front of the compound and we started talking with the UNHCR delegate from Nairobi. Finally he promised to report the situation, immediately, to his superiors. We followed up with another meeting, in the afternoon, with the camp committees, the Nairobi delegates, Dr. Camara and a police officer. While all this was happening Mohammed, the field officer, was at the border purchasing refugees. The meeting was long and difficult. Most of the talking was done by the UNHCR delegates and a police officer who threatened us. We had to remain calm no matter what they said. The delegates at least had spoken with refugees before their return to Nairobi but the meeting was in vain.

It was a few days after this incident that, adding salt to the wound, a bus, which travelled between Moyale Kenya and Marsabet transporting Kenyan citizens, stopped at Walda camp for lunch. On the bus was an Ethiopian prisoner who was hand cuffed and being escorted by police. He began speaking with refugees, in Amharic through the bus window. After a few short conversations the refugees rescued him from the bus and took him to one of the refugee 'hotels' (made of UNHCR issue plastic sheets). The police who escorted him fired a few gun shots into the air and then left with the bus. He was kept hidden in a 'hotel' until dark. When it was dark he was taken to a location in the ex-military part of the camp. Around 7pm I was called to the UNHCR compound, along with other community leaders. When we arrived we were received by an angry police officer from Marsabet. The meeting was regarding the Ethiopian who had escaped from the bus with the aid of refugees. The police officer said that he did not come for a discussion but to take back the criminal, or, if we couldn't deliver him that night, to return to Marsabet and bring back army police to search the entire camp. I asked him to give us a few minutes to discuss the situation. After a few argumentative talks we agreed to hand the Ethiopian over. This created a rift in the leadership team as some people in the team played a role in hiding him. I said to the leadership team that this can't happen, the prisoner was not a refugee after all, he was not our concern and we had to hand him over. Finally we agreed, as community leaders, to pretend that we didn't know where he was and that at 8.30pm we would call a meeting of all refugees in front of the compound and we would ask the refugees to hand him over. So we called the meeting and a few refugees went back pretending to look for him before we handed him over to the police officer, so that the police would not know that the community leaders were involved. Later we heard that he was arrested in Moyale, Kenya while the Kenyan police were looking for a burglar with a similar physical description. By the time he was taken to court in Marsabet the real burglar was found. The Ethiopian was sentenced to a few months in prison, only because of his escape from police. At Kakuma camp the rumour was spread that I was the one who had handed him over to police.

One day the issue of Mail distribution to refugees in the camp was raised. Mail was coming to the refugees through the UNHCR office in Nairobi. It arrived every Tuesday and was given to one of the refugee clerks, who was also dealing with vegetable and meat distribution and who had a close link to Genet Gebekiristos, the Deputy Representative of the UNHCR in Kenya, he called her 'Shenkore, meaning elder sister. This refugee clerk was opening every piece of mail and checking whatever he wanted to check in his shelter at the UNHCR compound. I had collected evidence of opened and discarded letters from the rubbish bin in the compound several times. Some of them were sponsorship forms that were sent to refugees from the U.S.A, Canada and Australia. The reason some of the mail went missing was because some of it contained money or cards informing them of parcels that could be collected from the Nairobi post office. We organised a meeting with Dr. Camara with the aim of taking over the mail distribution by assigning one person, to be selected by the refugees, for this specific duty. After a long battle we succeeded in taking the mail distribution duties off the dishonest clerk. Later the former mail clerk and the security officer who attacked refugees with a chain were sent to Nairobi to work for the UNHCR. The mail clerk was put in charge of a transition camp for medical resettlement cases in Langata, a suburb of Nairobi. Eventually he was resettled, along with the other, chain wielding, refugee. Neither of them has spoken to me since.

Eventually Dr. Camara and Mohammed left Walda. I discovered later that Dr. Camara had become a foreign minister representing his country, Sierra Leone. I never discovered what happened to Mohammed.

Walda camp was a living nightmare. Typhoid, malaria, malnutrition and hepatitis were rife and bandits killed many refugees. Between 1991 and 1993 more than 3,700 refugees died. Seventy five percent of them were women and children. This, of course, was only the recorded figure, which is cross referenced with the distribution reports. It was not unusual to see refugees being transported by other refugees in wheelbarrows, wrapped in blankets, to a tent marked 'hospital.' Sometimes the refugees carrying other refugees collapsed on the way. It was heart breaking to see human beings being pushed in a receptacle for soil, stone or rubbish. As a kind of joke some of the wheelbarrows had "Ambulance donated by UNHCR" painted on the side of them. I was one of those, transported by 'wheelbarrow' to the hospital having collapsed with malaria and typhoid. After admission I had to have a drip in my arm for two weeks. One of the good things about being in the camp was that the refugees all took care of each other, those who could afford it donated and prepared food for me, those who couldn't helped to transport the donated food to patients in the hospital. I recovered and was discharged after two weeks but it took me several more months to regain my physical strength.

It was approximately the beginning of 1993. One night three young Ethiopian refugees were slaughtered and left naked in the bush surrounding the camp, bound together. It was one of the most horrible things that had happened to us. All of the refugees were devastated and outraged, and scared. Their funeral was held in the camp cemetery, everyone cried openly. The smell of their bodies didn't disgust anyone. Everyone wanted to carry the coffins and was emotionally devastated. It seemed at that moment as if all of us had gone mad in that scorching sun.

At the same time there was open war taking place between the Borena and Geri tribes. Most evenings they fought with heavy machine guns and ammunition. The camp looked like the front line at night and in the morning it seemed like nothing had happened, except that a few more people were killed or wounded.

The other puzzling thing was the arrival of an Ethiopian at Walda camp, running for his life. A few days later he was found in the camp near a small bridge, hanged in one of the acacia trees. Opposite his body was a syringe. His death created a dilemma as he had left a lot of money and his passport in a suitcase at his friend's shelter. He had been anxious since arriving saying that the Ethiopian Government would follow him to Walda and kill him and everyone believed that, that had been the case. There were also many unidentified refugees whose bodies had been found near the camp but were badly mutilated by wild animals.

In the camp, especially Walda, many things happened that were interwoven with global politics. At the time of our arrival, in 1991, there was a woman who arrived at the UNHCR office in Nairobi as a representative of the UNHCR Deputy Representative for Kenya, the rebel group who held power in Ethiopia. She held a meeting every two weeks in Moyale, Ethiopia, the border town between Kenya and Ethiopia, which was situated 125 km from Walda camp, with an American called Jim. They would cross the border into Ethiopia to meet with Ethiopian Authorities. Even though it was difficult to know the aim of these meetings it was obvious that the main agenda item was us. Every second Thursday morning the head of the field office would come with a list of Ethiopian names, he would ask the refugees who worked in the compound if they recognised any of the names on the list and if they were currently in the compound. Based on this it was obvious that there was some kind of plot against the refugees. The entire time that Jim worked at Walda camp he never shook a refugee's hand. He also never sat next to a Kenyan driver preferring to sit in the back seat alone. He never removed his sunglasses in front of people. No-one could be sure if he was even looking at them. Once I asked him why he wouldn't shake hands with me, he didn't respond he just left me standing there wondering.

Once Jim left the camp, after a few months, the meetings with Ethiopian officials, across the border in Moyale, stopped. Whether this meant it was 'mission accomplished' or not no one knew. It remained a puzzle, like most things in refugee life.

It was after Jim left Walda that a delegation from the UNHCR, headed by Roberto Contero Marino, at the time senior protection officer in the branch office at Nairobi, who later became head of the sub office at Kakuma camp, visited the camp with three Ethiopian officials in a land cruiser. I was called to a meeting with the other community leaders. At the beginning of the meeting we were introduced to Mr Contero and the other delegates. The Kenyan police chief was also there. It was against our protocol for the police chief and the Ethiopian officials to be there. They had come to discuss repatriation of Ethiopian refugees to Ethiopia. Once we found out who the other delegates in the meeting were we refused to take part. We asked the police chief to inform the delegates that they needed to leave the camp immediately, that the repatriation issue was none of our business; we were not willing to discuss, encourage or discourage any refugees on the issue of repatriation. It was not our issue. The district police officer supported our position and he assured us that he would send the delegation, with a police escort, back to Ethiopia. We made a formal complaint to the UNHCR and the Kenyan Government about this security breach and the fact that the violation was made by the very people who were supposed to protect us. We never received a response.

Later the former Archbishop of the Ethiopian Orthodox Church arrived at Walda camp. With him were two, young, Ethiopian Deacons. All three were running for their lives. A few days after he arrived he was called to the UNHCR compound. That same day a UNHCR plane arrived carrying deputy representatives of the UNHCR, a representative of the Kenyan Government and the US Ambassador to Kenya. They went to the small cottage in the UNHCR compound, which was used to hold meetings with refugees, (if they were lucky enough to get access to the compound.) After a few short words between the Archbishop and the Kenyan Government representative in Amharic, while she was translating for the US Ambassador, they called in two Kenyan police men. They escorted the Archbishop to a vehicle and left for the airport at Sololo, 20kms from Walda camp. The two young Deacons were told to go back to the camp. After this incident I never managed to find out what happened to the Archbishop and I never saw the two young Deacons, who were supposedly left in the camp with us, again. I was able to observe all of this because, at the time, my job was to record the mortality rate in Walda camp. Each day I had to count graves for the UNHCR. In order to collect the paint to mark the new graves and get transport to and from the grave site I had access in and out of the UNHCR compound, any time I liked. Especially that day, I had to start late due to the visitors arriving from the airport so I had a good chance to observe everything.

The UNHCR began a new shelter construction programme at the camp after an influx of new refugees from the Geri and Borena tribes. The new constructions were intended to be permanent shelters, with cement floors and roofs of corrugated iron. Each shelter was to be large enough for one family. The contract for these new shelters was given to a private, German contractor called Claude. He had one refugee working for him as a supervisor and around one hundred more as construction workers. The location chosen for the new shelters was not chosen very carefully, it did not have good drainage and once the rain started it became very swampy. All of the new houses were flooded. Almost one thousand new shelters were unliveable. One day Claude was seen dismantling his camp ground, without paying anything to the one hundred refugees who worked as labourers for more than three months, he and the refugee who worked as his supervisor escaped together. We tried to secure money for the refugees who had worked as labourers but we were unable to do so. Later I learned that the refugee 'Supervisor' who escaped with Claude was resettled, with help from Annette Ludeking, the social services officer at the UNHCR in Nairobi. Recently I heard that he is highly regarded in the Ethiopian community where he was resettled.

Not long after Jim left Walda an Italian arrived by the name of Adelmo. He was Jim's replacement. It was about that time that security levels at the camp deteriorated dramatically. Everyday refugees were being killed in the camp and both day and night became very dangerous. We all started losing sleep and jumping at our own shadows. We had several meetings with Adelmo and the Kenyan police demanding the camp be relocated. Both agreed that the camp was no longer safe, especially as some shootings and murders had already taken place uncomfortably close to the police compound. It was clear that the issue had spread beyond the refugees; the camp was no longer safe for anyone.

KAKUMA REFUGEE CAMP

After all the ups and downs Walda camp was finally closed and we were shifted to a new camp called Kakuma. It was during the shift that I was called to Nairobi for a resettlement interview with the Australian High Commission, along with some other refugees from the camp. One of the refugees I was being interviewed with had worked as a distribution clerk in the camp. He used to sell a lot of food and non-food items, illegally, that CARE had donated. He also befriended a Senior Resettlement Officer named Nathan Robbie. He used to wine and dine Nathan when he came to visit Walda to discuss resettlement issues with the money he had made selling stolen food items. The name that this refugee, and others like him, gave to this style of theft was 'business.' My interview at the Australian High Commission was unsuccessful and I was rejected. I was handed over to a UNHCR officer who organised another resettlement interview for me, this time with the Canadians but they didn't like me either and I was returned to Kakuma. Kakuma camp was a very depressing place. The weather, the wind and the dust were terrible; in short Kakuma was where nature played its ugliest games.

Kakuma camp held more than eighty thousand black African refugees from all over Africa. Some of them were 'urban' refugees, academics who had suddenly found themselves thrown into a camp in the middle of nowhere. In the new camp we never knew what was happening and we were desperate for a decent meal, a comfortable bed and to walk free from the camp. We didn't have any means of communication with the outside world. Perhaps because of the scorching heat or the isolation from the rest of the world, some people began to go crazy with the not knowing, but most people were fighters and a common saying in the camp was "we are stronger than steel." I began to wonder what was happening in my homeland, Ethiopia, and I began contemplating my fate and the fate of those around me. I began digesting the reality of refugee life. I began asking myself, how did I get into this situation? What is happening in the world? Who is responsible for all this? Where is my proper place in the world? What is my future? Questions I was never able to answer, even after resettlement.

At the beginning of April 1993 there was an incident in the camp that almost started the worst refugee conflict you can experience as a refugee. There were some refugees who were former military, from the

Ethiopian military regime. They were drinking local Ethiopian alcohol in one of the camp bars. The owner of the bar was a former military intelligence officer. While they were drinking they claimed that he had an Ethiopian passport, that he had shown it to them, (no one was able to verify this claim,) they claimed he threatened them with a gun. After an hour news of the incident had spread like wild fire through the camp and caused a lot of anger, particularly in the Ethiopian section of the camp. The majority of the refugees began to to gather in front of the library and demand retribution. The chairman of the community was unable to calm them down. A 'mob justice' scenario would have been very dangerous and bloody and threatened the security of the entire camp. From experience I knew how to calm the mob and bring the situation under control. I stepped in and started speaking on behalf of the mob, the community leaders began to agree with what they were saying and it calmed the mob down. Their anger was targeted at a particular group of refugees, the Tigrean's, a group of exiles from Ethiopia who had supported the current regime.

Once everyone became calm and began to listen I told them they were right to be angry but if we became emotional and began a fight we would be playing into their hands. They could claim they were victims of ethnic violence and we could be forcibly repatriated to our homelands for creating a security situation in the camp. I proposed that a small committee be formed, including current community representatives, and that the committee collect names of people who had committed violence or been disruptive. That these people be brought, peacefully, to the library for an interview and an explanation. After that the committee would select people whom they believed were a genuine danger to the community and produce a list to present to the UNHCR and the Kenyan Government. Without any further protest the mob accepted this idea. Around one hundred refugees were brought to the library. From this number only eleven were included in the list, which was handed over the UNHCR with an accompanying letter. The rest were told to go. One of the eleven was a former deacon of the Ethiopian Orthodox Church. This created a great deal of protest from the church followers in the camp. I had to attend a meeting with church leaders and other elders to explain the reasons for his inclusion and to bring peace and reconciliation. I also told them that being ousted from the camp might help their case for resettlement, if they explained that they could not return to the camp for fear to their personal safety. I told them that I personally did not believe the accusations but to avoid further conflicts within the camp this was the best option. No one was hurt by this even though those eleven people were removed from the camp and may have been relocated against their will. For the time being they were safe under UNHCR protection. I also asked the community chairman to read the letter we had submitted to the UNHCR out to the camp. The letter stated that the committee representing the Ethiopian community had no hard evidence against the eleven but believed their lives would be in real danger if they remained in the camp. Therefore it was in their best interest and in the interest of maintained peace within the camp that they be removed into UNHCR protection. The reading of this letter and a few further hours of discussion helped to calm the situation.

This situation was ignited by emotion and frustration; there was no other way to calm the situation down. You cannot approach this kind of crowd with anger or tell them they are wrong. A desperate crowd, who are just waiting for an excuse to create drama. This kind of approach would only incite violence and serve to escalate the severity of the situation. I couldn't just stand back knowing what might happen, I would have felt too guilty, knowing the potential outcome but doing nothing. The first thing I did was to listen to the crowd, listen to their anger and frustration. When they said things like "we will kill them," "we will cut them to pieces," I simply stood back and let them vent their anger, then before they could begin planning their retribution I stepped in and started by saying "you are right," repeating and affirming all they had already said. Then I explained to them the reasons why we shouldn't go through with what they wanted to do and that we should be wiser than the criminals they despised. I raised the idea of the list that we could then give to the UNHCR. I explained that I was happy to help with some support from others, including the community leaders. We agreed on this and I was able to prevent the camp from being turned into a field of genocide.

These types of incidents were not the only events to increase anger and frustration in the camp. There was also the ongoing issue of have nothing to do, day or night, the hardship of life. The visible difference in living standards within the camp, the economic wealth of some refugees compared to others, the scorching sun and other emotional issues all helped to increase tension amongst the refugees. The incessant hot weather heightened people's emotions and resulted in people losing their temper more easily. I was just proud that I was able to prevent the worst happening to me and my people, my fellow refugees.

Shortly after this particular incident three student leaders arrived at the camp from Addis Ababa. They were from the university in Ethiopia and had fled to Kenya. They were brought, by the UNHCR, to Kakuma camp. As soon as they arrived they began a hunger strike, claiming that Kenya was not safe for them. They attracted a lot of attention, especially from the Ethiopian refugees. This made the UNHCR uncomfortable with their presence in the camp so they were kept in a tent inside the UNHCR compound and were only allowed to have meetings with Ethiopian community leaders. A few days into their hunger strike the UNHCR decided to relocate them to another camp. On the day that the three students were scheduled to leave the camp, it was windy, dusty and exceedingly hot under the scorching sun. We staged the biggest protest rally we had ever held in the camp to show our support for them, we were joined by many other communities in the camp including Turkana's carrying the Ethiopian flag. We condemned the international community for supporting the brutal regime of EPDRF in Ethiopia. We were also protesting against the UNHCR for violating its duty and failing to protect refugees. We continued the rally until the students left from the Kakuma air strip in a UNHCR plane. I was unable to find out what had happened to the students after they were taken from the camp.

I have been criticised for my actions in the camps since leaving. This criticism has followed me all the way here to New Zealand. I have tried to explain my logic and reasons for doing what I did. I did it for my people who asked me to represent them. I have no guilt or regrets. Some of my ideas, I believe, saved lives--that was my main reason for getting actively involved in camp politics. I did not expect to be praised and did not do it to be a hero. For instance, a refugee day celebration that I organised was criticised by a refugee article in *Kanebu,* (Kakuma News Bulletin, a refugee produced camp newsletter,) it said that it was inappropriate to celebrate and dance as it only made the UNHCR and other NGO's look good and made it seem as though refugees were happy with their lives in the camp.

Back when I was in Nairobi, attending my interview for resettlement at the Australian High Commission, I met a young Ethiopian lady whom I knew when I was in Walda camp. I knew I wanted to marry her and begin a family, resettlement or not. The desire for a relationship, sexual and otherwise, in the camps is very strong. After many years stuck in the camps like a god damned hermit, dreaming of beautiful women, to be in a relationship is not just a physical need it is also an emotional one. After all I love women even though I would not say I was a womaniser. We agreed to get engaged. She told me she could not be in a relationship with me unless we were married because of her protestant faith. I believed her and foolishly included her name as my fiancé when completing forms to be resettled in Canada. She asked me to also include her brother's name on the resettlement form so that they did not have to be separated. Later I discovered that this man was not her brother at all but her boyfriend. Finally we had our interview with the Canadian officials, her, me and her 'brother.' It was only after the interview that I learned she had deceived me. It turned out that this type of deception was not uncommon in Nairobi. Some refugees targeted others who looked as though they had a good chance at being resettled and after resettlement left them. This made some unsuspecting refugees lose their minds.

After my return from Nairobi I began working for the LWF (Lutheran World Federation) as a sanitation worker, spraying toilets in the camp, carrying twenty five litres of disinfectant back and forth five days a week, eight hours a day, in the scorching sun, on foot. The incentive was 1000 Kenyan Shillings, which is almost $15 USD a month. My main motivation behind taking the job, however, was to keep busy; it would also give me access to the UNHCR and NGO compounds to observe things. Later it inspired me to begin a refugee news bulletin. I wrote a proposal and handed it around hoping to find an NGO who was interested in funding the news bulletin. After many ups and downs the LWF manager and the camp manager, a Swede named Steven, agreed to fund it locally by supplying paper and typists every month. They asked me to find people to work with me on the bulletin, including an editor and administrators. After shaping the structure the bulletin would take we published our first issue in September 1993. It was a small publication, manually duplicated and stapled together. I was very happy to at least start the bulletin; after all you have to start somewhere.

We were preparing to celebrate the Ethiopian New Year, which is on September 11, in 1993. I had volunteered to take an acting part in a drama, which was written, composed and directed by Abebe Feyisa, an artist, writer and psychologist, a very talented and unique human being. I was given one of the lead roles, which was written to reflect our life in Walda camp. It included the story of the three young refugees who were murdered in the camp. I was feeling unstable at the time due to the woman whom I thought was to become my wife leaving me in Nairobi. That night during the show I removed all my clothes in front of the audience and went crazy, yelling and screaming I ran through the audience. It remained one of the more memorable events during our New Year celebrations. After that we celebrated Ethiopian New Year every year.

After scrubbing toilets I moved up to Social Worker for the LWF, this raised my monthly pay to 1500 Kenyan Shillings, equal to $21 USD a month. I also got approved time to work on the news bulletin each day after midday. One day I got talking to an LWF delegate from Japan who was visiting the camp. During our conversation the idea of beginning a photography programme was raised. I told him that for that I would need a camera, he promised to send me one. A short time later the camera arrived, as promised, at the camp. With the camera in hand I became fully engaged in the bulletin project, my monthly wage doubled to 3000 Kenyan Shillings, about $42 USD a month. I loved the work and was happy, more or less, for a time.

We named the bulletin *KANEBU* and being the photographer gave me a lot of access in and out of the UNHCR compound. It also enabled me to meet many people visiting the camp, from many parts of the world. This also helped me promote the bulletin. I would collect people's business cards and send them copies of the bulletin as it was produced. LWF covered the cost of postage and for the first time *KANEBU* had worldwide distribution. Every Tuesday, Thursday and Saturday I would get copies ready for postage and seal them in the mail pouch, which was forwarded to the LWF office in Nairobi. In return for the bulletin we asked people to send us books for our library. I received books from most people who received the bulletin. The library was located in the Ethiopian part of the camp and was an initiative of the members of the Ethiopian community.

KANEBU fast became a means of communication with the outside world by raising issues of concern to refugees and encouraging refugees to contribute short stories, poems and articles for inclusion in the bulletin. KANEBU gave refugees a voice in many ways. During the demeaning 'head count' episode, by the UNHCR, KANEBU published an article, penned by a refugee, which said "we are not cattle to be counted and forced into an enclosure by the UNHCR." One issue of KANEBU (issue 20, 1997,) published the following acronyms given to agencies by refugees. This outraged not only the UNHCR but also the Kakuma Social Services Officer, Walla Kuoy:

IRC—International Robbers Community

LWF—Life Without Food

WFP—World Food Problem

RADA BARNEN (Swedish Save the Children)—Refugee Blood (Sack the Children)

JRS—Jesuit Refugee Spoilers

UNHCR—United Nations High Consumption of Refugees

ICRC—International Cross of Refugee Confusion

These are just a few I could mention.

Around April 1995 I received an official letter from Mr Bob Koepp, LWF's (Lutheran World Federation) Emergency Operations Coordinator in Nairobi, congratulating me and the KANEBU editorial team for the good work we had done and were doing. I replied to his letter and asked him to sponsor the second anniversary edition in September of that year. We wanted to publish five hundred copies with a publisher in Nairobi and also needed money for a few days accommodation and so that I could travel to Nairobi to oversee the publication; I also asked if we could include an interview with him in the issue. To my surprise he replied within a few days saying that he would be happy to sponsor the issue and to make the necessary arrangements with LWF staff at Kakuma camp. At the end of August I went to Nairobi for three weeks and stayed in a three star hotel, each week I was given 5000 Kenyan Shillings as a per diem. I did my job as well as treating it as a bit of a holiday. I bought some second hand clothes and more books and movies. After this *KANEBU* moved one step closer to being a professional publication. Instead of being published manually in the camp it was now being published in Nairobi, instead of monthly it became a quarterly publication. Every three months I flew to Nairobi to oversee the publication. I was given a budget of 250,000 Kenyan Shillings a year to publish 300 copies of the bulletin with the Nairobi printers; this sum included my accommodation and other expenses. By the time I left Kakuma camp in 1997 we had published twenty regular issues and eight special issues of *KANEBU* over three years.

We distributed issues of KANEBU to NGO's and the UNHCR, both in Nairobi and elsewhere. Two copies per issue. We sent four copies each issue to the refugee library in the camp and individuals working for the NGO's could purchase a copy for 20 Kenyan shillings, other interested individuals could buy a copy for 10 Kenyan shillings. The LWF decided to contribute money made by KANEBU back to KANEBU to incentivise and continue the good work.

KANEBU, as mentioned, was financed by the LWF. Their contribution to the publication came from donations made to LWF for the Kakuma project and was not taken from money allocated by the UNHCR. However *KANEBU* became an issue for the UNHCR, particularly for Wall Kuyou, acting head of the sub office for the UNHCR in Kakuma. He wrote a strong letter to the LWF stating that *KANEBU* had become too single minded, being headed by one person, me, and that it should be run by a committee appointed by the UNHCR, selected from UNHCR staff, NGO staff and the refugee community. This letter was also sent to LWF and UNHCR offices in Nairobi. The LWF camp manager at the time, Zaka, showed me a copy of the letter asking for my opinion. I told him that the publication was my idea and that, had I not been a refugee, I would have owned it outright having secured all the funding myself. I said that the UNHCR had no right to centralise or control it; it was not food or allocated supplies for distribution therefore did not fall under UNHCR jurisdiction. I told him that if they wanted to they could begin their own news bulletin. The LWF agreed and refused their advice on the matter. When the new head of the UNHCR sub office for Kakuma arrived, called Ortega, the issue of *KANEBU* evaporated. Ortega was more supportive of the idea of having a refugee news bulletin, by refugees in the camp.

In each issue of *KANEBU* there was a permanent column called "Focus on Organisations." The column involved doing interviews with different NGO's and heads of the camp, including UNHCR officials. One of the officials whom I interviewed was Aurelia Brasilia, the US Ambassador to Kenya, while she was at Kakuma for a two day visit. With her during her visit was Alan Peters, the UNHCR representative for Kenya and Somalia, based in Nairobi. I went to the airstrip when they arrived with the LWF and my camera so that I could take photos for *KANEBU*. It was my usual practice to cover every visit to the camp by taking photos. I hung around waiting for them by the swimming pool while they had some tea. When they emerged there was chaos, the drivers were hurriedly ushering people into cars, some people were running. The UNHCR driver told me to sit in the car with him, it also happened to be the car carrying the ambassador, Alan Peters and some other embassy staff. When Alan Peters discovered that I was in the car with him he was outraged. He shouted at the driver and told him to stop the car, then he told me to get out and find another car. I was able to find another car and follow them back to the camp. Apparently refugees were not supposed to sit in the same vehicles as the UNHCR.

It was on June 20, 1996, on world refugee day, that I organised a photographic exhibition in the refugee library. The exhibition included around one thousand photographs depicting camp life. Inspired by the exhibition we had the first group of Camp Sadako (volunteer students, named after the former UNHCR High Commissioner, who came to stay at the camp for six weeks) came to the camp. This group of students were form Australia; there were sixteen of them in total. Two of the students, Carl Solomon and Naomi Flutter, showed interest in *KANEBU* and decided to hold a writers workshop. They invited writers from throughout the camp to attend. After they departed the writers workshops were continued by an Italian named Fabio Germano as a vocational training programme in the camp. Fabio helped us all gain a lot of knowledge and experience; he also took over editing *KANEBU* until his time came to leave the camp. It turned out that, before they left, Carl and Naomi had written a letter to Fabio asking him what he thought about publishing a collection of writings by refugee writers in Kakuma. This idea was proposed to us, by Fabio, during one of our workshops. We all agreed in principal but asked that we received, in writing, verification that we would retain copyright of all our work and that any money raised would be used to fund projects in the camp of our choosing. We were sent a copy of a contract stating that we retained ownership of the copyright in the publication, each writer would receive $20 USD for their contribution and two copies of the book. Any money raised would be sent to Kakuma to support projects the writers approved of, one of them being the ongoing costs of *KANEBU*. Happy with this arrangement we sent around one hundred contributions for the book. From the one hundred we sent them they selected twenty eight to be included in the book one of which was a poem of mine. The book was launched in Canberra at Parliament House as part of the 50 year celebrations of the creation of the UN (United Nations), attended by the Australian Prime Minister and other officials. When our copies of the book were sent to Kakuma they were accompanied by Nicole Delaney, who brought two copies of the book for each of us and $20 USD, as agreed. Nicole had also organised for a media crew to cover the story, which was lead by Mohammed Alamin, the producer of the famous television series *Focus in Africa*. This TV programme was aired in most African countries, including Ethiopia. I and another refugee writer were interviewed for the programme. So the UNHCR received positive publicity without actually having anything done anything for the project. Nicole Delaney stayed in the camp for a further six weeks. Nicole now works in Geneva for the aid agency which is dealing with HIV/AIDS and Tuberculosis.

The book was titled *Tilting Cages: An Anthology of Refugee Writing*. However, despite our contract ownership of copyright for the book was awarded to Carl and Naomi, which shouldn't have happened. The first print run was for five thousand copies. The publishers didn't spend any money on the publication; the costs were paid by AUSTCARE (an Australian NGO). But Kakuma didn't see any further money, other than our $20. We didn't know what had happened to the money until one day I was called to a meeting with a gentleman named Carl. Carl was a new employee of the UNHCR who had been hired to create adult education projects for refugees. He had come to Kakuma to conduct research. Carl had organised a meeting with me and other members of the refugee writers group. He suggested that *KANEBU* should be run by committee, by all members of the writers group and not just by one person, me. He told us that unless I handed over control of *KANEBU* the earnings from *Tilting Cages* would not be released for use in Kakuma. I told him that I was happy for him and the writers group to use the money to establish another bulletin but that *KANEBU* was my brain child and I would continue to run it until the day I left Kakuma. After several tense arguments it was clear that we were not going to come to a consensus and the meeting was concluded.

I saw Carl once more after that, when I was in Nairobi, he was still working for the UNHCR. Sometime later a woman from AUS-TCARE came to visit the camp. She approached me about organising another book. I told her that after what happened with the first one that was simply not going to happen. She was surprised to hear that we never received the proceeds from the book and assured me she would investigate what had happened to it when she returned to Australia and get back to me. I never heard from her again. While I was living in Nairobi a group of Japanese students went to stay at Kakuma, they translated *Tilting Cages* into Japanese and were able to raise money from the translated version. They sent $10,000 worth of proceeds from the book to Kakuma; the money was used to renovate the refugee library and to buy solar panels to power lights in the Library.

After I was resettled in New Zealand I planned to take the UNHCR to court. I was furious about the kinds of people the UNHCR had employed and sent to the camp, the fact that they robbed us and were able to get away with it. Particularly in regards the proceeds we never received for the first book. I enquired as to the whereabouts of Carl through the UNHCR resident representative based in Auckland. His name was Hans. One day, out of the blue, Carl called me from Canada. He told me that he had the proceeds from the book in a bank account and that he was still working for the UNHCR. He told me he had got my contact details from the UNHCR. I was unsure how he had got my contact details, perhaps Hans had given them to him. I didn't want to talk to him in detail. After the entire book was first published in 1995 and this was 2001 and at that time the money raised by the book had still not been sent to Kakuma.

However, some good news I discovered at that time was that *KANEBU* was still going. After I left Kakuma in 1998 publication dropped off for a while but recently it had been picked up again. In 2004 the *KANEBU* website was established and is published in English and Japanese. Proceeds from *KANEBU* are now used to train refugees to use computers. There is also an online discussion group, which I joined. I have also learned that the editors and reporters working on *KANEBU* now have a computer, printer and photocopier. This news makes me very happy. I contacted the *KANEBU* editors and the refugee library and discovered, to my dismay, that the proceeds from *Tilting Cages* had still never reached the camp.

Teshome was among the first of the Ethiopian refugees to enter Kenya in 1991. He was first in Oda camp, then Walda and finally Kakuma. He was an active member of the church, charismatic, out spoken and well respected. He had been a civil servant back in Ethiopia. He always smiled, would talk to anyone who approached him and was a very good advisor but slowly he began to isolate himself. He locked himself in his shelter. Friends discovered him a week later. A case like this, of self enforced isolation, was previously unknown in the camp. Later it was discovered that the UNHCR introduced a refugee head count by placing invisible ink on refugees' fingers and then made them pass through a dark room and fenced enclosure. Teshome did not want to be part of the head count. He refused; in fact he locked himself away days before the head count. After a while his shelter disintegrated on him, he didn't have anything to eat or any clothes to wear. He was taken to the hospital on several occasions but he didn't like it. He hated life and lost hope. Finally he died and was buried in Kakuma. Like many other refugees in the camp Teshome died of lost hope and slowly going crazy.

Of all the things I could tell you about Kakuma the thing most worth mentioning is the creativity of the refugees. The creativity they displayed in an attempt to improve their lives in the camp. Like decorating their shelters and furnishing them with brick 'sofa beds' decorating their walls, brick beds and sofas with decorative papers and turning the wheat flour into a glue to stick them to items.

One of the worst things worth mentioning was the snake and scorpion bites, which added another layer of suffering to our daily lives.

One afternoon an Ethiopian refugee, who was referred to Nairobi for emergency medical treatment, went crazy in front of the UNHCR office, stripping off his clothes until he was naked with a catheter still attached to his penis. He was removed from the camp by force while crying and screaming for help.

Zemed Liben was another young Ethiopian refugee who became very sick in the camp, finally the camp hospital referred him to Nairobi hospital but only after he slipped into a coma. Shortly after he reached Nairobi he passed away. He is buried in the Langata cemetery in Nairobi.

The perimeter of the UNHCR compound in Kakuma was fenced by three fences; the entrance through the main gate had three doors. All the compound fences were electrified. It was more secure than the central prison in Ethiopia or Guantanamo Bay in Cuba.

While in the camp I managed to make a little extra money by carrying visitor's luggage up to the compound for them. They would pay me in tips and it gave me a chance to observe what was going on in the world of refugee charity.

When I think on Kakuma camp I think of so many people who came to stay at the camp as volunteers, students and researchers. People who treated the camp as their laboratory and us black African refugees as caged monkeys or lab rats. I think of the pharmaceuticals that were donated to the hospital but had their expiry dates removed. Our source of suffering was a source of adventure for many westerners who came to stay in the camp, that wrote their books, shot their documentaries and used us as their raw material. A commodity to help them quantify the mystery of suffering, some of them made enormous profit from their creations and were hailed as 'experts' on refugees, credited with knowing more about us than we knew about ourselves.

For this black African refugee the camps felt like a laboratory for the west where they could experiment and discover what worked and what didn't. To discover whether we were rats or monkeys.

I always laugh when things are tough. I laugh during the worst times, the bad times, the ugly times, I laugh at my own weakness, when I brain storm, when I find out how things are tangled and interwoven I laugh. I remind myself that fire also laughs when it is burning. When I am abused and mistreated I laugh. As a result of all my laughter, my shaky right hand, my blurted speech and my cerebral palsy many people in the camp thought I was mentally impaired, including other refugees. As a result no one bothered to hide anything from me or check themselves around me; no one thought I would remember anything I had observed and everyone 'enjoyed' seeing me around. This helped me to have access to a lot of information and situations perhaps I shouldn't have, in the camps and later in Nairobi. I observed carefully, listened, watched without being taken seriously. I made mental notes and now 90% of my writing is based on those years of refugee life and observations. I ensured I was liked and, although I am approaching my fifties, my memory is still very good. This may seem shrewd of me but on all my reference letters from NGO's and the UNHCR it is mentioned that I was well liked by the entire staff and would be missed.

When I was in Nairobi, in March 1997, working on the publication of *KANEBU*, I was introduced to a young, beautiful Ethiopian lady, by some friends I trusted and had met in Walda camp. I agreed, through my friends who acted as mediators, to marry her if she agreed to move to Kakuma with me. We went to the JRS office in Nairobi, where the UNHCR officer's interview refugees and we were told to return the next day for an interview. The following day we were interviewed and given a protection letter to go to Kakuma. Her name and photo were added to my file and she was issued with a letter which listed her as my dependent and had her photo on it. I was excited to finish my work in Nairobi and return to Kakuma. I went back quickly and she followed after a few days. The LWF staff thought it odd that I was anxious to leave Nairobi. I left as quickly as I could which meant catching the bus back to Kakuma rather than flying. The LWF staff also thought this was unusual. After arranging my shelter in Kakuma she arrived. We stayed together in my shelter at Kakuma until, a few weeks later, I was asked to go to the UNHCR office in the camp. I was told that I had to report to the UNHCR Social Services office in Nairobi in a few days. I was told that my travel documents were all arranged and expenses were covered to travel by road. I couldn't figure out why I might be needed in Nairobi. I considered a number of factors. Perhaps *KANEBU* had become a problem? Perhaps they were going to offer me a job in Nairobi? A few days later I travelled to Nairobi, as requested, and was received by Dr. Whande, the senior Social Services officer, originally from Zimbabwe, whom I first met when she travelled to Walda from Geneva. I also met her several times when she visited Kakuma. Also there was Annette Ludeking, the Social Services officer for Kenya, originally from Denmark. They offered me a job.

Since I left Kakuma, especially since I arrived here In New Zealand, the camp has changed. Change is to be expected from humans living in one environment for a long period of time, negative or positive. I have followed the situation in Kakuma closely since coming to live here. One thing that never changes, however, is that it is still a refugee camp, a human prison with no predictable future. As always it is still full of conflict, confusion, and contradictions for my fellow black African refugees. They are still frying, years later, in that scorching sun, in the middle of nowhere.

NAIROBI, WORKING FOR THE UNHCR

My job at the UNHCR in Nairobi was to work at the branch office as a transport assistant. I surprised myself by accepting the job without any hesitation. I was asked to start immediately but I told them I needed two weeks to hand over *KANEBU* and the photographic project to someone who was willing to take them over from me. I also needed time to say goodbye to everyone. So we agreed that I would start mid May, 1997. On these terms I returned the following day to Kakuma. When I reached Kakuma the first person I broke the news to was the young woman who had started living with me in the camp, to my surprise she told me that she already knew I would be offered this job. I asked her how she knew, she didn't reply. At that moment I felt excitement to leave the camp, confusion and also sadness to leave all my friends. Later on, when things fell apart with the young Ethiopian woman, I discovered that I had been tricked.

When I went to Nairobi I stayed for a while with a couple who were living at JRS House in Mountain View, a suburb of Nairobi. I stayed with them for two weeks while I waited for my accommodation in the JRS House to be ready. I didn't take anything with me to Nairobi except my books and a few clothes in one small bag. The director of JRS, Father Eugene Birer, gave me everything from a bed to sleep on to basic furniture items, utensils and manchester. For me staying at JRS House was like staying in a palace. While I had lived in the camps I had never slept on a bed except one made of bricks, filled with sand and covered with plastic.

Moving to Nairobi was the beginning of a complex, difficult and scary period for me, which lasted for the next two and a half years. My being invited to work for the UNHCR in Nairobi surprised and puzzled everyone, including me. My main job at the UNHCR was to organise the transport of refugees, from and to camps, from protection, to resettlement and social services. I had a desk on the second floor, next to the National and Regional East Africa Officers. Their Regional Social Services Officer had his own office; the rest of the officers had their own desks with computers. I also had my own desk but no computer. My desk had a drawer in which was kept the key for a safe, which was located in the Senior Officer's toilet. The safe contained my budget for transport, which at that time was around $1000USD. The transport job I was given was too much work for one person but like all work that involved refugees it was not unusual to be overloaded. The National Officer for Social Services was a woman from Denmark; she had worked for the UNHCR for over ten years, in the Nairobi office. She was my immediate boss with another Kenyan guy who was my supervisor. His job was to cross check all my transportation requests and assigned budgets before it was approved and then sent to finance for processing. Once a request was processed I would have to go to a bank to cash a cheque for the amount requested. The cheque was always made out to whoever drove me to the bank, as I was a refugee I was not allowed to cash cheques. Once at the bank I had to witness the driver receive the money and count the money to ensure the right amount was given. I then had to transport the money back to the office. Sometimes the drivers would be given other errands to run and I would have to go with them and wait until they could drop me back at the office again, sometimes this would take hours making my day much longer. This process was repeated daily and never ending. As a refugee I was paid monthly for my work at the UNHCR. I earned approximately $350 a month. This was enough to get by in Nairobi. The funny thing was, because I was a refugee, I had no job description, no specified working hours and no overtime or holiday pay. There were many times I ended up working late into the night and returned home tired and hungry at 2am. Sometimes having not eaten since 6.30am the previous morning.

One day, it was a Friday; I was called by the Senior Protection Office and told to go to the airport, with another Kenyan gentleman from logistics. Our task was to collect Eritrean refugees who were stranded at the airport and transport them to Kakuma Camp. According to the Senior Protection Office they were ready and willing to go to the camp. However, when we reached the airport the scene was quite different. These Eritrean's were victims of the Ethio-Eritrea war and had been expelled from Ethiopia. When they arrived at Nairobi airport they began a hunger strike. By the time we arrived they were into their second day and they did not want to go to the camp. They asked for assurances that they would be re-settled in Kenya and until they received it they refused to leave Nairobi and would continue their hunger strike. After we had spent some time at the airport I decided to try and get permission to talk to them. We were taken to the area where they had been detained since their arrival and began a conversation. I could see that their talks with the Kenyan officials had broken down so

I asked them to leave so I could talk to them alone. They agreed and retired to the next room. I began speaking to them in Amharic, the official language of Ethiopia and my first language, it was also the first language of one of the young expelled Eritrean. I introduced myself and told him my story, from the time I had left Ethiopia to that day. I told him about Kakuma Camp and, when and how I had started working for the UNHCR in Nairobi and I showed them my ID and my UNHCR protection letter. I did this to remove any suspicion he may have of me and to make them trust me. I told them that for now the best option for the group was to go to Kakuma with the UNHCR, get registered there as refugees and work from within the camp to be resettled. They agreed and a transport and police escort was organised. I asked them to eat some food and end the hunger strike. Finally some food was provided for them at 9pm. In the meantime the transport that had been organised for them had left and a new bus had to be found, by the time this bus arrived the police escort had disappeared. Finally after midnight we contacted the Senior Protection Officer at her residence and she told us to return and report to her residence. We arrived at her residence and spent half an hour briefing her on the events of the day, we lined our empty stomachs with soda and finally arrived home at 2am. The next morning I was too tired to return to the airport so I hid when a driver came to pick me up. I learned the following morning, Monday, that the Eritrean refugees had been transported to Kakuma over the weekend.

There were times, at the UNHCR office that I had to spend my weekends doing piles of training or conference documents, photocopying, binding and packaging. This was usually if there was a conference or seminar coming up in Nairobi or one of the camps. In addition to this work every time a group a refugees came to Nairobi for resettlement, medical treatment or when they had chosen to come to the city to protest about conditions in the camp they would usually camp outside the UNHCR office. We nicknamed this 'Chiromo Camp' after the street that the UNHCR offices were located on. Sometimes UNHCR officials would get sick of seeing the camp through their office windows, especially after the head of sections meeting every Friday. Before the office would officially close for the weekend, on a Friday afternoon, one of the officers would decide to send these refugees back to Kakuma. Without any discussion with them, or consent, a bus would be organised and they would be taken by shuttle to the bus depot and dumped there. This always required a great deal of financial processing, the bus company would invoice the UNHCR based on the number of people they were transporting so numbers needed to be recorded, each refugee had to have travel documents on them, I had to ensure that each refugee had enough cash on them to pay for the final leg of the journey. The whole reason for this was that the UNHCR did not like refugees loitering in Nairobi over the weekends. This whole process was very time consuming and often I would not finish on a Friday until 8.30pm. So I began to arrange for these transports early on a Friday morning, I would go to the bus company offices at 12noon to make bookings for regular travellers and make arrangements for the transport. I would anticipate and do all this early so that I could return to the UNHCR offices and finish at the same time as all the other staff.

Other days I would often spend my time between police stations with people from the Refugee Protection section of the UNHCR. We would undertake mass refugee round ups, interviews and work to convince these refugees to return to the camps. Then we would arrange transports for them if they agreed. I learned quickly that my job at the UNHCR was not restricted to refugee transportation but to do everything and anything the other staff wanted me to do. Running up and down from office to office, serving tea and coffee, doing shopping, paying bills, running to buy cigarettes, doing black market money exchanges; this was the job I loved the most because I always got a tip at the end of it.

While doing all this if anyone wanted to send refugees back to the camps urgently and I didn't have money in the safe ready for them, because I hadn't had time to place a formal request with the financial services team, it was me who would be to blame.

A few weeks after my arrival in Nairobi things got ugly at home. The girl who was living with me as my wife had been spending most weekends in Eastleigh. I discovered that she had a husband there and that the two of them had planned for her to marry me as they believed it would speed up their resettlement. They knew before I did that I was going to be invited to work for the UNHCR and had used this information to trap me. The person who introduced me to this girl was a good friend of mine, he was also from the same area with her and we had been through Walda and Kakuma camps together. I considered him a very close friend. When I realised the game and how I had been trapped I decided to approach him and tell him my suspicions of this girl. He told me that she was no better than a prostitute and that I should get rid of her. He said he would bring his sister to Nairobi to marry me instead. Even though I knew that he was the one behind the whole thing I didn't show any signs that I knew of his involvement and said "ok", but first he needed to help me calmly and peacefully separate from this girl. He did help me and finally the girl left.

Unfortunately before she left she decided to try and make my life hell. She contacted my boss at the UNHCR and another Ethiopian guy who worked at the UNEP (United Nations Environment Programme), who was a colleague of my bosses husband and a friend to the girl, and tried to get me fired. It didn't work. My friend also didn't succeed in getting his sister to Nairobi for me to marry and slowly I cut off communication with him. Sometime later he gave my name and office number at the UNHCR to an Ethiopian lady in America who phoned claiming to be his sister. She said that she would pay me whatever I wanted to help resettle her brother. I told her I didn't know anything about this kind of illegal processing and not to call me again.

Not only was life complicated at home it was also complicated at work. My boss, Annette Ludeking, was not happy with my appointment. I was appointed to the newly formed position of 'Transport Assistant' by Dr. N. Whande, who was the Regional Social Services Manager. It turned out that Annette had also applied for the position of Regional Social Services Manager. I was recommended for the position and brought from Kakuma by Dr. Whande. I was the first person to ever have been appointed to a UNHCR position from a refugee camp. Any refugees who had been picked for previous positions were living in Nairobi and were members of a political organisation that had been rallying against Ethiopian Political Regimes for more than 30 years. Annette was an ardent supporter of this organisation. When I appeared in the office and began working for her she made it clear that she was not happy about my appointment. I began hearing from local staff in the Social Services division that my appointment was not approved by Annette.

After my 'wife' left I had a kind of emotional breakdown. Everything seemed complicated. I was afraid of what might happen to me next. I felt lonely, I was surrounded by people who were meant to be my friends from Walda and Kakuma Camps but they had become obsessed with resettlement and thought that I could and should do everything and anything to help them. I felt that none of my friendships were pure anymore. I was not interested in seeing them anymore and to make things more complicated I felt trapped in a complex chain of corruption within the UNHCR system. I observed that there was a global chain of money for resettlement.

I also observed people arriving in Nairobi everyday from the horn of Africa, especially Ethiopia, who were accommodated in refugee accommodation in Nairobi straight away and within a few days or weeks, had already begun the resettlement process. Many without ever having been to a UNHCR office or having to stay in a camp.

It was around this time that twenty Ethiopians arrived direct from Ethiopia. They carried Press ID's. I learned that this ID could be obtained on the black market in Addis Ababa quite easily. At that time the Ethiopian Regime was cracking down on Journalists who represented the free press. The victims of this brutal action were poisoned, tortured or disappeared, often kidnapped by Government forces and executed. Many of them were unable to escape. From this group of twenty 'journalists' perhaps four of five of them were actual journalists. We knew that several of them could not be journalists because they were unable to read and write. Most of them were eventually sent to Norway. Meanwhile many genuine cases were suffering for years in refugee camps. All of this was managed and co-ordinated by the UNHCR office. When the Norwegian Embassy in Nairobi was conducting their resettlement selections it was actually my boss, Annette Ludeking, who was completing the selection process for them and advising embassy staff as to who they should or shouldn't take. At this time Annette was no longer an official UNHCR employee; her contract had not been renewed but she was given a three month contract by the Nairobi office to find and recommend the best NGO (Non Governmental Organisation) to represent urban refugee cases. She was given the title of Senior Resettlement Officer, the last person in the post was a guy named Mark who didn't know what was going on right under his nose in his own department. After he left Protection, Resettlement and Repatriation services in Nairobi where all combined into one section. This gave a lot of power and control to one person under the title of Assistance Representative. It was obvious to me that Annette would recommend that an NGO replace the JRS

(Jesuit Refugee Service.) After I arrived in New Zealand I discovered that Goal Ireland was approved as an urban NGO, to work alongside the UNHCR. I was not surprised that Annette had looked far outside Africa for her selection and recommendation and she was appointed as director of this new NGO. I learned, a while later, that the funding requested to run Goal Ireland far exceeded any funding ever given to the JRS in Nairobi. Later Annette lost her job at Goal Ireland.

Shortly before I left for New Zealand a new Social Services Officer was appointed in Nairobi. He was from Eritrea and had worked with the UNHCR in Kosovo. He was a great support to me and worked hard to help genuine cases. The office was a highly difficult and corrupt environment to work in so he couldn't move as fast as he would have liked. The time between his arriving and my leaving was very short so we had only had time to begin the process of getting to know each and building a friendship.

Life in Nairobi had many ups and downs and temptations. There were many refugee ladies who would do anything for a chance at resettlement and from experience I did not want to get involved with the wrong woman. I went to Eastleigh, a refugee suburb in Nairobi, to visit a girl who I grew up with in Ethiopia, also to eat traditional Ethiopian food and to buy Mira (quat) a leaf that, when chewed, helps to calm you down or can act as a stimulant improving concentration, it is highly addictive if you use it too regularly. While I was visiting my friend I saw a beautiful, but shy, lady, who had come to borrow coffee cups from people in the neighbourhood. I asked my friend about this lady, she said she was alone; she had lost her husband in an accident in Nairobi. Since that time she had been single and was not interested in seeing anyone. But she agreed to introduce me to her if I was interested. The following week I went to Eastleigh and was introduced to her, I invited her and my friend to my house one weekend for lunch. From there our closeness developed and I was upfront with her and told her that I wanted to marry her but that I would give her time to make her decision. She asked me if I would be happy to take an HIV/AIDS test with her, I said yes. We had the test done a few days later and we were both negative. A few weeks later I asked her to move in with me and she did.

A few months after she moved in with me I asked her to marry me and she said yes. We registered our intention to marry at Shera House in Nairobi. We had to pay around $25USD and the date was set for Friday 20 February 1998. We decided on a weekday because if you get married on a weekend the cost jumps to $150USD, which we couldn't afford. The wedding preparations went well and we received a great deal of support from UNHCR staff and refugee friends. I chose my best men, two refugees and one Kenyan protection officer. One was a refugee who lived near me in the Refugee Compound in Nairobi, the second was a lawyer and I wanted him there in case an issue arose involving my previous 'wife.' The third was also a refugee; his wife grew up near me in Ethiopia. He had a new outfit for me to wear to the wedding, which his sister bought him in Canada and fitted me very well. The wedding went very well, we were surrounded by around 70 friends, mostly refugees whom I knew in Walda and Kakuma who were either living in Nairobi or had managed to get to Nairobi for a short time. The UNHCR loaned us a bus so we could transport all the guests to a picnic at Shera House, during the picnic the photos were taken. Except for missing my parents it was the best refugee wedding an Ethiopian man like me could have dreamt of. For my wife it was even better as she had some cousins and nieces in Nairobi and they were able to attend. For me it was just wonderful to have all my refugee friends there.

I was always amazed at the excitement in the UNHCR when news spread that a new influx of refugees were coming across the border. More refugees meant more money, emergency funds would be released in Geneva and staff assigned to address the emergency would receive duty allowances on top of their already fat salaries. I felt that the reason a lot of these people joined aid agencies in the first place was for the money. The irony was that these people were crossing the border into a foreign country to save their lives while the people in the aid agencies were excited, even happy, thinking of the additional money they would make from the refugees' plight.

I lost many good friends in Nairobi, people who expected me to help them, by any means, be resettled. They didn't realise that I had no power unless I joined the chain of corruption, the international criminal gang of resettlement. The refugees who were living in the compound with me, whom I knew very well and was very close to in Walda, Kakuma and Nairobi wanted to make friends with Annette and other staff in the UNHCR office, they thought it would help their case for resettlement. Several UNHCR staff would have friends and family come to visit Nairobi, I would invite them to my house. Annette's parents visited three times in one year from Denmark. My wife became very close to them, Annette would also come to visit with me sometimes and see the other people that lived with me in the compound. However I tried to prevent my house from becoming a place of contact between the UNHCR and refugees. This did not make Annette or my refugee friends happy and by the time I left Nairobi some of them were no longer talking to me.

I was sure that corruption and bribery was taking place inside the UNHCR Resettlement office. At one time I decided to try and infiltrate the corrupt group, but I needed to have a back up within the office if things went wrong. With this in mind I approached the Senior Protection Officer, Pia Pure Pia, asking her opinion and for protection if something went wrong. I raised the issue with her and she asked me in a strange way, "Why would you want to do that? This is Kenya." Right then Peter Alingo, the Kenyan Protection Officer and her deputy stepped into Pia's office. I left the office, knowing that he was one of the key figures in the corruption ring.

Another corrupt figure was Joseph Cavalerie, from Italy, who was a resettlement officer and a close friend of Annette's. All resettlement decisions were predominantly made by the two of them. Joseph's wife would often come into the office to sell gold from Dubai, Somalia and Ethiopia. When I saw all of the gold jewellery that she wore in the office, big chains, rings and heavy bracelets I realised that they were bribes from Ethiopian and Somalian refugees for resettlement. This business was done in broad daylight as she moved from office to office. She didn't try to hide it from any staff members. Later I heard news of an investigation into the conduct of Joseph and Peter and that they had been expelled from Kenya. I was not surprised to hear this news but I was surprised to hear that besides Joseph, Peter and a few other clerks, no other international staff were investigated.

My final task before leaving Nairobi was to find two translators to work for the UNHCR. One who could translate Amharic and one who could translate Oromo. I managed to find two good people. Both of whom were refugees and had been in Walda camp with me, one of them had also been in Kakuma camp. He was a good man and after a few months could not abide by the corruption and resigned after writing a letter to the Senior Protection Officer. I tried to track both him and his letter down but was unsuccessful; he had disappeared from the refugee scene. The other man had a beautiful baby, his wife got a scholarship in Nairobi to study dress making and he followed her to Nairobi to look after the baby. He stayed in his position as a translator. As I was leaving Nairobi he gave me a gold chain and my wife a gold ring as gifts. I told him we couldn't accept I knew he couldn't afford it but he said "no problem." A short time later he was accepted for resettlement in Norway, but to my surprise he managed to change his resettlement country to the USA, not just for him and his wife and child but he managed to resettle his sister and sister in law from Ethiopia. I heard it was his sister-in-law and her boyfriend who brokered the resettlement deal, according to my sources. He also managed to buy a house in America on his arrival. He is not on good terms with the refugee community in America, he avoids them.

By the time I left Nairobi I was experiencing severe health problems. I had become overweight, I was diagnosed with diabetes and every time I felt hungry I was eating too much. By the time I left Nairobi my weight had ballooned to 115kg. This was dramatic and alarming.

CONCLUSION

In no situation would I blame any refugee for their actions. We would still live in good countries if our country's situation had not deteriorated. If we hadn't become beggars, unemployed, if our countries were not war torn, rife with on-going war, massacres, genocides. Our countries, our people could have been the ones to feed the whole world. This and the human rights violations being carried out by our corrupt governments, collaborating with the west and looting our properties, made us look to the west for protection and survival. The west's pet dictators in Africa consume billions of dollars worth of food and other consumables while African's die of hunger, disease, war and conflict and while our labour and natural resources prop up the west, as it has done for centuries.

These are the dilemmas of life in an African refugee situation. Without knowing what is going on out there in the world, grieving for our destiny and the destiny of other black African refugees.

Being a refugee is a very difficult experience for any human being. Being a Black African refugee, especially in African refugee camps, is worse than being a prisoner. A prisoner knows how long he is going to be in jail. A prisoner has been to court, he has had a chance to testify in his defence, he has been handed down some kind of judgement. But if you are a refugee you don't know what is going to happen to you next. Tomorrow is not in your hands. It is in the hands of politicians, in the hands of agencies like the UNHCR and in the hands of superpowers who decide who should or should not rule your country. These selections are not based on yours and your people's best interests or choices, as in a democracy, but in 'their' best interest.

You just live for the day and the day is not satisfactory because of the food you eat, where you sleep, the sickness and the hardship you face, and the weather. Everything is traumatising, killing you mentally, physically, morally. You are not able to have a meaningful vocation.

There are some people who, when put into this situation, survive, overcome problems. These are very few. The majority feel helpless. Where the camps are located it is very hot. If you stay there very long you begin to lose your memory, your mental ability, you drain out. The sweet parts of your nature go away, only the bitter parts remain.

The puzzle of Black African refugee life is unbearable, particularly Black African refugees in African refugee camps. The every day events and activities connect and attach themselves to what has happened to us, to our families, to our people and countries they become interrelated, interwoven with strands of complexity. Human kind, god, the material universe, nature, civilisation the so-called international community and everyone turns against us. Even if we try to assimilate and integrate; mix and change our cultural make up. The machine of integration appears to be vomiting, ejecting us, thereby draining our pride and integrity. Every one of the power barons seems to show us cunning smiles full of dentures. Sometimes it is our own people treading on us, selling us for leftovers in western countries, in exile, in a manner similar to what they and others have done and are doing in the African refugee camps back home, on our skeletons.

We are identified as global 'beggars' even though we are a people of history, who are proud of that history, culture, natural wealth and ancient civilisations. When we are 'resettled' in western countries away from poverty, hunger, HIV/AIDS, genocide, ethnic cleansing, war, conflict, few of us are able to see the world as we had before, as a better place. For the world to be a better place, not just for a few but for all, all humanity must be included in our discourses and actions. Projecting one's own enclave as a model for the whole world and extolling one's own segment of a community as the whole of humanity, in all frankness, amounts to delusions of grandeur and serves no positive purpose. When the ideas of a few racially challenged and jingoist groups, that say that Africa should be 'erased' from the world map and be renamed as 'Continent X', are accommodated I cannot believe that there is any real commitment to peace and justice anywhere, save for a few written documents.

I strongly believe that a solution for Black Africa can only be achieved with Black African's full participation. Knowing that no-one else will try to force solutions to the problems of Black Africa.

Our continent has for too long been brutalised by the effects of colonialism as has been witnessed in other parts of the world. There has been no attempt to rectify the effects of colonialism, be it in the form of reconstruction or reparation. Instead, the newly dependent countries were left on their own to sort out the mess that had been created by others. The moment these countries began to recover from this trauma and destruction other colonialists appeared, bent on making it a testing ground for ideologies of communism, capitalism, tribalism and religious extremism.

Over the last century Black Africans have been denied their natural right to chart their own destiny and pursue development agendas as per their own economic goals.

During the cold war era African people withstood the worst of the bitter competition between the two camps. They withstood extreme human rights violations under the despots and the economic and social destruction they brought with them by being the client of either the west or the east.

With the end of the cold war the neo liberals appeared in Africa and left behind extensive damage and disintegration. This was as a result of the free market economy and the liberalisation mantras they forced their continental disciples to experiment with, even though the economic and social infrastructure of many countries was not ready for it.

The huge international debts that the continent is struggling with now were taken out mainly to prolong the lives of satellite states by purchasing military hardware and enriching the elite. Because of the recklessness of a few acting in foreign interests generations of Black

Africans are chained down by debt servicing obligations and foregoeing much needed health care and education services to meet those obligations. A meaningful life for any person worth the title does not necessarily reside in mere material possessions and physical comforts. The true worth of one's existence is measured in the degree of rootedness to a community, a true sense of belonging and a guarantee of continuity, among other factors, that can only be fully realised in one's own community and country.

To be exiled is to be left hollow, it is to be unwanted! In addition, it is a painful and traumatic experience. Instead of focusing on the symptoms of the current, unjust, global economic and social systems, as manifested in the increasing number of refugees, we need to focus on the root causes that are driving people away from their home countries. Only then can we achieve a world that is a better and more peaceful place for us all.

The white academics tell us about our history, what went wrong, what went right. While we know they are the source of most of our problems. They make money by writing a 'best seller,' by producing documentaries, they become 'famous' making profits out of our suffering.

They ask the question, "When does one stop being a refugee?" Especially at conferences, organised by the people who 'know what is best' for us. Sometimes I want to say to them "when you leave our continent and take back all the problems that you and your ancestors brought with you, when that happens we Africans will go back and rebuild our shattered continent, shattered by European settlers, colonisers and neo-colonisers. At that time we will stop being refugees." As if the title refugee is a title of achievement.

When you observe what is done to others in a similar situation to you it eats away at you, making your thoughts restless, shaking you up, unsettling your physiology, your psychology. Alienating you and outcasting you from everyone.

What refugees really want is a peaceful ordinary life, day to day, normal happiness. Freedom from human exploitation. To lead a small life in a small way. We didn't ask Europeans to invade and colonise, to reap the rewards of our continent, first by direct colonisation and then by neo-colonialism and imperialism.

The problems Africa is facing are based on the exploitation by the west since the era of slavery. The West profited and is profiting from the suffering of Africans. The irony is that some smart, ambitious western individuals are also capitalising on another angel of profit by writing books, by 'exposing' what has happened and is happening in Africa. We have a saying for this in Africa. It is "informing the friend or relative, the person who attended the funeral and who is in mourning that their loved one has died." They are using new media to tell us 'our story' and profiting from our misery while the story is told in a way that suits them. The real exposure should come from Black Africans, not from anyone who pretends to know what happened in our countries and presumes to tell us what is 'best' for us. The best and truest story will come from the brains and hearts of black Africans, not from the white man's sympathy.

The works or our past and present heroes, such as Nkrumah, Cabral, Lubumba, Achebe, Soyenka, Ngugi to name a few, are highly significant examples of the bright future of Black Africa. As times change we should take from their theories on non-violent struggle. Avoid any kind of bloodshed, war and physical conflict. If we do this we will achieve our ancestor's dreams of an Africa for Black Africans. Until we are able to achieve this we will never be free, we will remain the slaves of westerners, those Black Africans who are outside our homeland, in the west, bare the new slave name 'refugee.'

They hate us; they are disgusted by our black skin. What they need from us is our labour; they exploit us, suck our blood, our bone marrow and then throw us out. Bury us under the dust while we are still alive.

In my future writing, which will be titled *Outcast: The Plight of Black African Refugees, Part Two*, I will write extensively about the refugee experience in New Zealand.

Contributors

Dr Ramon Das holds a BA from Carleton College, an MA from the University of Wisconsin-Milwaukee, and a PhD from the University of Maryland. He has been teaching at Victoria University, Wellington since 1999.

Teresia Teaiwa was born in Honolulu, Hawai'i and raised in the Fiji Islands. She has a BA from Trinity College, Washington, DC, an MA from the University of Hawai'i and a PhD from the University of California, Santa Cruz.

Kathy Jackson is an experienced cross-cultural psychologist, currently employed at the Auckland Refugees as Survivors Centre where she is a Research Associate. In the past she has worked as a child psychologist and has also taught psychology and educational psychology at the University of Malawi, the University of Botswana and at Monash University in Melbourne.

Valerie Morse is a Wellington based peace activist, columnist and published author. She is a member of Peace Action Wellington and works to raise awareness of human rights issues.

Marion Maddox is director of the Centre for Research on Social Inclusion, Macquarie University, NSW, Australia. She holds PhDs in theology (Flinders 1992) and philosophy (UNSW 2000) and teaches religious studies and Australian politics.

Françoise Parent-Ugochukwu studied Classics and English before obtaining a Maîtrise in French Stylistics and a Ph.D. in French Literature (Grenoble 1974) and has lectured in Higher Education in Nigeria, France and the UK for the past thirty-five years.

Andrea Useem is a journalist who specializes in covering religion and politics. Now living outside of Washington D.C. Andrea served as a foreign correspondent in East Africa throughout the 1990s.

L. E. Scott is a Wellington-based jazz poet, performer, prose writer and reviewer. He was born in Cordele, Georgia, in 1947. Scott has so far published thirteen collections of poetry and short fiction. His work has been published widely in journals, magazines and newspapers in New Zealand, Australia, India and the United States.

Christopher LaMonica currently resides in Boston and until recently was Lecturer of International Relations and Development at Victoria University of Wellington, New Zealand. Prior to working in academia Dr LaMonica worked for the International Energy Agency at the OECD, the US Agency for International Development in Zambia, and the Harvard Institute for International Development.

Index